Peter Desbarats · Terry Mosher

The Hecklers

A History of Canadian Political Cartooning and a Cartoonists' History of Canada

MacPherson/Toronto/Star

McClelland and Stewart · National Film Board of Canada

Copyright © 1979 by
McClelland and Stewart Limited

All Rights Reserved

The Canadian Publishers
McClelland and Stewart Limited
25 Hollinger Road
Toronto M4B 3G2

Printed and Bound in Canada

Design: Michael van Elsen

Canadian Cataloguing in Publication Data

Desbarats, Peter, 1933-
    The hecklers

ISBN 0-7710-2686-2

1. Canadian wit and humor, Pictorial–History
and criticism.   2. Cartoonists–Canada.
I. Aislin.   II. Title.

NC1440.D48   741.5'971   C79-094274-7

Contents

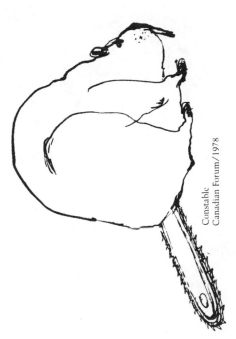

Constable
Canadian Forum/1978

Much of the early financing, research, and enthusiasm for this project was supplied by The National Film Board of Canada. Their initial sponsorship of this endeavour made this book possible. Particular thanks go to both Ian McLaren and Ian Mayer. Below is a description of the film made by The National Film Board:

"The Hecklers—Two Centuries of Canadian Political Cartooning" is a one-hour, 16mm colour film produced by The National Film Board of Canada, that brings your favourite political cartoons and their creators to life. The film takes a lively and imaginative look at Canada's history as seen through the eyes of her cartoonists, past and present. "The Hecklers" also takes a close look at the nature of the cartoonist and his world.

This film is available on loan, free of charge, from any National Film Board office in Canada.

Production and Direction:
Ian McLaren

Conception and Director of Research:
Terry Mosher

Script:
Ian Mayer

Narrator:
John Colicos

Preface

While researching this book, I was constantly on the lookout for an accurate definition of the political cartoon. During the heady days of the nineteenth century when the brilliant cartoonist Daumier was busily carving up the potentates of his time, the French art critic Champfleury defined these caricatures as "le cri des citoyens," or "the shout of the people." Most cartoonists working today are street-wise in that they have experienced the frustrations of the average individual in dealing with the suspicious factors that exert control over our lives. This experience hones the pen far better than a degree in political science. In Daumier's day, the targets may have been far more blatant– kings, cardinals and judges who embodied the differences between the haves and the have nots. Today the foe is far more nebulous, weaving its way through government, bureaucracy, and big business. But the target remains the same: Privilege.

Political cartoonists are generally considered public property. When they stray from the solitary confinement of their studios, predictable questions are often thrown at them.

"Where do you get your ideas?"

"How long does it take you to draw a cartoon?"

"Are your drawings censored by your editors?"

"How much money do you make?"

"Can I give you a terrific idea?"

Barron

FUNNY THING, LIFE...

One cartoonist I know always carries convenient, photocopied lists of answers, which prove invaluable at cocktail parties, bars, talk shows, bus stops–wherever he is expected to be as clever and witty as his drawings. However, many of us are at our worst in public, and it is often only while sweating over a drawing board that such ingenuity emerges.

Public curiosity is quite understandable, as political cartoonists are a very rare breed. In North America today, less than one individual in a million can claim to make a living from producing the configurations that appear daily on editorial pages. Curiously, and inexplicably, there are only two women who do so, both working in the United States.

Cartoonists themselves usually don't pretend to know what makes them tick. As the school doesn't exist that

can provide them with the necessary tools, cartoonists often brag that they went to all the wrong schools.

Getting started is the most difficult proposition, as there is never any visible calling for this particular occupation. However, if one knocks on a lot of doors, is extremely patient, and lucky enough to be in the right place at the right time, one just might get a chance to draw an editorial page cartoon for consideration.

After the first big break one discovers if he can deliver the goods again and again. An individual might be a competent or even brilliant, draughtsman, but he must be able to meet a regular and often monotonous deadline. Editors far prefer the latter talent to the former, as they are far too busy to nurture aspiring young cartoonists to fill up white space.

Pacing is another factor. Much like a professional baseball player who will stay in the big leagues if he can hit the ball three times out of ten, the cartoonist is doing his job if the readers react to his work, in one way or another, on a fairly regular basis, even though he cannot produce a drawing that will garner a maximum reaction every time.

Then there is the business of style. Any working cartoonist will admit to numerous early influences, usually the more the better. However a cartoonist working in Canada today will eventually have to generate his own particular 'look.' Otherwise he is likely to be dismissed as nothing more than an imitator.

This is an essential difference between American and Canadian political cartooning today. Individuality of style seems to be of little concern to many contemporary American cartoonists. Twenty years ago, most of them were drawing in a style that derived directly from Bill Mauldin and Herblock. Today, many use the styles of Patrick Oliphant and Jeff MacNelly. On the other hand, Canadian cartoonists take great pride in individual style. One can instantly tell the difference between a Macpherson, an Uluschak, a Berthio or a Blaine cartoon without having to check the signature.

This same individual flair is important in developing and communicating the cartoonist's own particular brand of humour. The wit and humour that one will find in a caricature by Ed Franklin is quite different from that found in the work of Roy Peterson even though both men are essentially caricaturists.

Because political cartoonists express the anxieties of a segment of the population, the medium is far from elitist. Nevertheless, the question is often asked, "Is political cartooning art?" Cartoonists are usually too busy to care and often express as healthy a cynicism about "Art" as they do of politics. However, the closest thing to an answer appears in Ralph E. Shikes' fine book The Indignant Eye. Shikes considers political cartooning art "when its draughtsmanship is superior and con-

trolled, the composition inherently striking, the impact of the conception immediate, the message of lasting interest—and perhaps when the artist's reputation is secure in art history books." One of the purposes of this book is to record the work of numerous long-forgotten cartoonists, many of whom had wide audiences in their time. Whether or not these cartoons are "art" is left up to the individual reader.

Another question arose during the work on this project: Besides entertaining the reader, do political cartoons ever have any "real" effect? I could only conclude that as a general rule they don't, but there have been occasional exceptions. Certainly a cartoon may give a reader a new perspective on a topic. Some cartoonists have pioneered attacks on politicans or policies that have been taken up by other members of the media. An excellent example is Duncan Macpherson's late 1950s Toronto Star drawings of John Diefenbaker. However, Macpherson himself maintains that, "a cartoon never hurt any politician. They manage to do that with their own mouths."

Daring cartoonists have changed our ideas regarding what is acceptable satire. During the days of Watergate and Richard Nixon, Bob Bierman of The Victoria Times was having a field day with the President's physiognomy. His editor discovered that Bierman was drawing Nixon's nose in the distinct shape of an erect penis, and threatened to fire him if he ever did so again. As cartoonists around the world were doing exactly the same thing, Bierman

drew the cartoon shown below, and it appeared, under a pen name, on the front page of the local university newspaper. Today, Bierman's cartoons of British Columbia Premier Bill Bennett appear regularly with erect noses, and, his readers and editors at The Times have come to expect this sort of thing from him.

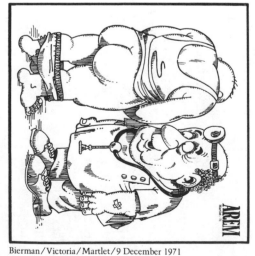

"You're right...It does look like Nixon's nose."

Bierman/Victoria/Martlet/9 December 1971

Traditionally religion was a touchy subject for cartoonists in Quebec, but this has changed in the last twenty-five years. In English Canada, the Royal Family was always considered unassailable. Ten years ago, the first drawing pictured here appeared in Maclean's and letters of protest poured in from across the country. Several years later, another drawing poking fun at the Queen appeared in the Montreal Gazette and drew more letters to the editor than anything that the newspaper had printed in its two-

Chapleau/Perspectives/1973

The Queen's Visit, or, How to see Canada without seeing Quebec

hundred-year history. That same year, Serge Chapleau's cartoon of the Queen's view of Quebec appeared in *Perspectives*, but the reaction of the French-speaking readers was highly laudatory. More recently, John Larter drew the caricature that appears on the next page for *The Edmonton Sun* during the Queen's visit for the Common-

Aislin/Montreal/McGill Daily/1969

wealth Games. The newspaper did not receive one protesting letter.

A problem in compiling this book was deciding, in some cases, whether or not a cartoonist's work fell into the category of political comment. Gag-cartoonists, comic-strip artists, sports cartoonists, illustrators and 'social' cartoonists such as Jimmy Frise, Henri Letondal, and Arthur Lemay, obviously are outside the scope of this book. But the work of Peter Whalley and George Feyer, who developed reputations as gag-cartoonists and illustrators in the

1950s and 1960s contained a cynical and satirical element that touched on both social and political topics, and it was felt that their work should be included. Indeed much of Feyer's best work has yet to be published as it was

Larter / Edmonton / Sun / 1978

considered far too scurrilous in its time as it often dealt with religious and sexual topics. Feyer had a rubber stamp made, which spelled out the word *horseshit* in Old English type. By using different coloured inks he would stamp the word on paper thousands of times to build images of cathedrals, popes, judges, statesmen, and any other subject that he felt warranted this specific treatment.

Several other individuals, although born in Canada, did little or no work here, establishing their reputations elsewhere. Trog, the well-known English political caricaturist, is the penname used by Vancouver-born Walter Fawkes. Boardman Robinson, the son of a Nova Scotia sea captain, worked exclusively in the United States.

He was also one of the few individuals who was capable of teaching cartooning. Three of his students from the Art Students' League, Edmund Duffy, Ross A. Lewis, and Jacob Burck won a total of five Pulitzer Prizes. More recently, Paul Szep, born in Hamilton, Ontario in 1942, became the editorial-page cartoonist for *The Boston Globe* in 1966 and won two Pulitzer Prizes over the next decade. Szep's debt to Duncan Macpherson is clearly recognized by his contemporaries.

In assembling these cartoons, we usually chose ones that deal with Canadian topics, even though our cartoonists comment on international affairs. We wanted to produce, not only a history of Canadian cartooning, but also a history of how Canadians have perceived themselves and their

LES ÉTUDIANTS EN GRÈVE

PAS DE PROBLÈME. JE LES TIENS PAR LES BOURSES.

LaPalme

Duplessis, of course, was an important figure in our history, but subjects for many others were not; any cartoons dealing with parochial or obscure individuals or topics were not included as they would require far too much explanation. This was found to be particularly true of Quebec cartooning, although a comprehensive study of Quebec cartooning alone would be very worthwhile.

French-language cartoons have been left intact with translation supplied where it was thought necessary. Often, because of various plays on words, however, some cartoons might only be understood fully by readers fluent in French. This cartoon by Jean-Pierre Girerd of La Presse is a good example. It pictures Quebec's education minister Jacques-Yvan Morin not concerned about students being on strike, as he holds their bursaries. But the French word bourses is also slang for testicles.

This book has been a long time coming—seven years to be exact. I remember along about year four, getting together with Duncan Macpherson, supposedly to discuss some aspect of the book, but really to consume numerous drinks. I mentioned that I didn't think I could face looking at one more drawing from 1924—not a terribly good

political institutions over the years. As an example, I spent an evening going through the work Robert LaPalme produced between 1945 and 1960. The majority of these cartoons were daily commentaries on the activities of Quebec Premier Maurice Duplessis. That one evening gave me a stronger sense of Duplessis the man than all the written material I had read on him over the years.

year for Canadian cartooning. Macpherson's reply was, as usual, prompt and to the point. "This is not the sort of project," said he, "that you give to Robert Thomas Allen and expect back the following Tuesday."

To a man, every working cartoonist in the country co-operated fully on this venture, and many became good friends in the process. Being a working cartoonist myself often proved advantageous as so much was already understood about the mechanics of cartooning. One problem that did arise, however, was how my own work should be handled. Therefore, at the outset, I left all of the final decisions relating to my material in the hands of co-author Peter Desbarats, and agreed to live with them.

Rosemary Shapley, Danyelle Fortin, Darrell Dickie, Sean Devlin, and Guy Badeaux all assisted in research at one time or another and their contributions proved invaluable. Among us, we looked at an estimated 800,000 cartoons in various newspaper offices, libraries, archives, and cluttered studios throughout the country. The final cartoons were chosen from an initial selection of 7,000. For the interested student or historian, copies of all the cartoons we considered and all papers relating to this project will eventually be filed with the National Archives in Ottawa.

Despite this exhaustive research, in-

Rodewalt/1978

formation on some of the earlier cartoonists is still quite sketchy. There may also be the odd unintentional omission. More information may exist, but because of the expense involved in tracing individuals and the final self-imposed deadline, some could not be pursued any farther. One mythical cartoon was supposed to have appeared in the Calgary *Eye-Opener*. It portrayed a small farmer standing in the middle of his vast wheat field during a blistering hail-storm. The cut-line simply reads, "God damn the CPR!" We checked through the existing microfilm of *The Eye-Opener*, but could not discover the cartoon. Perhaps this, and other such material might surface for possible updated editions of this book. In the meantime, I feel we have made a concrete beginning.

One of our first humour publications, *La Scie* carried the motto *Castigat Ridendo Mores* or "laughter corrects abuse." With this in mind, read on . . .

Terry Mosher
Montreal
June 26, 1979

Introduction

As many of us in childhood drew rough caricatures of teachers, parents and playmates, caricature was a private, family or tribal pastime from the beginning of human society.

Collections of prehistoric art often are punctuated by small figurines that seem to laugh or leer at the solemn faces outside the museum cases. Among the artifacts produced by the Salish Indians of British Columbia, for example, are small carvings that bear an uncanny resemblance to the little clay effigies of the great French caricaturist of the nineteenth century, Honoré Daumier, or to the papier maché studies of the contemporary British cartoonist, Gerald Scarfe.

Despite this ancient lineage, caricature as a consciously developed art is less than four hundred years old. It began in Italy as one of the lesser products of the Renaissance, stimulated, perhaps, by a national talent for elaborate insult. In the middle of the seventeenth century, the Italians described this distinctive art form by the term *caricare*, meaning to load or surcharge a line or drawing with exaggerated detail.

The term *cartoon*, in its modern sense, wasn't commonly used before it appeared in the English humour magazine *Punch* in 1843. Caricature as a popular political weapon reached maturity only in the 1700s, which came to be known as "the century of carica-ture." Political cartoons became regular newspaper features in the United States and Canada only in the 1890s, later in European countries. The political cartoon as we know it today, in newspapers and magazines, came of age in our own century. A product of art and journalism, it is now a conventional form of political and social comment. Presumably it will endure in its present form as long as newspapers remain important channels of political information and opinion.

Modern political cartooning began at roughly the same time as the political beginnings of the modern Canadian nation. With the founding of *Punch–The London Charivari* in England in 1841, the satirical magazine became a natural vehicle for political cartoons,

Blaine/Hamilton/Spectator

11

and several imitative and derivative magazines appeared in Canada.

Canadian cartoonists were relatively few in the nineteenth century compared with the numbers working in the United States, England and Europe. Their publications had to compete with imported journals and the expanding daily press, which only later would provide outlets for cartoonists.

Competition also produced benefits. American, British and French illustrated journals stimulated early Canadian cartoonists, who found in their emerging nation a rich source of political and social material.

Referring to their own country, American cartoon historians Allan Nevins and Frank Weitenkampf wrote that "political caricature can flourish in a new and immature country; social caricature cannot." In the nineteenth century, the political pressure needed to bring together independent British colonies into a new federation brought all of Canada's racial, cultural, social, and regional differences into focus.

The first Prime Minister of Canada, Sir John A. Macdonald, was a godsend for our cartoonists. His angular profile, ungainly figure, intemperate habits and the blatant corruption of nineteenth-century politics created a popular image that could be traced even by cartoonists with little natural talent for caricature.

In those days, artistic excellence was valued less highly than "punch." Cartoonists were expected to be direct and forceful. The body blow that could knock the wind out of a political reputation was appreciated more than deft brushstrokes. Many of the crude early

Canadian cartoons exhibit, to modern eyes, an enviably uninhibited joy of political combat.

Christopher Morley described American cartoons of the same era as a "remarkable panorama of sketches scrawled on the blackboard of America's schooldays." The Canadian slate was even more primitive, but many of the images have survived with unusual clarity. Many Canadian cartoons of a hundred years ago, with a few minor updatings, could be published in the newspapers of today; many of them

are, in fact, in revised versions, over and over again.

To a greater degree than in many older countries, Canada's image of itself has been shaped by political cartoonists communicating with mass audiences in the years when illustrated magazines and newspapers were at their most influential; there can be few other countries where the work of early political cartoonists has remained so relevant and vital because political and social preoccupations have remained so constant over such a long period of time.

Dominion Day

Something for the Father of Confederation to think over.

Sir John: "My dears, I congratulate you on the twelfth anniversary of your glorious victory. What can I do to add to your happiness?"

Mademoiselle Quebec (vigorously): "Mind your own federal business, and permit us to manage our local affairs to suit ourselves, according to the terms of union, that's what you can do, Sir."

Bengough/Grip/1879

Canadians are still occupied with the same political problems that beset their nineteenth-century ancestors: the differences between Canadians who speak English or French, competition for political power and wealth among various regions of the country, and the struggle for national identity of a new and relatively weak nation with large and powerful neighbours and allies.

Dennis O'Toole: "And what be you afther doin', Michael Fogarty?"

Michael Fogarty: "Je souis monsieur Fogarté, maintenant. Bedad! Dennis, I had to turn Frinch. Why, since the clargy have started diggin' at the Frinch in town, I didn't sell enough boots to pay for me water tax."

Charlebois/1914

"Of course it's difficult for outsiders to grasp the subtle complexities of the situation here in Quebec."

Aislin/Montreal/Gazette/1977

Enduring Canadian traits, major and minor, are clearly recognizable in early cartoons. Ambivalence about Canadian nationalism is evident. When they considered Canada, the pioneer cartoonists swung wildly between an embarrassingly adolescent boastfulness and an even more distressing inclination to exaggerate national shortcomings. The conflict between puritanical laws and backwoods drinking habits, illustrated in many cartoons about Sir John A. Macdonald, is still reflected in the political debates of provincial legislatures.

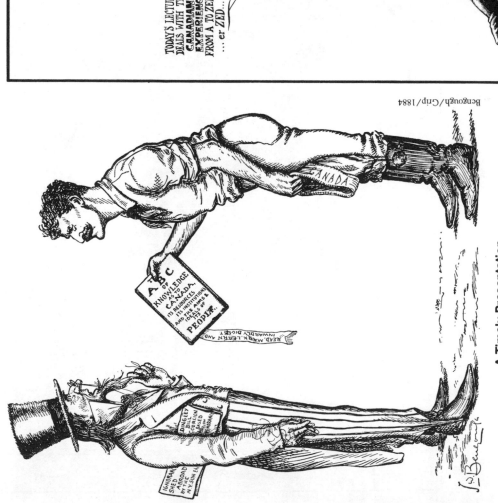

A Timely Presentation

Jack Canuck: "Neighbour, what chiefly ails you is ignorance. Accept this little work, which, if duly studied, will save you in the future from making yourself quite so ridiculous."

16

The Aid of a Glass!
Gordon B.: "Ah! You're right, Sir John; looking through *this* medium I do see factory chimneys in every town and village in the country."

Bengough/Grip/1881

"... the law was bound to catch up with him and his reckless habit of standing up with a glass in his hand to toast the Queen."

Norris/Vancouver/Sun/22 October 1969

Emerson described caricatures as "often the truest history of our times." The work of Canadian cartoonists forms an unorthodox history of Canada that completes and sometimes contradicts the conventional versions of this country's development.

William Murrell, the author of a recent history of American graphic humour, has contrasted "dry official or historical reports" with the work of cartoonists portraying "the situation as it appeared to a gifted and irreverent man in the street." In our own time, the skepticism of Canadian cartoonists has been provoked by the solemn politics of a struggle for national unity.

At a time when Canadians tend to take an apocalyptic view of current events and to ricochet between blind optimism and impotent despair about their national future, the heritage left by their cartoonists brings Canadians down to earth, restores their equilibrium and, most important of all, helps them to laugh at themselves.

Today, as in the Confederation period of the nineteenth century, a moment of decisive political struggle has thrown the character of the country into sharp relief, and political figures again have become somewhat legendary.

Luckily, this political ferment has coincided with the appearance of the

most gifted generation of Canadian cartoonists. The man best qualified to judge contemporary work is cartoonist Robert LaPalme who, since 1963, has directed Montreal's annual International Salon of Caricature and Cartoon. He has said that Canada, taking its relatively small population into account, has "the greatest and best group of cartoonists in the world."

Not only is the political scene rich in material for cartoons, but the larger Canadian newspapers have started to treat their cartoonists as independent commentators rather than simply as staff artists who draw funny pictures to illustrate editorials. The trend, established by Duncan Macpherson of *The Toronto Star*, has been toward giving cartoonists the status of columnists, whose every opinion does not necessarily reflect the judgement of the editorial pages.

This gradual but important shift in the cartoonist's role appears to have gone farther in Canada than in the United States, where cartoonists are usually tied more closely to the editorial policies of their newspapers.

"Of all artists," wrote William Murrell, "the cartoonist is closest to the people, and in America he is, almost without exception, one of them."

Canadian society has always been less egalitarian than that of the United

Racey/The Moon

A. G. Racey: Self-portrait

States. Birth, education and social connections have traditionally been important in Canadian business and politics, the two mainsprings of Canadian newspapers. They were often influential in the selection of editors, but cartoonists usually came from more ordinary levels of society.

Like the majority of journalists who worked in the same newspaper offices, cartoonists were rarely educated men. They earned salaries that enabled them to belong, at best, to the middle class. They also drifted from one newspaper to another, but perhaps less so than reporters because only the largest newspapers hired cartoonists and job opportunities were scarce.

Often the only difference between these cartoonists and journalists was the medium of expression, which wasn't always seen as an important distinction at the time. The difference becomes striking only with the passage of time as the men themselves fade into the past while their work survives. The cartoons often stay alive long after the dense columns of print have lost their relevance for all but a few historians. The words fail, but the pictures still speak.

"In each of us there is a trace of primitive, magic belief, which causes our imagination to obey the call of a picture more readily than that of words," claimed Werner Hoffman. He believed that, at its most cutting, caricature enacts the actual physical wounding of the victim. He was referring specifically to what he described as the "shrill, aggressive intensity" of English caricature during the Napoleonic Wars. While modern political cartooning is a muted and conventional echo of that art, enough of the savagery remains to distinguish it from other forms of journalism.

The difference between words and images lies at the root of the traditional hostility between editors and cartoonists. "Caricature means skepticism," Hoffman claimed, "doubt that logic and reason are capable of giving a full interpretation of the things of this world."

When Freud explored the relationship between wit and the unconscious, he distinguished between "harmless" and "calculated" jokes, describing the latter as a means of liberating primitive

or aggressive impulses in an acceptable form.

Speculations such as this provide insights into the special and often uncomfortable role of cartoonists in modern journalism. They often find themselves at odds with their editors because of the obvious difficulty of tailoring their own graphic form of expression to the literary conventions of written journalism. On modern newspapers serving mass audiences, editors no longer blindly serve as the partisans of a political cause. More often they seek to explain and reconcile differences. In their news and editorial columns, they try to make sense out of chaos and to indicate the way to rational compromise.

Cartoonists, however, thrive on confusion. The craziness of life is their inspiration. Their work illustrates the illogical contradictions of human behaviour, sometimes in a whimsical fashion but often by confronting us brutally with images of man's inhumanity. They don't want to reconcile political differences or social conflicts but to expose them.

Cartoonists are frequently as confused and cynical about their own role as about the world in general. One of

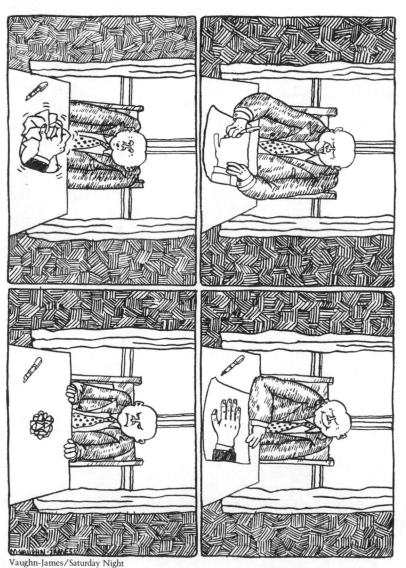

Vaughn-James/Saturday Night

the most famous British cartoonists of this century, Bill Pappas of *The Manchester Guardian*, once said that "cartoonists are just parasites—they knock everybody else." The contemporary American cartoonist Bill Mauldin has written that "every editorial cartoonist is a moralizer at heart, a sort of ink-stained, self-ordained preacher with a drawing board for a pulpit."

Once it was almost that simple. In the eighteenth century, the cartoonist or caricaturist created his design, often engraved his own plates and worked in close association with the print-seller who retailed them to the public. The cartoonist has never since enjoyed such independence or such direct access to the public.

In the following century, magazines and then newspapers brought the cartoonists' work to a mass audience. In the early stages, the slow process of engraving plates by hand on copper or wood preserved the independence of the cartoonist as artist-craftsman. His signed work was purchased and prominently displayed by editors as a special feature of their publications. When photo-engraving made it possible to transfer drawings quickly and cheaply to the printed page, cartoonists lost much of their independence. They became simply another part of the magazine or newspaper staff. Someone else owned the pulpit and often wrote the sermons.

Since then, cartoonists have struggled to work within a contradiction. The validity and ultimately the popularity of their cartoons depend on their sense of moral outrage, but unlike au-

thentic revolutionaries, they are supported by the established order. Even their victims generally applaud their work. Few contemporary cartoonists in Canada have ever received threats, bribes or even mild complaints from politicians; all have received many requests from politicians who want original cartoons of themselves to hang like battle trophies on their office walls.

The former Premier of Newfoundland, Joe Smallwood, a colourful politician often ridiculed by cartoonists, once admitted candidly, "I've never seen a cartoon about myself that I didn't like . . . cartoons, friendly or unfriendly, are so good that I'd hate to see them wasted on my opponents."

Well, better luck next time, Frank!

Franklin/Globe and Mail/3 November 1971

Smallwood after losing a close election

FREE LOAD By Feyer

EDITOR

Feyer/Maclean's/1 December 1952

If the cartoonists' savagery has been gradually tamed, the process contains the seeds of its own reversal. Newspaper editors will always try to domesticate their cartoonists, but they also realize that tame cartoonists satisfy neither their newspapers nor their readers. Newspapers need spirited cartoonists because, in the words of Draper Hill, the American cartoonist and cartoon historian, "like the carved figure-head at the prow of a ship, the editorial cartoon can be the leading edge of a newspaper's identity."

Thirty years ago, with some notable exceptions, Canadian cartooning had reached a pause in its development. Cartoons on editorial pages were, in the words of one cartoonist of that time, "polite little adornments." A Liberal government had been in power in Ottawa since before the Second World War under the leadership for most of that period of Prime Minister Mackenzie King, a rotund and seemingly lacklustre little man whom cartoonists found difficult to caricature. Some of the larger Canadian newspapers were experimenting with syndicated cartoons, in the belief that the time had passed when every newspaper of a respectable size had to have its own cartoonist.

Within a few years, changing political conditions and the influence of a new generation of cartoonists drastically altered this. New names, ideas and styles appeared on editorial pages as cartoonists explored new territories created by political events and changes in public taste. At a time when everyone least expected it, Canadian cartooning experienced a renaissance whose influence is still being felt in the 1970s when the leading spirit of this rebirth, Duncan Macpherson, can refer truthfully to his space on the editorial page of *The Toronto Star* as "a platform to yell back at the machine."

Peter Desbarats
Ottawa
June, 1979

1: Tracing the Background

The first Canadian cartoonists of the nineteenth century didn't start to work on a blank page. Their pens were influenced strongly by the cartoons that they saw in American and overseas publications.

The work of Canada's early cartoonists can be appreciated only if it is viewed against the background, even sketchy, of the development of political caricature and cartooning elsewhere, particularly in the United States and England.

By coincidence, one of the key figures in this process is also a minor figure in Canada's national history: Brigadier General George Townshend, third in command of the British forces that conquered Quebec in 1759.

In most respects, Townshend was a typical product of his time and breeding. Born in 1724, he was christened in honour of his godfather, George I. Toward the end of his career he was Lord Lieutenant of Ireland where, according to one historian, "George managed to achieve an unpopularity which would serve as a model for future Anglo-Irish relations."

As a young officer in battle, he saw a shell take off a Prussian colleague's head, spattering his own uniform. "I never knew," yawned Townshend, delicately brushing the debris from his tunic, "that Sheiger had so many brains."

Townshend could never resist the

1st Marquis Townshend by Thomas Hudson, 1759

cal caricatures on small panels about the size and weight of playing cards. From the start, they had an "amazing vent," according to the memoirist and letter-writer Horace Walpole, who reported in 1756 that Townshend "adorns the shutters, walls and napkins of every tavern in Pall Mall with impromptu caricatures of the Duke of Newcastle, William Duke of Cumberland, etc."

His work was popular because it was not only clever but novel, and every modern cartoonist is, to some extent, the descendant of this unpleasant aristocrat of keen eye, acid wit, and sharp pen.

The tides of war in 1758 brought Townshend up the St. Lawrence River to Quebec where he became the first cartoonist in what eventually would be known as Canada. General James Wolfe, the leader of the expedition, was younger than Townshend and, in Townshend's opinion, his inferior in every other respect. Soon after they arrived before the walls of Quebec, Townshend was circulating caricatures of Wolfe among his fellow officers.

During the seige of Quebec before the decisive battle on the Plains of Abraham, General Wolfe was meticulous about sanitation in the British camps, ordering new toilets to be dug every three days. Townshend drew cartoons about his commanding officer and the latrines.

temptation to be clever, but what distinguished him from contemporary wits was a gift for caricature. Many people found the combination detestable; many more thought it was irresistible. Starting in 1756, Townshend and the London artist-engraver Matthew Darly produced a series of politi-

Wolfe's mania for latrine inspection is ridiculed

Townshend/McCord Museum/1759

"If we live," threatened Wolfe, according to the later recollections of one of his other officers, "this will be inquired into."

Townshend replied by criticizing Wolfe's tactics and threatening to bring him before a Parliamentary inquiry when they returned home. It wasn't necessary. The General died on the field of battle, mercifully spared the sight of Townshend accepting the surrender of the French forces.

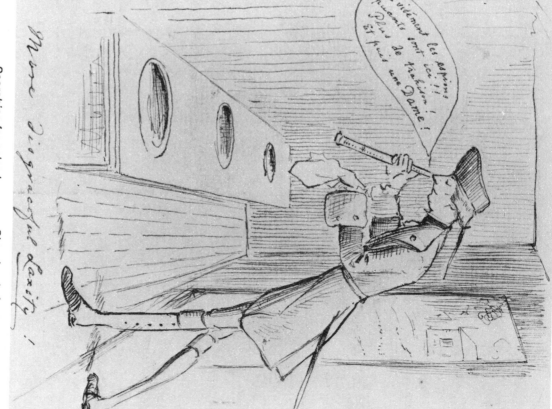

Searching for spies becomes Cherchez la femme

Townshend/1759

Even in death, Wolfe wasn't safe from Townshend's pen. During the seige, the General occasionally had invited women prisoners to dinner and his gallantry wasn't unnoticed by Townshend. Camp gossip was illustrated after the battle by a Townshend drawing entitled: "The Irish Venus Mourning General Wolfe."

After the British victory, Canada was briefly at the mercy of this autocratic cartoonist until he returned to the seige of London high society.

"He has dealt grotesque cards from house to house, from Town's end to Town's end," according to a letter in *The Public Advertiser* in 1765. "Is there a great general of highest rank and most eminent military abilities? If the size of his person as well as face should be larger than ordinary, this malicious libeller at three strokes of his pencil scratches out his figure in all the ridiculous attitudes imaginable."

Townshend's work stimulated and fed a British craving for political caricature. In 1766, a caricature on the American Stamp Act sold 2,000 copies in four days despite a price that was equivalent in today's money to at least several dollars.

Caricature also became a popular pastime for many amateurs who lacked the social connections and talent of the venomous Brigadier. Lessons in etching and caricature were given by Mary Darly as part of the print-seller's business. In 1763, she and her husband published a little guide to the art, engraved by herself, which included examples of the work of her pupils and clients, including Townshend.

In the introduction to her book, Mary Darly attempted to define the difference between what was then called *character*—the portrayal of human types in art—and caricature. "Caricature is the burlesque of

Character," she explained.

The distinction that Mary Darly tried to make between caricature and art has troubled artists, cartoonists and critics ever since. Townshend's sketches, for instance, appeared toward the end of the career of William Hogarth, whose work portrayed a variety of English types and often conveyed a political or moral message. Some say that

Hogarth's work approached caricature, but the artist himself saw a clear difference.

"I have always considered a knowledge of character, either high or low, to be the most sublime part of the art of painting or sculpture," he wrote in 1758, "and caricature as the lowest, indeed as much so as the wild attempts of children."

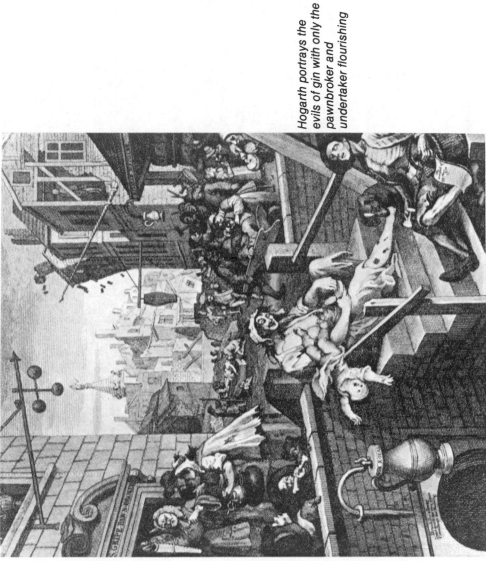

Hogarth portrays the evils of gin with only the pawnbroker and undertaker flourishing

Gin Lane by Hogarth, 1750-51

23

Even Hogarth, however, was fascinated by the graphic shorthand of the clever caricaturist. He recalled seeing "a famous caricature of a certain Italian singer that struck me at first sight, which consisted of a straight perpendicular stroke with a dot over it."

The debate about the artistic merits of caricature, and how to classify caricature that approaches art or art that smacks of caricature, has continued for centuries. The experts can't even seem to agree on what many consider to be the oldest surviving caricature—a sketch of Ikhnaton, the father-in-law of King Tutankhamen, drawn about 1360 B.C. The fact that Ikhnaton was reputed to be an extremely ugly man has left the experts in doubt as to whether the work is a caricature or a portrait.

The ancient Egyptians also drew men as animals, but for religious, not comic, purposes. From the classical periods of Greek culture have survived burlesqued figures in terra cotta and on vases, taken from popular comedies. Even the gloom of Romanesque and Gothic architecture was relieved by gargoyles and other whimsical figures on stone capitals and wooden miserere seats that still communicate a sense of man's ingenuity and playfulness.

It wasn't until the seventeenth century, in Italy, that drawings appeared that are recognizable instantly as the ancestors of modern caricature. Artists began to distort human features for deliberate effect, as in the work *On the Human Physiognomy* produced by Giovanni Battista Della Porta. His contemporaries, the brothers Agostino and

Annibale Caracci, drew caricatures of types encountered in Bologna and published them in 1646. Annibale Caracci's caricature sketchbook is the earliest example of this kind of personal work recorded.

Twenty years later, the sculptor Bernini introduced the art from Italy to France and became "probably the first artist to pass on to posterity caricatures of particular individuals."

Pier Leone Ghezzi is said to be the first artist to make a living from portrait caricatures. By the time of his death about 1755, caricature and political satire were growing in popularity throughout Europe.

The first modern cartoon campaign was launched by the English and Dutch against the absolutism of Louis XIV of France. The prints, made in Holland and sold cheaply, stimulated a vast production of cartoons toward the end of the seventeenth century.

Martin Luther drew caricatures, believing that he "maddened the Pope" with his pictures. In turn, his enemies caricatured his relations with Katharina von Bora.

In 1740, the English printmaker, Arthur Pond, helped to pave the way for Townshend when he published an album of twenty-five caricatures by different artists. By that time, the new art was popular enough to have its own detractors. In *The Spectator* of November 12, 1712, an essayist defended *The Dignity of Human Nature* by attacking "... these burlesque pictures which the Italians call *caricaturas*: where the art consists in preserving, amid distorted proportions and aggra

vated features, some distinguishing likeness of the person, but in such a manner as to transform the most agreeable beauty into the most odious monster."

James Gillray was the first master draughtsman to devote himself to the regular production of political satires. Gillray was born in 1757, the year before Townshend sailed for Quebec, and died in 1815, insane and alcoholic. For twenty years, he was England's favourite caricaturist, creating a body of work that has inspired cartoonists ever since.

Like many cartoonists of more recent times, Gillray is survived by a multitude of drawings but few details about his life. Only sixty years after his death, one of his biographers, Thomas Wright, was struck by the lack of contemporary records.

"The man who bequeathed such admirable materials for the reconstruction of his contemporaries," he complained, "strange as it may seem, was treated by the chroniclers of his own time with so much reserve that it is difficult to seize on the satirist as he may have presented himself personally to the world."

From the records and personal recollections that did survive, Wright succeeded in constructing a verbal portrait of the caricaturist at work that many modern cartoonists will recognize. Unlike Townshend, who mixed socially with the aristocratic politicians whom he caricatured, Gillray was a soldier's son trained as an artist in England's new Royal Academy, founded in 1768. He was forced to sketch his subjects on the run, on small cards that he carried in his pockets. Two centuries later, the great New Zealand-born cartoonist, David Low, used the same method in the same London streets.

"The pieces of card," according to Wright, "are of the ordinary playing size, and are pencilled on both sides with clear, slight outlines—which are full of character—of the notorieties he sketched in the House of Commons, in the lobby, in the parks, in Bond Street, at the club windows, and wherever the subjects for his satire might be encountered."

Gillray lodged for much of his productive career with his publisher, the print-seller Mrs. Humphrey, who exhibited his plates in her shop window at the corner of Bond Street and St. James's Street.

A French émigré in London in 1802 wrote that "they are fighting here to be the first … to see Gillray's latest caricatures."

"The enthusiasm is indescribable," he testified, "and when the next drawing appears, it is a veritable madness. You have to make your way through the crowd with your fists."

The cartoons that Gillray produced were politically savage. Unlike modern cartoonists, Gillray had no hesitation in portraying the personal weaknesses and the private affairs of political figures, including royalty. He was sickened by the French Revolution and produced a flood of cartoons vilifying the French and Napoleon. One memorable cartoon commemorating the Revolution shows a typical French

A View in Perspective.

The Zenith of French Glory; — The Pinnacle of Liberty.
Religion, Justice, Loyalty, & all the Bugbears of Unenlightened Minds, Farewell!

Gillray/12 February 1793

The execution of Louis XVI in Paris on 21 January was followed on 1 February by a declaration of war against England.

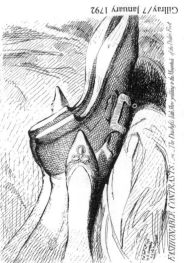

Gillray/7 January 1792

FASHIONABLE CONTRASTS; — or, — The Duchess's little Shoe yielding to the Magnitude of the Duke's Foot

Fashionable Contrasts: Or, The Duchess's Shoe yielding to the Magnitude of the Duke's Foot

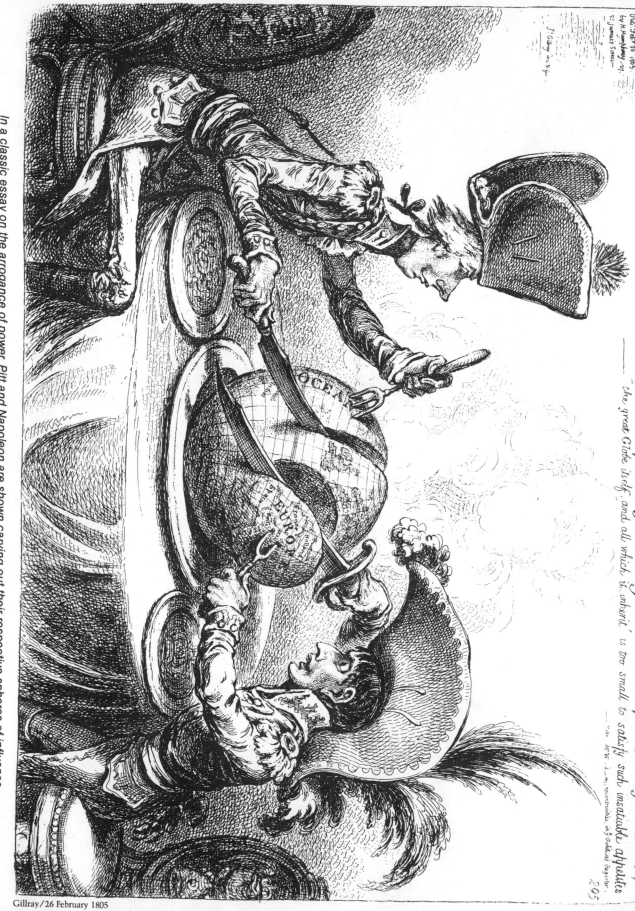

The Plumb-pudding in danger; — or — State Epicures taking un Petit Souper.
— "the great Globe itself, and all which it inherit," is too small to satisfy such insatiable appetites

Gillray / 26 February 1805

In a classic essay on the arrogance of power, Pitt and Napoleon are shown carving out their respective spheres of influence.

"Poor France! The branches are broken but the trunk still holds."

Daumier/Charivari

family sitting down to consume a meal of recognizable parts of the human body.

Gillray and his contemporary, Thomas Rowlandson, another graduate of the Royal Academy, were the professional artists who perfected what the amateur Townshend had begun. As the first cartoonist to systematically use speech balloons and horizontal banks of framed pictures, Rowlandson was one of the precursors of the comic-strip artist. Like Gillray, his personal life was tragic. He gambled and drank away an inheritance as a young man and died in penury.

About the time that Charles Philipon started his weekly *La Caricature* in 1830, Paris succeeded London as the liveliest centre of political caricature. Philipon launched *Le Charivari* in 1832, a daily publication that promised to supply its readers with a new cartoon in every issue.

One of Philipon's artists was Honoré Daumier, the great master of

Daumier/Charivari/9 February 1871

This has killed that.

social comment with and without political content. During his lifetime,
Daumier produced more than 4,000
lithographs as well as paintings, drawings, woodcuts and sculptured caricatures. In Daumier's case, the distinction between art and caricature
became meaningless.

Daumier was imprisoned for six
months in 1832 for his political cartoon *Gargantua*, a caricature of King
Louis Philippe. Philipon, an artist as
well as a publisher, also spent time in
jail, for drawing this caricature of Louis
Philippe showing his head being transformed by stages into a pear.

Political cartooning was transformed
during this period by a technical development that enabled cartoonists to
reach mass audiences: the invention of
lithography about 1795 by Alois Sene-
felder, a Bavarian. Caricatures no
longer had to be laboriously hand-
engraved on wood or metal plates, but
could be drawn directly on the printing
surface.

The first lithographed political cartoon appeared in 1829. The new pro-

ductions were immediately popular in
Europe and the United States. Currier
and Ives in the US ultimately produced
more than 80 political cartoons by lithography, with some editions running
up to 100,000 copies.

In 1841, *Punch—The London
Charivari* made its first appearance,
destined to develop the weekly political cartoon into a magazine institution
and to long outlast all its early competitors. In July, 1843, *Punch* published a satirical drawing of a ragged
crowd inspecting cartoons or sketches
of work commissioned to decorate the
Houses of Parliament. It was entitled
Cartoon No. 1 and from that time on,
the word was used more and more

John Leech's
Mr. Punch

Leech/Punch

Philipon/Charivari/1832

Tenniel/Punch/1890

Tenniel's famous cartoon at the time of Bismark's retirement

Dropping the Pilot

Tenniel/Punch/August 1857

The British Lion's vengeance on the Bengal Tiger

often to designate political cartoons.

While Daumier railed against social injustices in France, John Leech produced for *Punch* a series of drawings of London street urchins—*Portraits of Children of the Mobility*. Leech drew 3,000 pictures for *Punch* and critic John Ruskin credited him with producing "the definition and natural history of our society, the kind and subtle analysis of its foibles."

Sir John Tenniel, the illustrator of *Alice in Wonderland*, was chief cartoonist at *Punch* for more than forty years and is remembered, apart from *Alice*, as the developer of the lion as the symbol of the British Empire.

By the Victorian era, British cartooning had moved so far away from the lusty savagery of the previous century that Gillray's work was regarded with embarrassment. "Our respectable ancestors had not the least notion of what we call decency," chirped a Victorian cartoon historian in 1877. "Many of [Gillray's] works could not now be exhibited."

The start of cartooning in Canada coincided with the appearance of *Punch* and other early comic journals in London. The first North American magazines quite openly copied these models, in appearance, literary style and cartoons. Comic journals in the United States such as *American Punch* and *Southern Punch* also showed the same influences as *Punch in Canada*. In the second half of the nineteenth century, as British cartooning abandoned the vicious snarl for the genteel smile, cartoonists in the United States developed a tougher and more distinctive style. Because this was more compatible with the tenor of Canadian politics, the influence of US cartooning rapidly became dominant in this country, at least for political cartoons.

29

The first cartoon to be published in the territory now known as the United States was by Benjamin Franklin and appeared in his 1747 pamphlet *Plain Truth*. It was a woodcut, as was the first North American newspaper cartoon published in *The Pennsylvania Gazette* in 1754: a drawing of a broken snake with the motto *Join or Die*. These bore little resemblance to modern cartoons and their early appearance did not establish cartooning as an element of American journalism at that time.

Nothing comparable, however, could have been published in the French colonies of North America during the same period because these colonies lacked even a printing press.

The War of 1812 against Britain produced a burst of political cartoons, many of them by William Charles, a Scotsman who was the first widely acclaimed political cartoonist to work in the United States. Yet American cartoon historian Frank Weitenkampf has counted only 78 political caricatures issued before 1828, while cartoons in newspaper and magazines appeared even less frequently.

The introduction of lithography in 1822 triggered an explosion of cartooning in the United States. Lithograph cartoons on separate sheets enjoyed fifty years of popularity. More than six hundred prints from that period have survived.

Among the artists who pioneered lithography in the United States was an émigré from Quebec, Napoleon Sarony. He was born in Quebec in 1821 and was said to have done signed

In 1848, the engraver Frank Leslie arrived in the United States from England; in 1855, he launched *Frank Leslie's Illustrated Newspaper*. Leslie discovered and employed Bernard Gillam, originally from England, and the German-born Thomas Nast and Joseph Keppler, three of the most prominent cartoonists during the decades when weekly magazines enjoyed undisputed primacy.

Harper's Weekly began in 1857 and *Vanity Fair* in 1859. Joseph Keppler began to publish *Puck* in English in 1877, after starting with a German-language version, and by the early 1880s, its circulation had risen to 80,000. *Puck, Judge* and the original *Life*, launched in 1883, became the great triumvirate of late nineteenth-century humour magazines in the United States.

Magazines remained the most im-

Franklin/1754

work for lithographic houses from the age of thirteen. In 1838, he issued nine small lithographic cartoons for a political allegory entitled *A Vision of Judgment* which portrayed statesmen as animals.

portant vehicle for political cartooning until the last decade of the nineteenth century. After the *New York Evening Post* cartoon of 1814, no cartoons appeared in US newspapers until 1839. Newspaper cartoons were still an oddity in 1867 when the *New York Evening Telegram*, a sensational newspaper printed on pink newsprint, attracted even further attention by publishing a large front-page cartoon every Friday.

At that time, technical difficulties prevented the widespread use of cartoons in newspapers. Their production was too expensive and too slow for newspapers whose pages were filled with narrow columns of dense type and occasional woodcuts.

The first fully illustrated newspaper in the United States was *The New York Daily Graphic*, launched on March 4, 1873, by a company organized by George E. Desbarats, the Montreal publisher, and backed by Canadian and American investors. Using a photo-engraving process developed by the engraver William Leggo of Quebec, and employed successfully by Leggo and Desbarats in *The Canadian Illustrated News* in Montreal since 1868, the *Daily Graphic* reproduced cartoons in the 1870s and the 1880s until, after successive changes of ownership, it succumbed to competition in 1889. American cartoon historian William Murrell has stated that the *Daily Graphic* "taking advantage of the latest steam engraving and printing equipment . . . created a new field in journalism."

The second half of the nineteenth

century is remembered today as the classical period of political cartooning in the United States, with Thomas Nast as its greatest practitioner.

Nast was born in Bavaria but came to the United States at the age of six. Leaving school at fifteen, he went to work as an illustrator for *Frank Leslie's Weekly*. Nast joined *Harper's Weekly* in 1862, quickly becoming the most popular and influential political cartoonist in the United States.

In the 1870s, his cartoons against the municipal regime of William Marcy "Boss" Tweed in New York had a political effect that no contemporary cartoonist could hope to match.

"Stop them damn pictures," howled Tweed. "I don't care so much what the papers write about me. My constituents can't read. But, damn it, they can see pictures."

Tweed once offered Nast half a million dollars to "study art" in Europe. At one time, the cartoonist was said to be earning almost as much as the President; but the man who gave the popular image of Santa Claus to the world, and the Republican elephant and Democratic donkey to American voters, was almost penniless toward the end of his life. As a charitable gesture, President Theodore Roosevelt appointed him Consul General to Ecuador in 1902,

but within six months Nast had died of yellow fever at the age of 62.

Among the readers of *Harper's Weekly* during Nast's early years on the magazine was a young compositor in a small town near Toronto. *The Whitby Gazette* had no method of reproducing the cartoons that John Wilson Bengough drew in his spare time, but he sent one of his drawings to Nast with a letter filled with admiration for his "elaborate and slashing full-page attacks."

Nast replied with a letter and an etching of a self-caricature. Years later, when the two men met for the first time at the Canadian Club in New York, Nast probably still looked much the same—"a dapper little man," as Bengough remembered him, "with a hooked nose, bright eyes, a curled moustache and a beard trimmed to a fine point at the chin."

The young Whitby compositor, by then, had become Canada's first great political cartoonist.

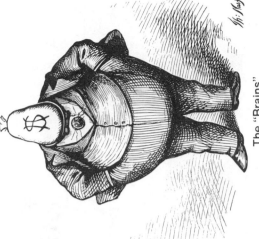

The "Brains"

"WHO STOLE THE PEOPLE'S MONEY?"—DO TELL. N.Y.TIMES.

'TWAS HIM.

Little Guys – Big Guys

In the cartoonists' history of Canada, the durable hero is the average tax-payer, the little guy; the perennial vil-lain is the average politician, the big guy. They march together through the years, the big guy's hand in the little guy's pocket, antagonistic but insepara-ble.

The two main characters of the car-toonists' history represent opposing sides in a form of class warfare. Their persistence, decade after decade, indi-cates that the conflict is very real al-though governed by convention and tempered with humour.

Canada has escaped civil war, revo-lution, and severe social unrest; but it has suffered from political corruption, social and economic inequality, and injustice toward its weaker citizens. Cartoonists have been closer to these aspects of our society, and more sensi-tive to them, than have many of the writers and journalists who have left behind records for historians.

"Congratulations!"

Bengough/Grip

Franklin/Globe and Mail/14 June 1976

"Bring out your dead... Bring out your dead..."

Their pictorial record enables us to see our ancestors struggling to change the inequities of Canadian society, or reluctantly conforming to them; it almost allows us to hear the sounds of this effort: the tolerant chuckles, the sarcastic laughter, occasionally cries of outrage, and sometimes the speechless silence of sheer astonishment at the audacity of human predation.

The little guy has dozens of disguises, but is always instantly recognizable. No character is closer to the cartoonist's heart, and everyone recog-

nizes himself, to some extent, in the little guy who is dwarfed and victimized by human institutions.

Always conventional in his own time, the symbol of mediocrity, the little guy's power to move us sometimes gains strength over the years. The clenched fist and menacing club of J.W. Bengough's brawny nineteenth-century Canadian, in toque and jackboots, expresses a sense of pioneer democracy that still attracts and saddens us. We have lost much of that naive confidence in the strength of public opinion.

Fitzmaurice/Vancouver/Province

Mallette/Globe and Mail/1978

... THREE SHIRTS, TWO SWEATERS, FLEECE LINED THERMAL UNDERWEAR, TWO PAIRS OF PANTS, FOUR PAIRS OF WOOL SOCKS, ASSORTED SCARVES, HATS, EARMUFFS AND TOQUE, A HOT WATER BOTTLE, DOWN FILLED ARCTIC TUNDRA PARKA AND MITTS, THERMAL LINED BOOTS ... BUT I DON'T WANT TO OVERDO.

By the early years of our own century, Bengough's self-reliant "Canuck" had been replaced by the milquetoast that J.B. Fitzmaurice drew for *The Vancouver Province*. Fitzmaurice's "Mr. Common People" became one of the prototypes of the little guy of our own time, as did Archie Dale's character representing "The People" who appeared in *The Winnipeg Free Press* in the 1930s, with his straw boater on the back of his balding head and his comic-strip dog to cheer him up.

In 1945, Robert Chambers combined the bowler and spectacles of his conventional little guy with the physique and club of Bengough's "Canuck," but it was only to create, as the caption said, a "Giant for a Day." The next day, after the election, the little guy shrank back to size and cringed in the palm of the politician's hand, a furled umbrella his only weapon.

Kyle/The Moon/1900

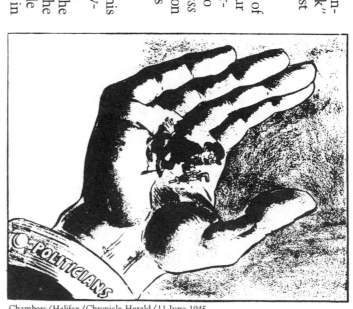

Giant for a Day

Chambers/Halifax/Chronicle-Herald/11 June 1945

Back to Normal

Chambers/Halifax/Chronicle-Herald/12 June 1945

In recent decades, John Collins of *The Gazette* in Montreal clothed his little guy in a barrel beneath an over-sized bowler and christened him "Unowho"; Albéric Bourgeois of *La Presse*, before Quebec's quiet revolution of the 1960s, discovered his little guy in Baptiste, an impudent habitant farmer; Duncan Macpherson's version of the same character in *The Toronto Star* is a pudgy, bespectacled tramp; Len Norris of *The Sun* in Vancouver created the supreme suburban slob in George Phelps; and virtually every other contemporary cartoonist has a character at the tip of his pen, often nameless, to embody the little guy in his own heart who jeers, rages, and thumbs his nose at the system.

34

Bourgeois/Montreal/La Presse

Macpherson/Toronto/Star/1976

Collins/Montreal/Gazette/2 April 1979

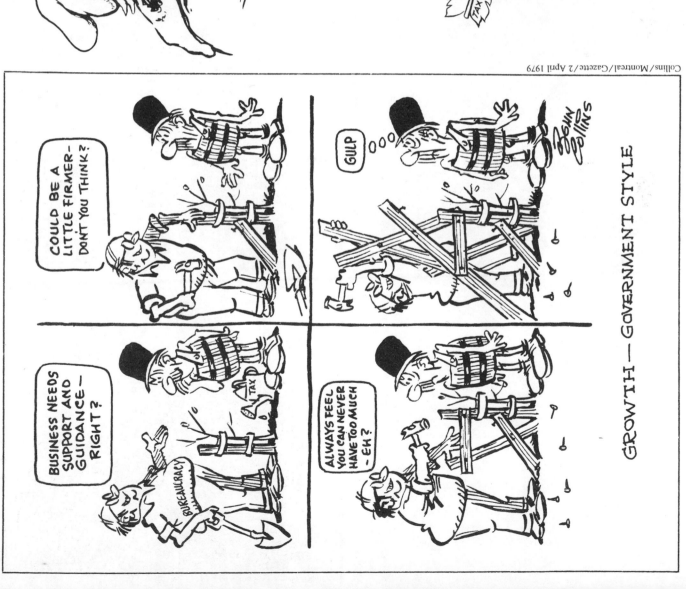

GROWTH — GOVERNMENT STYLE

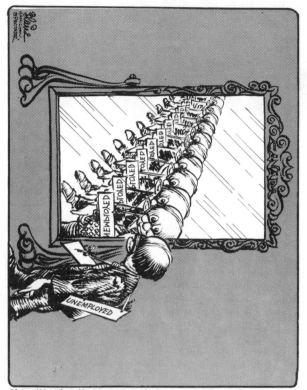

Blaine/Hamilton/Spectator

Norris/Vancouver/Sun/16 March 1968

"Buy gold! Buy gold! Nag, nag! Nag, nag!"

Bierman/Victoria/Times/4 September 1975

"...I hope you noticed we are 0.3 per cent less deep in it..."

"...No, I'm sorry. I don't have any opinions on capital punishment, censorship, drug addiction, women's lib, minority government, Quebec, food prices, professional hockey or American take-overs...I've given up thinking about anything for a year..."

In his own heart, the little guy cherishes an image of the big guy that finds expression in a companion cartoon convention. Sometimes these figures are as anonymous as the "Men of Weight in Parliament" that Edward Jump drew for *The Canadian Illustrated News* in 1872; more often, they are as identifiable as the political "godfathers" that Serge Chapleau drew in 1973 to portray Quebec's party leaders. In the cartoonists' history, the big guys of politics are idle and venal egomaniacs, careless of the public good

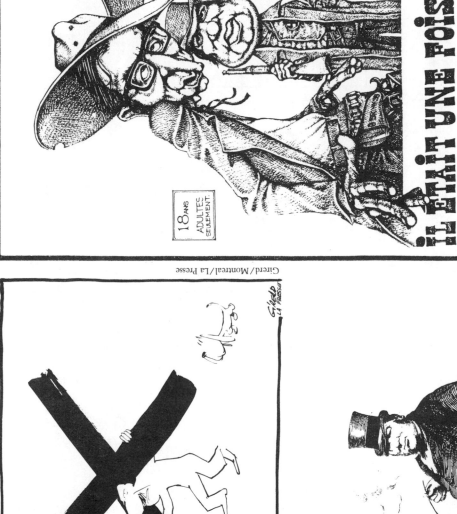

Chapleau/Perspectives/1973

Elections as "Spaghetti Westerns"

Girerd/Montreal/La Presse

Jump/Canadian Illustrated News/18 May 1872

Men of weight in Parliament

38

and energetic only in pursuit of their own narrow interests. The durability of this caricature reveals a belief among cartoonists that their sacred duty is to wage a never-ending assault upon the dignity and public reputation of all politicians.

This eternal campaign is so single-minded and even simple-minded that its persistence would be boring in the extreme were it not for the fact that

The Official Opposition

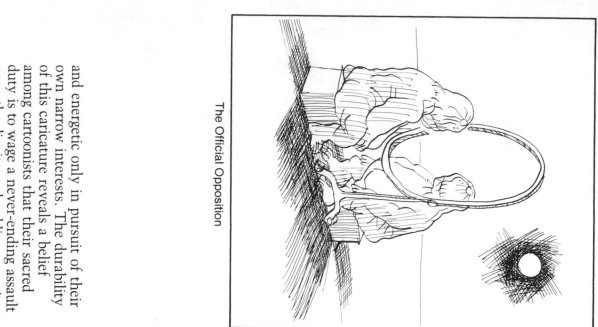

Whalley/Phap

Alberta's Premier Aberhart salutes.

Cameron/Calgary/Herald/26 June 1937/Provincial Archives of Alberta

Berta/Toronto/Sun

Monks/Windsor/Star

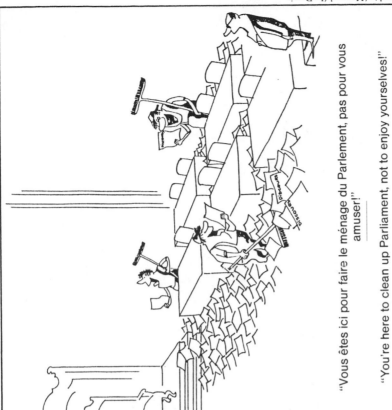

"Vous êtes ici pour faire le ménage du Parlement, pas pour vous amuser!"

"You're here to clean up Parliament, not to enjoy yourselves!"

politicians prove, over and over again, that the political grotesques of the cartoons are often more authentic than the more conventional portraits produced by journalists and historians.

In the long run, the little guy, the perennial loser, always wins in the cartoonists' version of history because, like Berthio's cleaners amid the litter of parliamentary debate, he always enjoys the last laugh.

SO WHAT ELSE IS NEW?

"...Gentlemen, modern research has found that the average taxpayer's clothes now contain 14 pockets..."

2: J.W. Bengough

J. W. Bengough: Self-portrait

Bengough/Grip

According to his 1923 obituary in Toronto's *Globe*, where he had once worked briefly, the townspeople of nearby Whitby still remembered how "Johnny" Bengough had made "funny chalk drawings of local characters on the board fences of the town."

Bengough doesn't refer to this in his own autobiographical writings, but he does recall a childhood interest in art and an early ability to sketch. When he won a prize for schoolwork a perceptive teacher gave him a book entitled *The Boyhood of Great Artists*.

It probably contained little encouragement for a youngster growing up in an obscure corner of the British Empire. Small-town Ontario in the nineteenth century was neither the place nor the time to dream of an artistic career of any kind, although technically, it would have been easier to become another Rembrandt in Whitby than a newspaper cartoonist.

When Bengough left school in his teens to become a compositor for the local newspaper, neither *The Whitby Gazette* nor the largest newspapers of North America and Europe had the facilities to publish political cartoons. These had only just started to appear in magazines and up to that time, the history of illustrated magazines in the Canadas had been brief and discouraging. When Bengough was born in 1851, it was only fifty-nine years since the first printing press had been estab-

lished in Upper Canada. Louis Roy, originally from Quebec, issued the first number of the *Upper Canada Gazette* in 1793 at Niagara, then the capital of the province. It wasn't until the end of the first decade of the nineteenth century that newspapers were established on a firm basis in Niagara, Kingston and York, as Toronto then was called.

The first comic journal to publish political cartoons on a regular basis was *Punch in Canada*, launched in Montreal on New Year's Day, 1849, by J.B. Walker, a designer and wood engraver who had emigrated to Montreal from Ireland with his father in 1842. Walker was only eighteen years old

when he went into business as the publisher and illustrator of *Punch in Canada*, promising in his first editorial statement to combine "spice and spirit" to produce a "first volume palatable to the taste of all."

Walker drew a full-page cartoon for each issue of the biweekly. Within three months, it claimed a circulation of 3,000. In the following year, it moved to Toronto and began to publish every week but the magazine lasted less than two years.

Although Walker occasionally adopted the *Punch* character from the British comic journal, and tried to adapt him to local conditions, his themes usually were taken from Canadian politics and his treatment was lively and imaginative.

The subject of many of his cartoons was the popular movement to annex Canada to the United States, which Walker strenuously opposed. Brother Jonathan represented the United States in most of Walker's cartoons but in October 1849, he drew a group of Canadian politicians as "naughty children" attempting to pawn the British flag to a pawn-shop keeper entitled Uncle Sam. This was one of the first appearances of this figure in a Canadian cartoon following its debut in an 1834 lithograph cartoon in the United States.

Punch in Canada also expressed racial attitudes with a nineteenth-

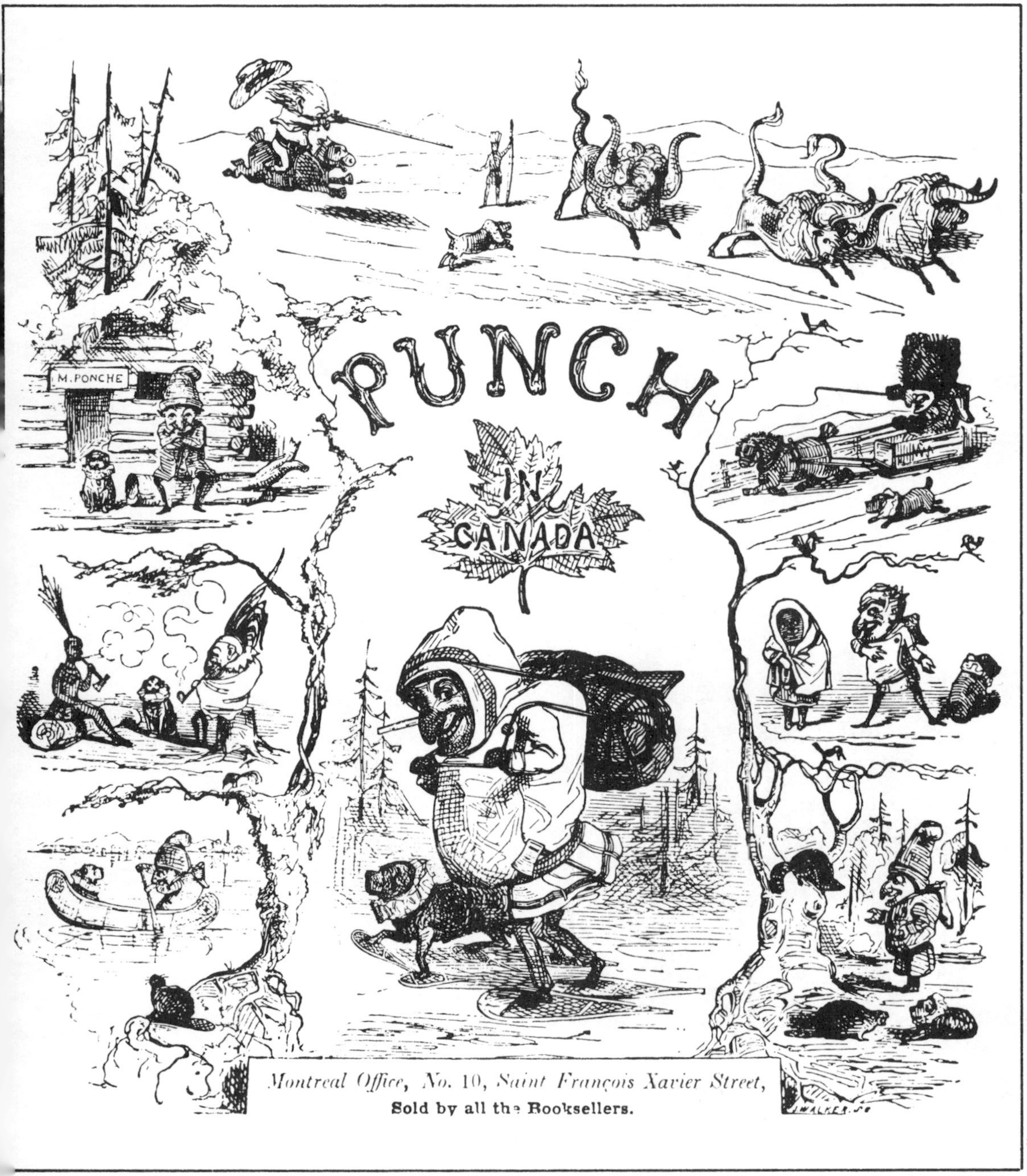

Walker/Punch in Canada/1849

Punch (in Canada) will hereafter appear every fortnight

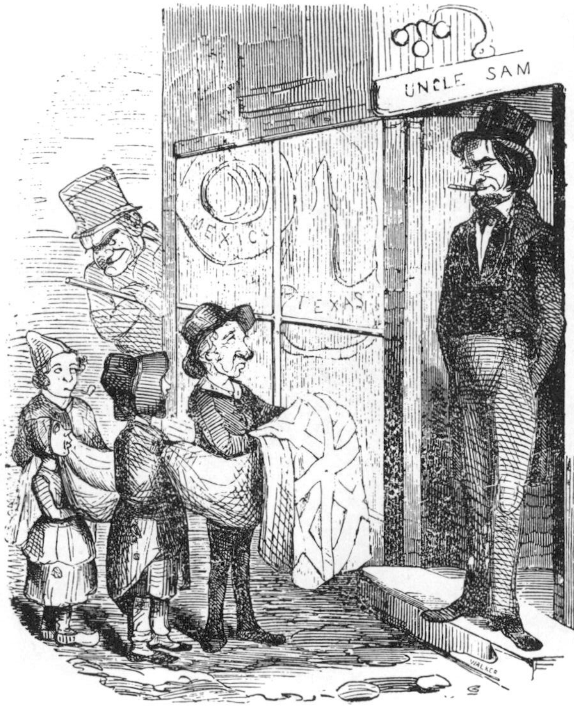

Walker/Punch in Canada/20 October 1849

Little Ben. Holmes

And some naughty children attempt to pawn their mother's pocket-handkerchief, but are arrested by policeman *Punch*, who was stationed "round the corner."

century frankness that brings the modern reader up short. In an 1849 cartoon, *Townships Colonization – A Settler*, a huge farmer of Quebec's Eastern Townships is looking skeptically at a diminutive Frenchman being presented to him as a prospective settler. The farmer scoffs, "Why there's lots of them chaps here already – in the mashes."

When Bengough reproduced this cartoon in his 1866 *Caricature History of Canadian Politics*, he explained that "the comparison of the newly-arrived Frenchman to the frogs is a time-honoured joke . . . ".

42

The antagonism between English and French was illuminated glaringly in 1849 when an English-speaking mob burned and looted the House of Parliament in Montreal to protest a law compensating victims of the 1837 Papineau rebellion. *Punch in Canada* reflected the bitterness of racial strife in Montreal during that period in cartoons that are among the most vitriolic expressions of racism ever produced in Canada. English-French rivalry has remained an enduring theme of Canadian cartooning ever since, but never

with the crude intensity of the early nineteenth century.

Punch in Canada was the first of a number of comic and literary journals published in English in the nineteenth century, with such titles as *Nonsense, The Jester, The Wasp, Diogenes, Stadacona, The Gridiron, The Sprite, The Free Lance, The Bee, The Dagger, Paul Pry and Grinchuckle*. Not all of them were humorous. *The Grumbler*, when it appeared in 1859 or 1860, was said to be "the first successful literary paper Canada had and the best," published in opposition to *The Poker* which was "well named for it had no more wit or humour in it than a poker."

The 1837 Rebellion (illustrated later)

Tiret Bognet/Le Monde Illustré/1890

The Houses of Parliament, Montreal.

Taken while burning on the night of the 25th of April 1849; it having been fired by an outraged and Loyal British populace, three hours after the Governor-General the Earl of Elgin, gave his assent, in the Queen's name, to the Bill for rewarding the rebels.

Walker/Punch in Canada/5 May 1849

Rebellion Losses.

Aha! dey have giv me *une poche* full of money for lose my vife, and I vould have sell her myself any time for two dollare!

Walker/Punch in Canada/1849

The history of these publications is often obscure. Most of them rarely used cartoons and when they did, the quality of the work was uneven and the artist is often unidentified or unknown.

In the late 1860s, cartoons were a feature of *Diogenes*, published by Walker and edited by George Murray, an Oxford graduate who was known in his day as an accomplished scholar and poet. The question of annexation to the United States remained a favourite subject with a cast of characters that included Brother Jonathan or Cousin Jonathan and John Bull or Mrs. Britannia. Canada was usually represented either by a demure young thing entitled "Miss Canada" or by a strapping and aggressive young man labelled "Young Canada."

A typical cartoon published in *Diogenes* in 1869 showed two women seated on a bench in a garden while nearby, picking his teeth with a penknife, lounged a flashy but obviously disreputable American. Miss Canada is indignantly denying Mrs. Britannia's suggestion that she might have encouraged the advances of her "cousin Jonathan."—"Certainly not, mamma. I have told him we can *never* be united."

In the same year, Young Canada appeared in a cartoon in Walker's *Grinchuckle* kicking Uncle Sam down the stairs of a structure entitled Dominion House, with a grinning John Bull on the doorstep, saying, "That's right, my son. No matter what comes, an empty house is better than such a tenant as that!"

From its start in 1868, *The Canadian Illustrated News*, and its French-language edition, *L'Opinion Publique*, published political cartoons that reached a comparatively wide audience. Many of these early cartoons were unsigned, but in the early 1870s, the magazine started to publish the signed work of Edward Jump, an itinerant caricaturist who came to rest in Mon-

Uncle Sam: "I can almost hear them singing 'The Star Spangled Banner' in Ottawa, Be gosh."

McConnell/Toronto/Daily News

Young Canada: "We don't want you here!"

John Bull: "That's right, my son. *No matter what comes*, an empty house is better than such a tenant as that!"

Walker/Grinchuckle/23 September 1869

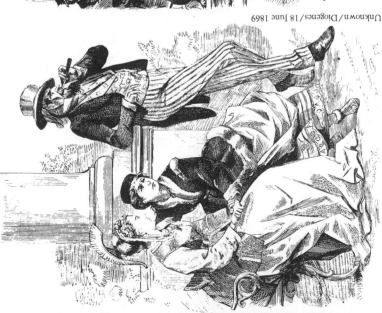

A Pertinent Question.

Mrs. Britannia: "Is it possible, my dear, that you have ever given your cousin Jonathan any encouragement?"

Miss Canada: "Encouragement! Certainly not, Mamma. I have told him we can *never* be united."

Unknown/Diogenes/18 June 1869

treal for a few years between jobs in various parts of the United States.

Jump was born in France about 1831 and worked in San Francisco from 1856 to 1868. It was said that he got his start in graphic work by making labels for whisky bottles in San Francisco.

Jump drew a curious cartoon mocking the panic of the San Francisco earthquake entitled *Earth Quakey Times* that was, in the opinion of one critic years later, "a fair example of Jump's peculiar talent ... extracting and exaggerating the humorous aspects of a tragic situation."

About 1868, Jump was in Washington rooming in the same house as the celebrated author Mark Twain. He married a member of a visiting French opera company and soon became an established artist. At one time in Washington, he was said to be earning an income of $500 a week, mostly from his work as a portrait painter. Jump's French origin and, perhaps,

the influence of his new wife were probably instrumental in persuading him to move to Montreal where, from 1871 to 1873, he became an illustrator and cartoonist for *The Canadian Illustrated News* and *L'Opinion Publique*.

He was the most accomplished caricaturist to work in Canada up to that time. One of his most popular creations was a series of sketches in which he dressed Canadian politicians in the costumes and characters of classical heroes. Prime Minister John A. Macdonald, for instance, was *The Many-Counselled Ulysses*. The inscription written in Greek at the bottom of the cartoon and a quotation from Pope's translation of the *Iliad* indicates that Jump was a cultured man as well as a deft caricaturist.

Later in the 1870s, Jump returned to the United States where he worked for Frank Leslie's magazines in New York. He died some years later in St. Louis; he was said to have committed suicide.

In the same year that Jump arrived

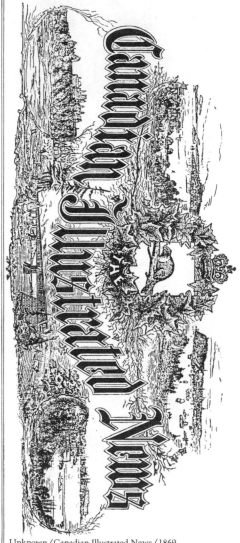

Unknown/Canadian Illustrated News/1869

Canadian Illustrated News

MONTREAL, SATURDAY, OCTOBER 30, 1869.

[SINGLE COPIES, TEN CENTS
$4 PER YEAR IN ADVANCE.]

in Montreal, "Johnnie" Bengough travelled a much shorter but more significant distance when he moved from Whitby to Toronto to join the local reporting staff of the *Globe*. Even as a compositor and occasional contributor for *The Whitby Gazette*, he was a compulsive caricaturist whose work passed from hand to hand around the town.

Every week, he purchased *Harper's Weekly* at the local bookstore to study the cartoons of Thomas Nast. "Nast had the field of political cartooning practically to himself for years," Bengough recalled, "and must have inspired thousands of boys as he did me. "I was full of enthusiasm over the fall of Boss Tweed and the Ring, and of course ready to endorse the prevalent opinion that this desirable result had been brought about chiefly by the Cartoonist's weapon."

While still in Whitby, the young newspaperman drew a cartoon "as nearly as I could in the Nast manner," showing the members of the Tammany Ring standing in a circle around the artist and paying him obeisance with uncovered heads. He sent the drawing to the editor of *Harper's Weekly* and received a note praising "the accuracy with which Mr. Nast's touch was reproduced." Later, Nast himself sent a complimentary letter and an etched self-caricature.

Because *The Whitby Gazette* had no method of reproducing cartoons, Bengough's first attempt at journalism was literary. Much to the annoyance of the composing room foreman, he would disappear into the editorial offices upstairs from time to time to write articles for the paper. At one point, he wrote a serial in daily installments entitled *The Murderer's Scalp, or the Shrieking Ghost of the Bloody Den* to fill space in a special four-page bulletin published for a time by his newspaper to meet its readers' demands for news about the Franco-Prussian War.

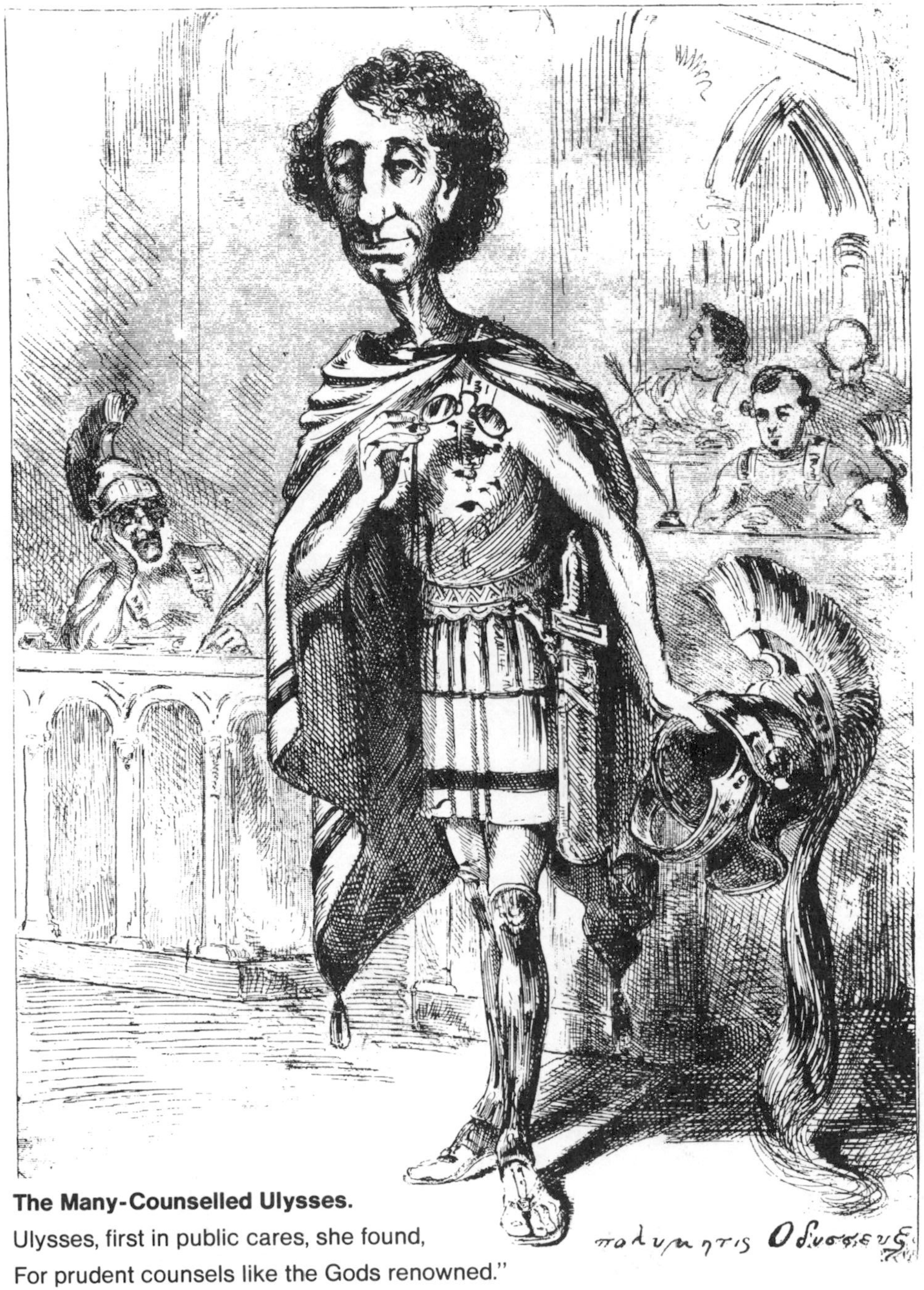

After he was hired as a reporter by *The Globe* in 1871, Bengough continued his artistic development at evening classes organized by the Ontario Society of Artists. He left before the end of his first term because "the copying of the placid countenances of Greek Deities in plaster casts proved too much for me."

More intriguing was the countenance of "Old Jimmiee" – Senator James Beattie, proprietor of *The Leader*, a Conservative newspaper. On summer afternoons, "Old Jimmiee" would establish himself in an armchair in front of his office on the shady side of King Street, "ready to receive the greetings of the faithful." Bengough decided that "Old Jimmiee" was "an irresistible subject . . . and on a memorable day, I produced a pencilled portrait."

The event was memorable for Bengough because it introduced him to lithography. Sam Beattie, the old senator's nephew and business manager of the newspaper, brought the drawing to a local lithographer who had it reproduced.

"The ease and accuracy with which the reproduction was done struck me with amazement," Bengough wrote, "but further, it gave me an idea."

The Many-Counselled Ulysses.

Ulysses, first in public cares, she found,

For prudent counsels like the Gods renowned."

(Pope, *Iliad*, II,205,6.)

Grip, a comic journal edited and illustrated by Bengough, made its first appearance on May 24, 1873.

"There was no great furor over the initial number," confessed Bengough, but unknown to him at the time political life in Canada was about to be rocked by the Pacific Scandal. Prime Minister John A. Macdonald had been re-elected in 1872 but the Liberals soon uncovered evidence of a $300,000 contribution to the Conservatives by Sir Hugh Allan of Montreal, the head of a railway syndicate anxious to build a new line to the Pacific coast.

"The whole country was at once aflame with interest and excitement," Bengough recalled, "and an absorbing theme adapted to keep Grip going for many issues had thus been supplied at the right moment.... The circulation increased rapidly, and the permanent success of the publication was assured."

Bengough quickly discovered why publications reproducing cartoons by lithography were rare at that time. It was one matter to reproduce a few hundred copies of a drawing on single sheets from a lithographic plate but it was quite another to attempt to use the same process for the rapid production of thousands of copies. After starting with lithography, Grip switched to wood-engraving, the process then used to reproduce Nast's cartoons in Harper's Weekly, and ultimately to zinc etching, which copied the original by a chemical process, as in lithography, but produced a durable plate that could be used alongside the hand-set type of the day.

During the twenty-one years of Grip's existence, Bengough was editor and virtually its only illustrator. From time to time, he would alter his style to create the impression that Grip had other artists on its payroll. Cartoons dealing with current political issues in Quebec, for instance, were done in what Bengough described as "a slashing 'French' style of handling" and signed L. Côté.

Soon after these cartoons started to

Bengough/Grip/7 November 1874

Mercier transferring the Crown

Bengough/Grip

appear, Bengough had a visitor at the *Grip* office. Thumbing through the current issue and discovering the new Quebec cartoons, the visitor became immensely interested.

"L. Côté," he cried. "That fellow can draw; no offence, you know, but you really ought to model yourself on his style."

Bengough resisted the temptation to confess his subterfuge, and the real identity of L. Côté remained hidden until Bengough revealed it years later in his memoirs.

Cartooning was only one of Bengough's talents and interests. One year after *Grip* appeared, he made his debut as a public speaker in Toronto's Music Hall at the corner of Church and Adelaide Streets. His main purpose was cartooning for his audience; the speech was only to provide a framework for his drawing. He commissioned a "literary genius" who had written comic pieces for the defunct *Grumbler* to string together a few phrases for him. Although the *Globe* critic the day after the performance said that the audience was "somewhat surprised at the ability displayed in the literary portion of the essay," the drawings were the main attraction. Bengough produced fifteen to twenty sketches on an easel on stage, using black crayons on white newsprint, and the caricatures were auctioned at the end of the speech.

The success of this first *Chalk Talk* encouraged Bengough to make a nine-week tour of Canada "from Rat Portage, Ont. to Victoria, BC, and thirty-four entertainment-starved communities in between." He continued

his public speaking for more than forty years, in all parts of Canada as well as the United States, Australia and New Zealand.

His routine, in smaller Canadian communities, was to arrive well before the hour of the speech to leave time to meet his sponsors and to discuss the "local hits," as he called his subjects. Bengough would then contrive to meet and study them. Sometimes he would work from a photograph, although he found this difficult, and he recalled once doing a sketch for an Ontario audience working only from a verbal description.

"As a general rule," he wrote years later, "the 'victims' enjoy the fun as well as their neighbours."

The violent exceptions to this seemed to occur mainly in the Maritimes. At Pictou, one of the "local hits" showed up at the railway station the next day with a club, only to discover that the cartoonist had left town on an early train. At Yarmouth, which Bengough reached by stage-coach, a retired sea captain accused a fellow citizen of helping Bengough to caricature him and the two men fought their way through the plate glass window of the shop where they had happened to meet.

Some of Bengough's speeches merely enabled him to display his virtuosity as a cartoonist, but in many others his sketches were used to help communicate a moral or political message. Bengough was an enthusiastic proponent of women's suffrage, prohibition, tax reform, proportional representation and free trade. His repertoire also in-

cluded a number of speeches for school children. Most of his texts today seem either pedantic or juvenile but it's difficult to evaluate them in isolation from their original context and without Bengough's lively presentation.

Bengough's interest in political questions made him a prominent member of the Public Ownership League and the Canadian Peace and Arbitration Society. He was President of the Single Tax Association and tested his political theories by serving as a Toronto alderman. In some respects, he was a Victorian predecessor of the politically aware journalists and cartoonists who appeared in Canada in the 1960s. His obituary stated that he had a "profound distrust of accumulated wealth and of the manufacturing class in general."

When Sir John A. Macdonald died in 1891, Bengough drew a cartoon which would be considered scandalous today, with its specific political criticisms, but his personal feelings perhaps were better expressed in a verse published at the same time:

And he is dead, they say!
The words confound and mock the
    general ear.
What! Can there be a House and
    Members here,
And no John A.?

Bengough had once called Sir John A. Macdonald "my chief stock in trade." He was fortunate not only to have such a colourful and distinctive politician in power during most of his career, but to work in opposition to him.

Bengough met the Prime Minister only once, during a brief interview in the Parliament Building at Ottawa. He wrote later that "the quality that impressed me most during those few minutes was his air of shrinking bashfulness!"

Nothing could have been less typical of the characteristics shown by the Macdonald of Bengough's caricatures. It was Bengough's ungainly, boozy and corrupt Macdonald that engraved itself

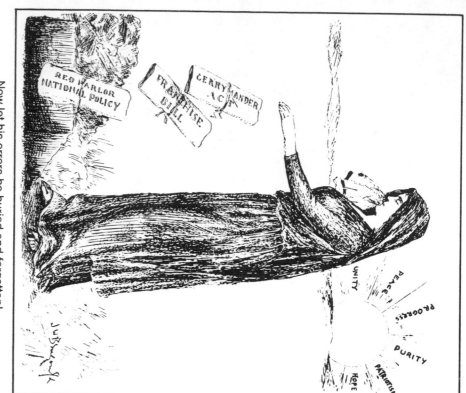

Now let his errors be buried and forgotten!

Bengough/Grip/1891

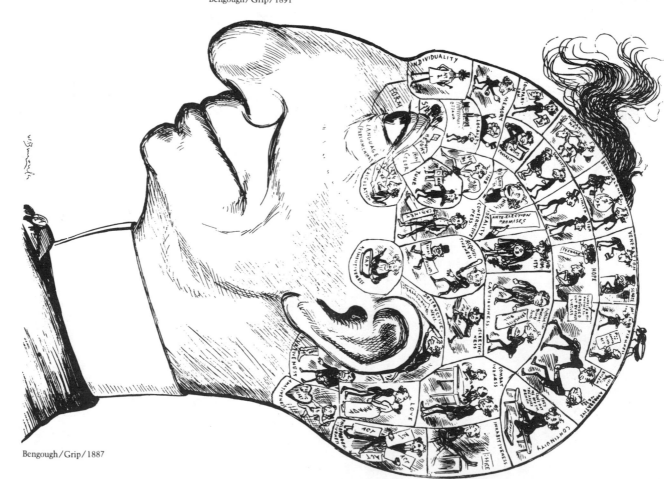

Phrenological Chart of the Head of the Country

Bengough/Grip/1887

Bengough/Grip/7 February 1874

Pity the Dominie! or Johnny's Return.

Canada: "Here's our Johnny for you again, Mr. Mackenzie. You'll find him apt enough, but frankly, Sir, he's full of mischief!"

on the public mind, particularly in the days before newspapers published photographs of politicians.

During his few years in Canada, Edward Jump had portrayed Macdonald as a sleepy if somewhat crafty idiot. Bengough, over a much longer period, developed Macdonald's frizzy hair, long nose and large mouth into national symbols. No other political figure came to life so vividly beneath Bengough's pen; no other cartoonists, even those who were far better draughtsmen, were able to capture Macdonald's style and mannerisms as effectively. The Prime Minister still seems to live, breathe and hiccough in Bengough's cartoons.

Often he was a showman, a carnival barker in high boots, checked pants and polka-dot shirt, his pockets stuffed sloppily with pamphlets and papers bearing satirical titles.

Macdonald's head on a schoolboy's body was ridiculously apt in a cartoon about the Conservatives returning in Opposition to the House of Commons under a new Prime Minister as if they were boys meeting a new teacher.

"Our Johnny" was presented to Prime Minister Mackenzie by Miss Canada, who warned Mackenzie: "You'll find him apt enough, but frankly, sir, he's full of mischief."

Year after year, John A. declaimed, winked, leered and cavorted through Bengough's cartoons as if he were a scrawny W.C. Fields. Even when he is pictured receiving his appointment to the Privy Council at the hands of Queen Victoria, Bengough's Macdonald can't refrain, in the act of bowing to the Queen, from reaching behind with his foot to kick a Liberal opponent in the stomach.

On the wall above Macdonald's head, in this cartoon, there is a sign reading *Privy Council–Great Statesmen Only Admitted.* Bengough's cartoons are filled with these editorial asides. A playbill advertising and picturing "John A. Macdonald in his original Shakespearian characters" is accompanied, at the bottom of the wall, by a small notice explaining that "owing to the expense of this engagement, prices will be raised all over the country."

Bengough's cartoons of Macdonald contain not only an element of good humour, but something approaching grudging admiration, despite the overt political intent of the cartoons. The classic Pacific Scandal cartoon of the Prime Minister with his boot on Miss Canada's prostrate figure, a bottle in his pocket, and a speech balloon emerging from his mouth bearing the words, "These hands are clean!" is as funny as it is savage.

Another familiar Pacific Scandal cartoon in the same vein shows Macdonald confronting a startled Mackenzie with his hands in his pockets and

Sir John's Crowning Victory.

Bengough/Grip

the remark, "I admit I took the money and bribed the electors with it. Is there anything wrong about *that?*"

Bengough wasn't afraid, on occasion, to let Macdonald laugh at him. After the Conservatives were returned to power in the 1878 election, Macdonald was shown carrying a "clean sweep" broom and a pre-election cartoon by Bengough that had predicted a Macdonald victory.

Grip, the talking raven, from his perch atop the artist's easel, promises to "retire from this prophecy business after this!"

Other politicians in Bengough draw-

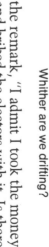

Whither are we drifting?

Bengough/Grip/16 August 1873

Bengough/Grip

The New Sir John.

Fine man, but hasn't so good a face as the old Sir John.

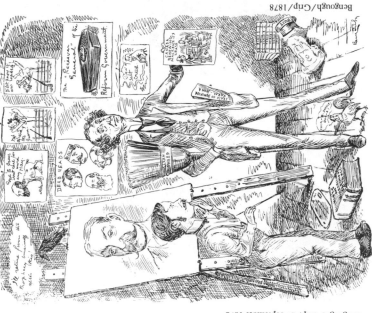

Bengough/Grip/1878

"I don't know, but it seems to me this picture of yours, my prophetic friend, needs a little 're-adjustment,' don't it, hey?"

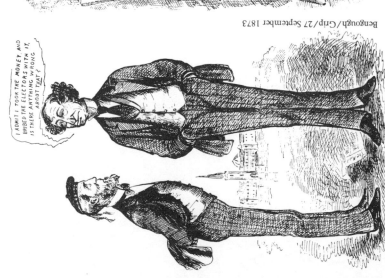

Bengough/Grip/27 September 1873

I ADMIT I TOOK THE MONEY AND BRIBED THE ELECTORS WITH IT, IS THERE ANYTHING WRONG ABOUT THAT?

"We in Canada seem to have lost all idea of justice, honour and integrity.—*The Mail*, 26 September.

ings usually play stock characters and assume symbolic postures. He was never able to breathe life into Alexander Mackenzie, the dour Scottish stonemason from Sarnia who succeeded Macdonald as Prime Minister in 1873. Bengough supported Mackenzie politically, but it was Macdonald who supported Bengough as a cartoonist. He seemed cast by nature for every role that Bengough imagined for him.

Subsequent Prime Ministers failed to provide the same inspiration for Bengough, as he confessed in a cartoon that showed *Grip* attempting to caricature "The New Sir John"–Sir John

Abbott who led the country briefly after Macdonald's death. The final blow to Bengough as a cartoonist was the victory of his own party in 1896. The following year, he produced the cartoon on the next page, showing the Liberal leadership of Wilfrid Laurier reconciling all the competitive factions in Canada. English and French were portrayed as cherubic youngsters perched on Laurier's shoulders in Bengough's most unmemorable cartoon, proving once again that cartoonists make poor propagandists.

Bengough severed his connection with *Grip* after Macdonald's death to

join *The Montreal Star* as cartoonist. He later worked briefly in Toronto for *The Globe* but his most productive years as a cartoonist were behind him. He died in 1923 at his home in Toronto, an unfinished anti-tobacco cartoon on his drawing board.

The New York Herald once described Bengough as "the greatest cartoonist on this side of the continent." He was hardly that. Bengough was influenced by Thomas Nast, but he never approached Nast's draughtsmanship or sense of composition. His cartoons often looked crude and even childish and many of his ideas were

51

copied from others. Their lasting quality lies in their zestful portrayal of Canadian politics during the early decades of Confederation and Bengough's forthright portrayal of the political, racial, and social antagonisms that divided Canadians at that time. A surprising number of the cartoons are still understood instantly by Canadians despite the disappearance of many of their principal characters from public memory.

"Grip's humour is his own," wrote Principal G.M. Grant of Kingston's University of Queen's College in 1886, in the preface to Bengough's Caricature

"HOME, SWEET HOME."

Bengough / Globe / 1 September 1897

History of Canadian Politics. "It has a flavour of the soil. It is neither English nor American. It is Canadian."

Grant described Grip as "the most honest interpreter of current events we happen to have." The honesty and authenticity of Bengough's work has kept it alive for Canadians who, to this day, form an appreciative audience for his cartoons.

"Grip not only generally hits the nail on the head but sometimes hits like a blacksmith," wrote Principal Grant, "and we belong to a race that loves to see a blow well struck."

Sketches for the
Caricature of a Nation

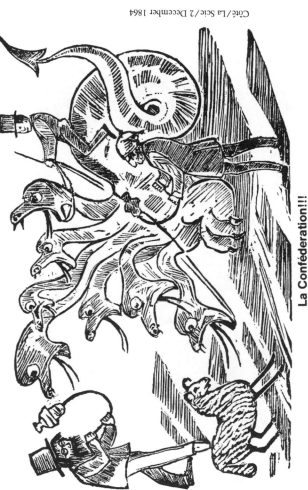

La Confédération!!!

Wafting incense on the many-headed monster of Confederation to make it agreeable to Quebec, the Lamb.

Côté/La Scie/2 December 1864

All the main features of national attitudes in modern Canada were sketched crudely in the first cartoons published in the nineteenth century. Canadians and their cartoonists since then have merely completed the national caricature in more detail.

Regular publication of cartoons in humorous journals began in the 1840s, a decade after disturbances in Upper and Lower Canada had threatened the peace and orderly development of the colony. The subsequent dispute over compensation for losses suffered in the rebellion in Lower Canada widened divisions between English and French. This antagonism inspired many of the first cartoons published in English-language journals and, in a less virulent form, it continues to provide the basic material for many contemporary cartoons.

French-Canadian cartoonists began to express the attitudes of their own group at a time when Confederation was being proposed as a system that would permit both English and French to collaborate in the development of a new nation. The scepticism and apprehension of many ordinary French-speaking Canadians was clearly expressed in some of these cartoons, now strikingly prophetic.

Within a few years of Confederation, political efforts to enlist Quebec support in projects of national development as well as during elections, provided a wealth of material for cartoons. Religion at this time was a complicat-

54

ing factor, with Catholic and Protestant factions constantly vying for political influence. This is the only major theme of nineteenth-century Canadian cartooning which has faded into the background in recent decades.

Inspired by cartoonists in the United States, and working with an abundant supply of native subject matter, the early Canadian cartoonists attacked political corruption with a directness that was then an accepted convention, but often seems libellous by modern standards. Politicians, including Prime Ministers, were often

The Peacemaker.

And the little boys who fought about their fathers.

Bengough/Grip/20 May 1876

Dundreary's "Widdle!"

Wh-why d-does the dog waggle the t-tail? B-because the d-dog is stwonger than the t-tail—otherwise the t-tail would wag-waggle the d-dog!

Bengough/Grip/10 November 1883

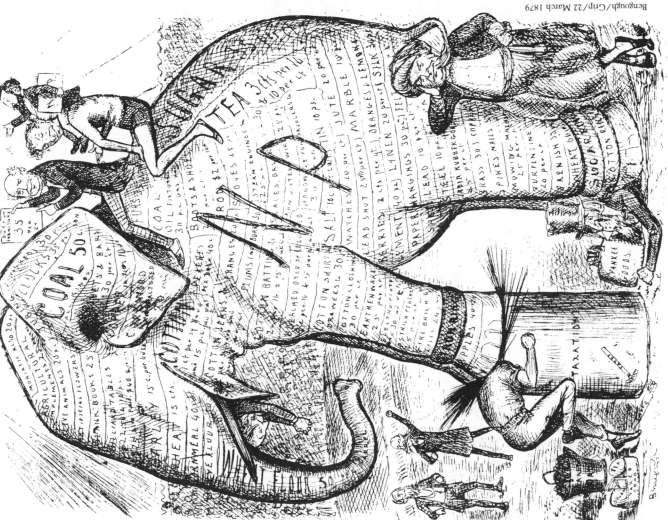

In the "Ring" at last!

The only satisfying picnic, after all!

shown slicing up huge patronage pies while patronage lists, railway contracts, and other incriminating documents spilled from their pockets.

An American import that failed to adapt itself to Canada was the elephant, which J.W. Bengough introduced to represent Prime Minister John A. Macdonald's national policy. Bengough was a great admirer of cartoonist Thomas Nast, the inventor of the Republican elephant in the United States, but he found that borrowed ideas and imitative cartoon styles had limited appeal in Canada, an axiom that still holds true.

The Confederation generation was fiercely nationalistic and protective about the new homeland, particularly

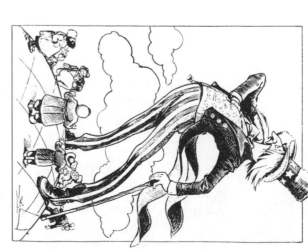

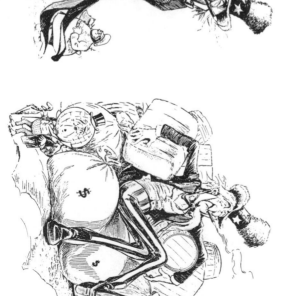

against American interference. Canada was often portrayed as an innocent young virgin in constant danger of being seduced by Brother Jonathan from south of the border. In Canadian cartoons, Jonathan or Uncle Sam was often shown as a crafty and somewhat disreputable Yankee carpetbagger. Britain, on the other hand, was Britannia or John Bull, generally benevolent sponsors of Canadian independence.

Pipe Dreams

1: A respectable old party was one day seen to enter a disreputable joint and to indulge freely.

Chic / Moon / 1901

2: He first sees himself as the greatest nation on the face of the earth.

3: Now he thinks he owns the largest, most powerful and finest navy that has been.

4: He next dreams that he controls the world's money and other markets.

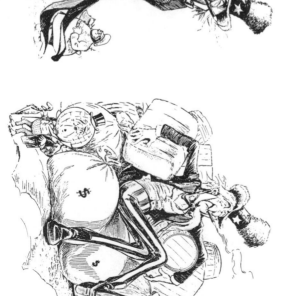

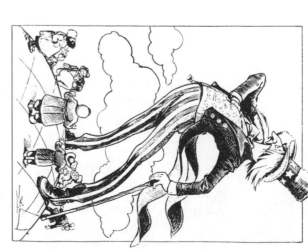

7: Now he thinks his army the finest, his daughters the most beautiful, his colleges the best, his statesmen, writers, artists, actors, athletes and possessions the greatest, his merchants the wealthiest and his constitution the grandest in the world. He gathers the world into his grip and is reaching for the other planets, when

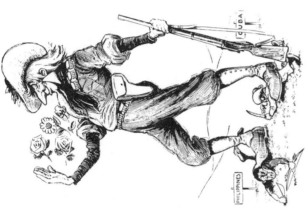

6: He dreams that he has licked all creation, and throws bouquets at himself.

5: He imagines that John Bull comes cringingly to his feet and begs permission to exist. His greatest ambition is realized.

8: He awakens and finds that he is the cause of much amusement.

In more aggressive moments, Canadian cartoonists drew their new nation as "Jack Canuck," brawny, virtuous, straight-talking, and something of an overgrown Boy Scout. He may have been naive, but he can be remembered wistfully today as the embodiment of an early and idealistic spirit of nationalism.

On domestic matters, cartoonists often produced a conflicting picture of a society oppressed by an unhealthy alliance of businessmen and crooked politicians. Liquor oiled the wheels of many political machines in those days and stimulated innumerable cartoons about the evils of drinking and the absurdities of liquor laws.

Quebec already was being caricatured as the unruly member of the national family, a domestic allegory that cartoonists would elaborate endlessly in subsequent years. French and English interests clashed in the new territories of western Canada, aggravated by two rebellions of French-speaking Métis, whose

Mackay/Canadian Illustrated News/1876 or 1877

Coming Home from the Fair.

Bro. Jonathan: "Adieu, fair Canada. I have long adored you, but never so much as now. May I not hope some day to claim you as my own?"

Canada (*kindly but firmly*): "Never. I hope always to respect you as my friend and well-wisher, but can never accept you as my lord and master. Farewell."

Willson/Canadian Illustrated News/12 August 1882

A Chip of the old Block.

Britannia: "There, John, I'm proud of him. A regiment or two of such fellows would do us credit in the East. Eh?"

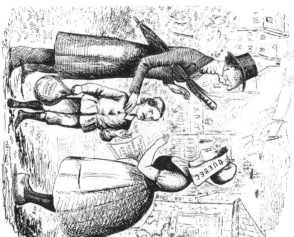

Bengough/Grip/12 August 1882

Madame Quebec's Wild Boy.

Mme Quebec: "It's so *kind* of you to take him, Sir John! He's nearly brought me to ruin!

Sir John: Have no fear, Madame; under *my* tuition he shall learn prudence, economy, industry, and thrift!

French and Indian ancestry and Roman Catholic religion attracted the interest and sympathy of many people in Quebec. The racial enmity that inspired cartoonists after the 1837 rebellions in Upper and Lower Canada flared up again after the Métis leader Louis Riel, elected to Parliament but

Something's got to go soon!

Bengough/Grip/29 August 1885

A Riel Ugly Position

Bengough/Grip/29 August 1885

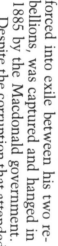

60

Bengough/1885

Berthelot/Canard/1885

forced into exile between his two rebellions, was captured and hanged in
1885 by the Macdonald government.

Despite the corruption that attended
the transcontinental railway and land
development schemes of Macdonald's
administration, the first decades after
Confederation saw the development of
a strong sense of national pride and re-

sentment of outside interference, particularly by the United States. This
emerging sense of nationalism, with all
its internal contradictions and adolescent boastfulness, was revealed with
embarrassing honesty in the works of
our first cartoonists. They show us as
we really were, not as we would often
like to remember ourselves.

3: Henri Julien

The only rail route from central Canada to the Canadian West, in 1874, was through the United States. The line ended at Fargo, North Dakota. In June of that year, a slender, adventurous twenty-two-year-old artist from Quebec stood on the railway platform at Fargo and looked out over the prairie for the first time.

"This narrow strip of planking was the dividing line between civilization and the wilderness," Henri Julien wrote later. "Behind us lay the works of man, with their noises. Before us stretched the handiwork of God, with its eternal solitudes.

"The first sight of the prairie is as impressive as the first sight of the sea. There at our feet it spread out, silent, immeasurable, sublime."

Julien spent the summer of 1874 riding across the prairie with 275 officers and men of the new Mounted Police, assigned to the expedition as artist-correspondent for *The Canadian Illustrated News*. It was the first trek westward by the force to set up posts and establish its authority from Manitoba to the foothills of the Rocky Mountains.

In Toronto that spring, Bengough, one year older than Julien, was launching a career as a public speaker that would take him to all parts of the country. Bengough later wrote about his travels but none of his writings has the power of Julien's description of the

Henri Julien

prairie. Bengough's prose, like his cartoons, was constructed according to the conventions of his time. Julien wrote as he drew, with the intensity of a poet. "This has truly been called the great Lone Land," he said of the prairies. "Its silence and solitude weigh on you like a mechanical power."

Bengough was a crude artist whose inventive political imagination and passionate convictions eventually would triumph over his artistic awkwardness to make him the greatest political cartoonist of his age in Canada.

Julien, by contrast, was almost apolitical in his opinions. He was a craftsman who regarded politicians simply as subjects for his pen, but the pen was gifted with its own energy. He was without equal during his time as a caricaturist and illustrator although he too seldom showed the irreverence that is an essential element of political cartooning.

Both his skill and his attitudes toward the public figures of his time originate in his family and social background. He was born into the printing trade, the son of Henri Julien, a foreman for the company founded in Quebec in the previous century by Pierre-Edouard Desbarats.

The large Julien family, with eight surviving children, moved with the company, taking the young Henri to Toronto in 1854, back to Quebec in 1860 and to Ottawa in 1867, where he attended university for a time. During those years he became fluently bilingual and acquired a breadth of experience unusual in French Canadians of his generation.

He also maintained contact with his roots in Quebec. Many of his childhood summers were spent with relatives on a farm near Ange-Gardien among the *habitants* who were favourite subjects in later years for his sketches and paintings.

By 1869, Julien was in Montreal working as an apprentice engraver under William Leggo, chief engraver for *The Canadian Illustrated News*. In 1868, *The Canadian Illustrated News* became the first magazine in the world to publish photographs as illustrations, using a halftone engraving process patented by Leggo. Julien was involved in improving this process as well as learning other types of engraving from Leggo.

His job as an engraver sharpened Julien's technical skill as an artist and made him familiar with the work of the best engravers and illustrators in the United States and Europe, frequently copied in the Leggo shop for reproduction in *The Canadian Illustrated News* and other journals published by George Desbarats. His own drawings started to appear in *The Canadian Illustrated News* in 1873 after caricaturist Edward Jump left the magazine to return to the United States.

Julien was the first native-born caricaturist of the first rank to appear in Canada; but like Bengough in Ontario, he had lively if less talented predecessors in his own society. His career coincided with a fertile period in comic and political journalism in Quebec that began about 1854 with the appearance of *Le Scorpion*, one of Canada's earliest French-language humorous journals.

The first comic journal to survive in Quebec for at least a few years was *La Scie – The Saw*, a bilingual publication that dated its first issue October 29, 1863. Illustrations started to appear in *La Scie* on November 25, 1864, and became a regular feature in the final version of the journal entitled *La Scie Illustrée*. At first, these were simple sketches printed from woodcuts, but

they developed into complete political cartoons, the work of a remarkable woodcarver who abandoned comic journalism early in his career to become one of the most notable religious sculptors in the history of French Canada.

Jean-Baptiste Côté was born in 1834 in the heart of the St. Roch ward of Quebec, a huddle of low houses and small shops beneath the cliffs of the ancient capital. It was a district of craftsmen: shipbuilders who worked in the yards at the mouth of the St. Charles River, printers, shoe-makers, ironworkers and tanners.

Côté himself came from a family of carpenters but he was one of those bright students from poor families traditionally selected by the Quebec clergy as likely candidates for the priesthood. He studied classics at the Séminaire de Québec, but ultimately chose to follow the family tradition by becoming an apprentice to the architect and carver F.X. Berlinguet. After he married the daughter of a St. Roch shipbuilder, he assisted Berlinguet in building churches in the Quebec region.

Details about Côté's career are sketchy. It isn't clear why he switched from architecture to journalism except that he had an obvious literary bent and a lifelong habit of doing what he wanted to do. Long after his death, one of his children remembered, bitterly, that "he did not try to work for money, only for his self-satisfaction. It meant misery for us all."

At first, Côté was one of the editors of *La Scie*, using his pen rather than his chisel on its victims. The

motto of the journal was *Castigat ridendo mores* – Laughter corrects abuse. Côté's woodcuts were simple and powerful. The first to appear in the journal, in 1864, was simply a picture of *Le Scieur – The Sawyer*, a man in a top hat but in his shirtsleeves applying a saw to the neck of a terrified victim. As Côté signed himself C.C. Lescieur in his journal, the drawing must have been a kind of self-portrait.

Côté had little respect for the Quebec conventions of the day, literary or political. While the print columns of *La Scie* accused Louis Fréchette of plagiarism, some years before he was recognized as the poet laureate of French Canada, Côté's cartoons attacked the British, the scheme for Confederation, lawyers and civil servants.

Confederation, in his view, was a many-headed monster that would de-

Côté/Scie/2 February 1866

Dragging the dead to the polls on election day

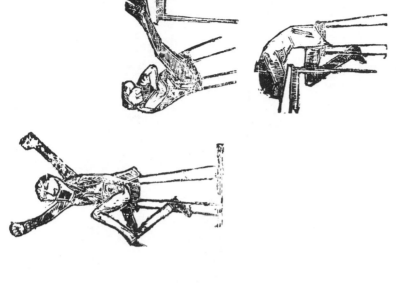

Côté/Scie/16 March 1866

A civil servant, Quebec, at his day's work. *Because of this cartoon, the artist was arrested.*

vour French Canada. He portrayed political organizers distributing liquor to prospective voters and dragging corpses to the polls. A distinguished Quebec politician was shown as a midget making a speech to the Commons in Ottawa so boring that everyone from the public in the galleries to the clerks on the floor of the House was falling asleep. He also drew a cartoon of a civil servant sleeping at his desk, which ended his cartooning career in 1868 when, according to one of his children years later, "He went too far with his pen and . . . was arrested by the police."

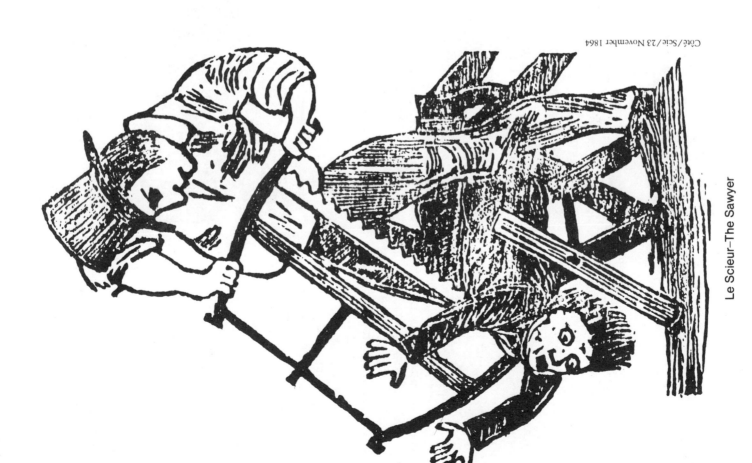

Côté/Scie/23 November 1864

Le Scieur–The Sawyer

After his brush with the law, Côté abandoned journalism and became a carver of ships' figure-heads, sign-boards, cigar-store Indians, ornate ink-stands and animals for the Christmas mangers of churches. His most significant work was religious sculpture, individual statues as well as elaborately carved panels showing such scenes as the Nativity and the Last Supper.

Côté's work, scattered originally among the parishes of Quebec, became in this century a valuable part of Canadian museum collections but by the end of his life, the sculptor was a pathetic figure.

"When I was a young boy," remembered a priest who had grown up in the St. Roch district, "I sometimes stopped to see him work in his shop. He was carving figure-heads—statues and nymphs. Of middle height, he already looked rather frail. Perhaps he did not earn enough to butter his bread. The poor fellow never knew how to make enough money."

Le Scorpion and *La Scie* were among the first of a constant succession of comic journals in Quebec. Most of them used little illustration and were aimed at an immediate political objective, often coming into existence and disappearing within the space of a few weeks or months.

Two other editors of Côté's time were, like him, cartoonists as well. C.-Henri Moreau, who started *Le Perroquet* in Montreal in 1865, was a Frenchman who graduated from the Ecole des Beaux-Arts in Paris before coming to North America. In 1860, he was an officer in the Union Army of the United States. He launched *Le Perroquet* to preach the annexation of Canada to the United States, but it lasted only a few months. Moreau returned to France, and died in 1867.

Hector Berthelot was a more durable rival to the more respectable Ju-

Unknown/Canard

lien during the three decades when he entertained Quebec as a journalist, humorist and caricaturist. Educated to be a lawyer, Berthelot went into journalism a few years after he was admitted to the Quebec Bar in 1865. He contributed to sixteen journals during his career and was known as "The Prince of Canadian Humorists" when he died in 1895 at the age of fifty-three.

Berthelot was described as "a bohemian disguised as a gentleman," although some of his contemporaries might have disputed the effectiveness of the disguise. His attacks on Senator F.X. Anselme Trudel, whom Berthelot christened "Le Grand Vicaire," so infuriated the Senator's two sons that they cornered the cartoonist in Montreal's Fortifications Lane and severely beat him. In 1887, Oscar Goyette, a former political candidate, successfully sued him for libel on the basis of an article casting suspicion on the manliness of Goyette, a bachelor. Condemned to pay a fine of $427.52 or spend three months in jail, Berthelot organized a public lecture to raise the money. It was so successful that it launched him on a new career.

Among the journals where Berthelot's work appeared were his own, *Le Canard*, which he founded in 1877 and sold the following year and *Le Vrai Canard*, which appeared in 1879 and which was followed by *Le Grognard* in 1881. Berthelot made another start in 1886 with *Le Violon* and when this disappeared, came full circle in 1893 by issuing a new journal with his old title, *Le Canard*.

He also worked, at various times, as

Julien/Canadian Illustrated News/9 September 1876

a photographer and as a translator and professor of French, but he was in his element sauntering along Montreal's St. James Street to trade rumours and quips with other members of the city's intellectual, political and artistic elites. In a parody of the five o'clock tea celebrated by some English-speaking Montrealers, Berthelot would invite his cronies to a "ten o'clock gin" on Sunday mornings to talk about new articles and cartoons for his publications.

When he died, he left $10 in his will to buy drinks at the Hotel Lumpkin for his friends who followed his hearse to Côte-des-Neiges cemetery on Mount Royal.

Henri Julien probably was among the mourners at the bar after Berthelot's funeral because he had contributed drawings to both *Le Canard* and *Le Vrai Canard* and because he possessed something of Berthelot's famed conviviality. Some years later, Julien responded to an invitation to dine at Reber's Palace in Montreal with a few lines scribbled beneath a quick self-caricature: "The above will be pleased to accept ...." Julien drew himself as a generous

British Columbia in a Pet.

Uncle Aleck: "Don't frown so, my dear, you'll have your railway by-and-bye.

Miss B. Columbia: "I want it *now*. You promised I should have it, and if I don't, I'll complain to Ma."

moustache and thinning hair, grinning at his host over a large tankard.

Julien was a born raconteur who entertained his companions not only with sketches but with political stories from the Press Gallery in Ottawa and perhaps, toward the end of the evening, with earlier recollections of the twenty-two-year-old who had travelled west in 1874 with the Mounted Police. His drawings, reproduced in *The Canadian Illustrated News* and *L'Opinion Publique*, gave many eastern Canadians a first detailed look at their new frontier and confirmed Julien's reputation as one of the leading illustrators of his day.

Eventually, Julien's illustrations reached a wider audience through *The Canadian Magazine* and *Grip* in To-

Berthelot/Canard/5 August 1883

Patronage in Quebec

ronto, *Harper's* and *Century Illustrated Magazine* in New York, *L'Illustration* and *Le Monde Illustré* in Paris and *The Graphic* in London.

In April 1888, Julien became chief cartoonist and illustrator for *The Montreal Daily Star*, at that time the most important of Canada's daily newspapers. He remained there for the last twenty years of a career described as 'successful, though not lucrative.'

His agreement with the publisher of the *Star*, Hugh Graham, stated that 'we will give you forty dollars a week to work for us exclusively and will provide an office . . . and keep you busy from nine to five, less an hour for luncheon.' In 1892, his salary was increased to $45 a week provided that he devote 'his entire abilities as an artist to the interests and work' of the *Star*. Julien needed the security that the *Star* provided. He and his wife, Marie-Louise, produced eighteen children. One of the eight who survived later remembered him as a devoted husband and father:

'He was too humble to speak of himself and his work. As soon as he arrived home, he aided mother and spent most of his time with the children. At night, he would get up to mind the youngest in the cradle; at times, there were two of them too young to walk. He had no time to rest, all his life.'

Affectionate at home, convivial at Reber's and other hotels in the city, Julien was punctilious about his duties and position at the *Star*. The recollections of one of his editors indicates, inadvertently, that the French-Canadian artist knew his place among the Eng-

lish-speaking staff and was sensitive about it. 'We were most intimate outside of the office,' wrote Brenton A. MacNab, 'but inside, Julien never forgot that he was under direction. His strict observance of such usage was often embarrassing.'

Julien produced not only cartoons but caricatures and many types of illustrations for the *Star*. When a famous surgeon visited Montreal, Julien was invited into the operating theatre to sketch him at work. As he left the operating room, he was stopped by a staff doctor who was unaware of the invitation. Infuriated by the artist's invasion of the operating room, the doctor asked to see Julien's sketches, then tore them to pieces before his eyes. Julien silently turned on his heel, walked back to his office and created a finished drawing from memory.

Every winter, during the parliamentary session at Ottawa, Julien would travel to the capital to sketch his political subjects in action. As a member of the Press Gallery, he was allowed to watch the politicians from the journalists' perch high above the floor. On one occasion, the Speaker of the Commons, acting on the suggestion of Prime Minister Wilfrid Laurier, broke the rules and allowed Julien to sit at the foot of the Speaker's dais to sketch the politicians at close range.

When the House adjourned, Julien would hurry from Parliament Hill to his room in the Russell House where he worked at his drawing board, a cheap alarm clock close by to remind him of deadlines. The drawings would be sent to Montreal on the train the

same night while Julien relaxed at Russell's with his friends from the Gallery, often still sketching on scraps of paper and the tops of tables.

During the winter of 1908, Julien suffered a severe attack of influenza in Ottawa. Before he was fully recovered, he went to Quebec to sketch the city's tercentenary celebrations. The following September, he had just left his office when he suddenly stopped on the sidewalk, threw his hands high over his head and collapsed, dying within a few minutes.

Critic Allen Jarvis, believes that 'Julien's peculiar talent was to produce, under the most intolerable conditions, drawings of contemporary events which stand up well even today.' Edgar Andrew Collard, historian and former editor of the *Montreal Gazette*, wrote in 1973 that he was 'a master of the black and white sketch, in many ways the greatest such master in Canadian art.'

Julien was the best illustrator that Canada had produced up to that time, creating memorable work for books as well as magazines and newspapers. He was also a good painter in watercolours and oils, depicting rural Quebec life in a style that often showed the influence of earlier work by Cornelius Krieghoff but that was more sympathetic in spirit. Krieghoff looked at Quebec through European eyes; Julien was, in the words of his friend and neighbour, the sculptor Philippe Hebert, 'the most essentially Canadian of all our artists.'

Among Julien's studies of rural French Canadians is a painting of a

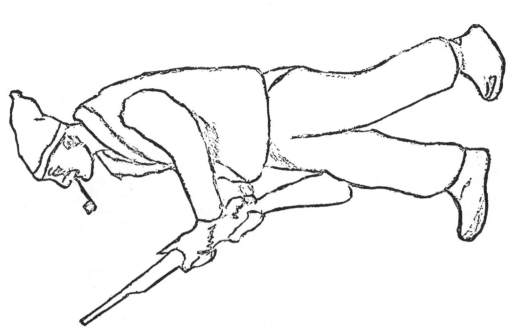

acter," wrote Hebert after Julien's death. "He did much fine work but he did not do what he could have done, what it was in him to do, had he had the opportunity. Given the chance and the training that comes to many artists, he would have equalled the best

Un vieux de "37"

Julien

gnarled farmer, toque on his head, pipe clenched between his teeth and musket in his hands, ready to defend his interests. This depiction of the spirit of the rebellion in Lower Canada in 1837 was adopted in the 1960s as a symbol of armed revolution the Front de

Libération du Québec. This use violated Julien's strong attachment to Canada but it testified to the strength of his portrayals of French Canadians and their Quebec homeland. "No one could approach him in the understanding of the Canadian *habitant* char-

67

Julien/Montreal/Star

Julien/Montreal/Star

painters of the present day in France."

Apart from drawing lessons suppos-edly taken from an Abbé Chabert, described by his biographer Marius Barbeau only as "an erratic French priest," Julien had even less formal art training than Bengough, but by his teens he was already a more accom-plished artist than Bengough could ever have become. His earliest sketch-es and cartoons were detailed produc-tions that rivalled the technique of Bengough's idol, Thomas Nast.

Julien's shortcoming, as a political cartoonist, was a lack of passionate conviction. Julien drew to order. Even when he took a strongly editorial posi-tion in a cartoon, his attack was never reflected in his caricatures of the politi-cians. They always retained something of the impersonality of state portraits.

Julien was remembered by his friends for his "lovable qualities." By temperament, he was perhaps too gentle to be a political cartoonist.

His early success brought him quick-ly into contact with Montreal's Eng-lish-speaking elite at a time when it dominated the city's business activities and, to some extent, its political life. The fact that he was hired and flat-tered by this group, his natural targets, might have taken much of the edge off his cartooning.

Among his most notable caricatures were the "Bytown Coons," a series started in the *Star* in 1897 and com-pleted before 1900. These were draw-ings of members of the Laurier cabinet portrayed as blackface minstrel per-formers with appropriate verses. They were reprinted in booklet form and were wildly popular, although both the drawings and dialect are now embar-rassingly dated. The Minister of De-fence, for example, was given these lines to conclude his performance:

"Oh, yo sho's hear me sassin'
"De Gen'ral w'en he's passin'
"Up an' down de ranks w'en on pa-rade.
"Well, he don't cut no figgah
"Wif dis yer gold-laced niggah;
"I'se de big buck ob de By-Town Coon Brigade!"

More original were the series of *Por-traits and Silhouettes* drawn in Ottawa, foreground caricatures of poli-ticians with their opponents silhouet-ted in the background.

Julien's artistry and industry would have been understood and appreciated by the craftsmen of St. Roch, where he was born. The same district also had produced Jean-Baptiste Côté but by the time of Julien's death, the skills and pride of French Canada's artisans were being weakened by industrial de-velopment. During his lifetime, Ju-lien's work recalled an earlier era of craftsmanship in Quebec, while his lack of political conviction expressed the alienation from Canadian political life of many members of a new genera-tion in French Canada.

Outlines of Canadian Nationalism

The most memorable national leader, after the death of Sir John A. Macdonald in 1891, was Canada's first French-speaking Prime Minister, Sir Wilfrid Laurier. He was a tall, slender, elegant figure, suave and urbane. For his contemporaries, he seems to have possessed something of the charisma that was projected more than half a century later by another notable Prime Minister from Quebec, Pierre Elliott Trudeau.

Laurier's political career was a model for Trudeau's, in some respects. He was an immensely popular Prime Minister, both at home and overseas. Making his first transatlantic voyage in 1897 to attend Queen Victoria's Diamond Jubilee, he was granted a knighthood and received a degree of public acclaim that reflected Europe's growing awareness of the transcontinental state created in North America by the union of seven former British colonies. This international renown, as Trudeau discovered in our own time, did little to conceal Laurier's problems at home. As time went on, newspaper cartoonists expressed the growing dissatisfaction with his government, particularly outside Laurier's own province of Quebec. Like Trudeau, Laurier lost the support of English-speaking Canada and, in defeat, found himself isolated within Quebec, his leadership a symbol of national division.

Wilfrid de Great.

W'en Queen Victoria call her peup's
  For mak' some jubilee
She sen' for men from all de worl'—
  Dat mean her colonie.

But mos' of all she sen' dis word,
  To dis Canadian shore,
"If Wilfrid Laurier will not come,
  I not be glad no more!"

Den Wilfrid sail across de sea,
  An' Queen Victoria's met,
An w'en she's see him, Ah! she is
  Jus' tickle half to deat'!

And w'en he's kneel, as etiquette
  Demand, for be correc',
She tak' a sword into de han
  An' hit him on de neck.

Oui, certainement, excep' de Queen
Herself, dat glorious day,
De greates' man on Angleterre,
Is Wilfrid Laurier!

Sir Wilfrid cross de Channel, den,
For visit la patrie
An' mak' fine spiches, two or t'ree,
In de city of Paree.

En bref, our Wilfrid capture France,
He's capture Anglan' too!
I t'ink he will annex dem bot'
To Canada—don' you?

Another Adventurous Inventor

Performer Laurier: "Yes, my friends, I'm going over in this machine—my own invention—I feel sure it will take me safely through."

Kahrs/Daily Mail and Empire/20 June 1896

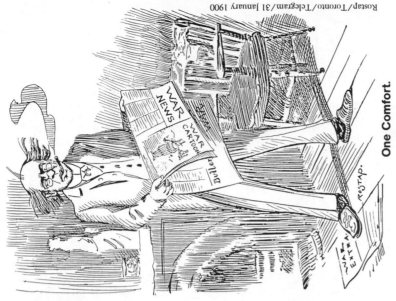

One Comfort.

Sir Wilfrid Laurier: "Thank hevings, the papers are so full of the war that they have no space for the failings of ME and my partners."

Rostap/Toronto/Telegram/31 January 1900

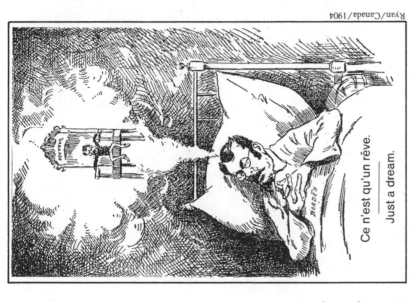

Ce n'est qu'un rêve.

Just a dream.

Ryan/Canada/1904

Le Cultivateur: (au chef tory): T'as beau te démancher de toutes les façons, t'arriveras pas m'emplir."

Conservative leader Borden fails to hypnotize a skeptical farmer.

Brodeur

There were other reasons for Laurier's unpopularity. Cartoons of the time show that Canadians were sceptical, then as now, about the motives of political leaders who crusaded for national unity. They suspected that differences between French and English were magnified at times to distract attention from government corruption and failures of government policy.

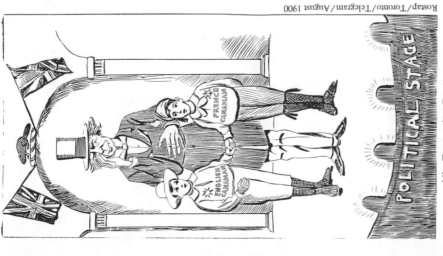

His Favourite Part.

Sir Wilfrid Laurier: "You're good friends, boys, and don't want to fight, but for heaven's sake, make a bluff and give me a chance to pick up votes on my figger as a peacemaker."

Rostap/Toronto/Telegram/August 1900

Although Liberals had exposed some of the patronage and influence-peddling involved in Macdonald's Canadian Pacific Railway, they discovered the same tendencies within their own ranks as Laurier sponsored the building of two all-Canadian transcontinental railways. Newspaper cartoonists kept the public aware of this alliance of capital and political power, and of the sordid realities behind the boldest schemes of national development.

Charlebois/1914

Hunter/Toronto/World/1907

Waiter: "Xcuse me sah, but I has to wait on some colonial conference genl'men now. Does yo' desiah anything mo'?"

The Country: "I got more'n I want right here."

The Growing Time for Trans-Continental Railways.

The Premier: "The people pay for and give you the Railways, and make you a present of the country; but what do they get as a quid pro quo?"

Chorus: "The people—as represented by the Government—will get our vote and influence, you know."

Canada: "Yes. It is a great scheme. The country needs it, and we ought to have it. But don't you think that if we pay for it, we ought to own it."

Ryan/Caricature-Politique/1906

Bengough/Moon/1901

That Canada was growing there was no doubt. At the outset of the Laurier period, Saskatchewan and Alberta joined Confederation to complete the union, apart from the eventual addition of Newfoundland years later. In the first decade of the century, the population increased from 5.3 million to 7.2 million, with more than half of the new arrivals settling in the western provinces.

During Laurier's political career, Canada progressively defined its relationship toward the two nations that had contributed most to its development, England and the United States, and revealed its own internal weaknesses in the process. The debate about trade reciprocity with the United States related to a question that continued to plague later generations: How much are Canadians willing to pay for independence from the United States?

Charlebois/La Conscription/1917

McConnell/27 July 1912

1911: Helping Uncle

McConnell/27 July 1912

1912: Helping Father

The future relationship between Canada and Great Britain was formed in the heat of political controversy over Canadian contributions to Imperial defence during the Boer War and the First World War.

Can He Hold It up?

Shields/Toronto/Telegram/1918

Make every ballot a bullet for Bill

Batsford/Manitoba Free Press/1917

Racey/Montreal/Star/19 May 1916

Laurier is accused of hesitating to march with England against the Boers.

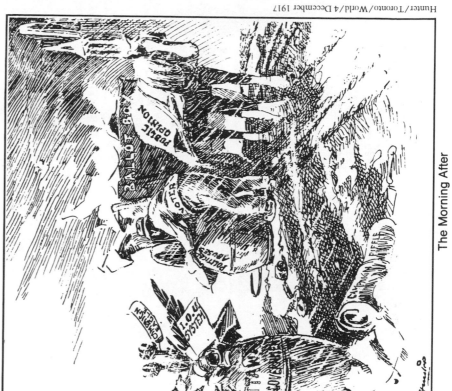

The Morning After

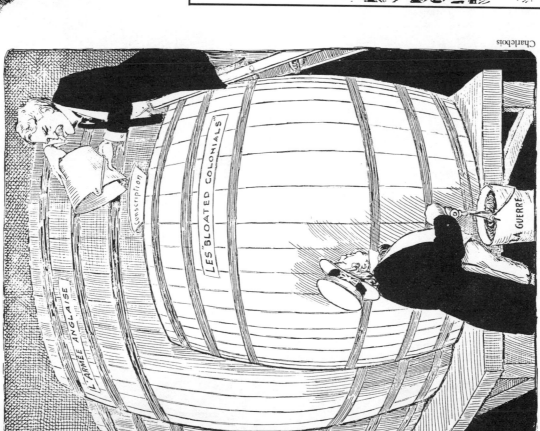

LES "BLOATED COLONIALS"

It now seems almost incredible that elections could be won or lost on the issue of a Liberal "red" or Conservative "blue" navy, but it was as meaningful a debate for Canadians at the time as the question, in our own day, of the languages used on signs outside post offices.

CLOSURE PROCEEDINGS!

Kyle/The Globe/12 March 1913

Whether Canada was to have its own navy or contribute to Britain's was a question that had all politicians in hot water.

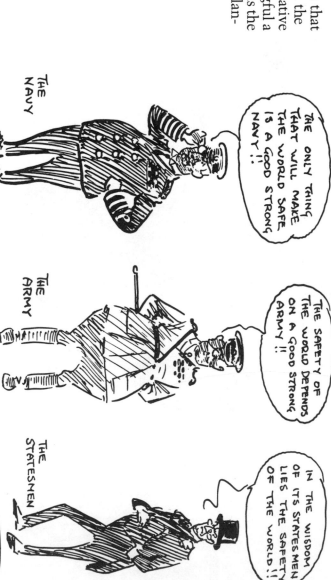

Vezina

"J'aime mieux une marine bleue qu'une marine rouge."

"Comment ça, Jos?"

"Avec une marine rouge, les enfants aurient été certains d'aller au guiâbe; avec une marine bleue, on va les envoyer au ciel!"

EVOLUTION

A NEW CANADIAN NATIONAL SPIRIT

4: Arch Dale

The legendary Arch Dale was once told that William Aberhart, the Premier of Alberta and one of his favourite targets, had referred to the cartoonist as a "common drunkard."

"I don't mind being called a drunkard," Dale is supposed to have replied, "but he used the word 'common'."

Despite the cartoonist's pretended irritation, Aberhart's description was inadvertently accurate. For his time—the middle period of Canadian history and Canadian political cartooning—Dale was representative of the common man, particularly in English-speaking Canada and even more specifically, in western Canada.

He was also typical of the political cartoonists who worked on Canadian newspapers in the first half of this century between the era of Bengough and Julien and the contemporary period that began in the 1950s with Robert LaPalme, Len Norris, and Duncan Macpherson.

Genial good nature is one of the characteristics that distinguished Canadian cartoonists of Dale's generation from their predecessors in Europe and the United States and, to a lesser extent, in Canada. When cartoonist Sam Hunter died in 1939, after a long career that began with Bengough's *Grip* in the 1870s and included more than twenty years as staff cartoonist with *The Toronto World* at the turn of the century, the obituary writer at *The Toronto*

Dale/Winnipeg/Free Press/1938

Star stated that there had been "no venom in his work . . . his cartoons have been good natured . . . they have reflected the shrewd but kindly personality of their creator."

The antithesis of Arch Dale in physical appearance and social background, Arthur George Racey of *The Montreal Star* looked on the world as kindly as Dale did although with a more genteel eye. Writing in a university magazine in 1935, S. Morgan-Powell, the *Star's* drama critic, paid Racey the highest

compliment of his time when he stated, "He is never vicious."

The son of a Quebec doctor, Racey went directly into cartooning from McGill University, joining *The Montreal Star* in 1899 and becoming chief cartoonist after Julien's death. He remained there for forty-two years to become, in the opinion of his contemporaries, the first Canadian cartoonist to gain international recognition. Racey's work was reproduced in newspapers and magazines in the United

States and England. In 1927, he represented Canada at a cartoon exhibition in Florence, Italy.

During the First World War, Racey raised $50,000 for the Red Cross through a series of lectures consisting of lantern slides of some of his war cartoons, and a running commentary.

"His viewpoint is neither Canadian nor anything else but cosmopolitan in regard to foreign affairs," wrote S. Morgan-Powell. In other respects, Racey was, in fact, very Canadian in outlook. His cartoon of the then highly respected RCMP cleaning up Chicago, or his rendering of Canada as an exploited fish, being sized up by a com-

Hunter / Globe / 7 December 1921

placent Uncle Sam, bear this out.

Elisha Newton McConnell's "six-by-four den right over the *Daily News'* front door" in Toronto lacked the spaciousness of Racey's genteel world but the outlook was similar. After graduating from the Ontario School of Art and Design in 1900, McConnell was chief cartoonist for the *Daily News* for fifteen years.

Before he went to the *Daily News*, McConnell participated briefly with other cartoonists in a short-lived but imaginative humour magazine called *The Moon*. Published in 1901 and 1902, it allowed its cartoonists to

express themselves with unusual freedom. McConnell drew the cover cartoon for its first issue showing the Toronto merchant Timothy Eaton with publishers of five of Toronto's daily newspapers leashed to a large sack of money labelled "for newspaper advertising." When *The Moon* set, McConnell joined the system he had caricatured but, according to contemporary reports, without ever succumbing completely to its values.

"He was a farm boy and remained a farm boy as long as he lived," his obituary stated. "All day long in his office he would have a procession of callers of all sorts and conditions, all calling him Newt ... farmers, mining men, politicians, tramps, drunks, artistic vagrants ...

"At half-past four, he would lean over his drawing board and begin to sketch. At five, he would carry down the finished cartoon. It was always accepted."

Timothy: "Well, the situation may be a bit unpleasant when exposed to the moonlight, but I can't see how it can be helped, boys; you're on my little strings, all right, so please don't talk, or I shall pull!"

McConnell/Moon/1901

Closer to Racey in his temperament and ambitions was Owen Staples who, under the name "Rostap," was an artist for *The Telegram* of Toronto for sixty years; for fifteen of these years he was also a cartoonist. Staples was still illustrating for *The Telegram* in 1947, two years before he died at the age of eighty-three. In addition to cartoons, he produced many etchings and landscapes of early Toronto as well as murals for churches and public buildings. His early caricatures of Laurier were as critical as any produced during that period, and were among his best work.

"Always apt, often brilliant but never bitter," was another typical obit-

uary judgement of the period, in this case for J.B. "Ben" Fitzmaurice, cartoonist for *The Vancouver Province* for more than fifteen years in the early years of this century and then, after a stay on *The Montreal Herald*, with the *Province* again after 1916.

An articulate supporter of the status quo who often used more than two hundred words in captions scattered throughout a cartoon, Fitzmaurice attacked Bolshevism and women's suffrage with equal gusto. His contributions to the war effort were Horace the Pig and Mrs. Carranza the Goat, inspired by government campaigns that urged Canadians to "Raise More Pigs" and to bring Mexican goats to Canada to increase milk production.

"It is my humble opinion," Fitzmaurice once wrote, "that if a man is to be

Rostap/Toronto/Telegram/12 January 1904

a cartoonist, it will just happen like cholera, typhoid or measles; but my advice is—don't be one—don't go out of your way to meet trouble."

Their few surviving comments indicate that many of these cartoonists didn't take themselves or their "art" too seriously. They were proud of their blunt approach. The editor of an Ontario weekly once said of McConnell's cartoons: "They were not beautiful but they were good." Fergus Kyle's obituary in 1941 said that the Hamilton-born cartoonist for *The Moon, The Globe, The Toronto Daily Star* and *Saturday Night* in the early decades of this century "was always more interested in people and problems than landscapes." He was said to have been "cold to mere decoration."

Although other cartoonists of the period were anti-Laurier, Kyle was very much on the Prime Minister's side. With the election of Borden in 1911, Kyle hit his stride by poking fun

Kyle/Globe/29 May 1912

Mr. Borden: "Go where I will, do what I may, that blamed ship keeps following me about."

Fitzmaurice/Vancouver/Province

Don't Let Our Visitors Miss Anything

at the naval policy of the Tories. His cartoon of a battleship following Borden through a wheat field was the talk of the country when it appeared in *The Globe* in 1912.

Cartoonists were prized in those days for "punch." It described a belly-laugh reaction rather than the brutal physical and intellectual impact of a cartoon by Gillray or Daumier. Canadian cartoonists of the period were encouraged to jab; roundhouse swings at their targets were felt to be bad form. Above all, they were supposed to entertain.

Life was harsh enough for many Canadians during the years between the great wars without having cartoonists flailing the nation's social, economic and political shortcomings. News-

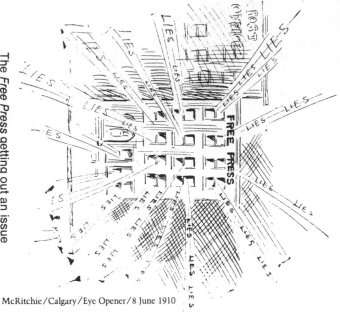

The *Free Press* getting out an issue

McRitchie/Calgary/Eye Opener/8 June 1910

papers had no desire to aggravate problems that seriously threatened the stability of the country. It was a comfortable time for cartoonists who dealt with human foibles and the conventional disputes of Canadian politics but a difficult time to raise more basic questions.

Publishers and editors controlled their cartoonists closely. As a result, their work revealed much about local and national political issues but said little about the economic and political forces that were unleashed in Canada during the years of economic depression.

Occasionally the sparks flew. Bob Edwards' *Calgary Eye-Opener* established a reputation for irreverence from 1902 to 1922. Edwards drew cartoons for the first few years of his notorious publication. Eventually he hired cartoonists of a more professional calibre, and Edwards had the insight to allow them free rein.

Donald McRitchie was among the cartoonists who worked for the *Eye-Opener*. A Maritimer who started cartooning in his spare time while working in the Boston office of the Dominion Coal Company, McRitchie had worked for *The Sydney Post*, *The Ottawa Journal* and for a newspaper at the Lakehead when Edwards' reputation attracted him to Western Canada. "In the fall of 1906," he later reminisced, "I was making people sizzle in Port Arthur with some pretty hot stuff, so much so that by the winter of 1907 I was in Winnipeg."

Several years later, he was back in eastern Canada, in Montreal. After

military service during the First World War, he settled down to become cartoonist and manager of the engraving department for *The Halifax Herald*, producing a series of strong cartoons attacking the federal government for ignoring the interests of the Maritime provinces.

Bob Edwards' inspired direction of the *Eye-Opener* helped to turn a former Calgary sign-painter, Charles H. Forrester, into a provocative cartoonist when he worked for Edwards about 1915. After the *Eye-Opener* ceased publication, Forrester reportedly abandoned cartooning.

Wading to the Bench

McRitchie/Calgary/Eye Opener/18 December 1909

Damfino!

Where in hell is Roumania?

ALSIFTON

BORDEN

AFRICA.

Sir Robert Borden, Canadian Delegate, Has Been Made Chairman of the Commission Appointed to Fix New Boundaries for Roumania and Greece.

BI-LINGUALISM

Forrester

Suicide?

Another promising start, toward the end of the *Eye-Opener's* run , was the appearance in Toronto of *The Goblin* , a magazine launched by University of Toronto students. Within a year it had the biggest news-stand sale in Canada, claiming a circulation of more than 10,500 copies. Richard Taylor, originally from Fort William, Ontario, drew his first cartoons for *The Goblin*. After it disappeared, he went to the United States where he became a regular contributor to *The New Yorker*.

Perhaps because of the newspaper

conventions that domesticated many Canadian cartoonists in the first half of this century, some of the most promising artists abandoned the struggle. Toward the end of his long and adventurous life, Jack Innes of *The Vancouver Sun* said bitterly that he would "rather sit in a damp morgue with every slab occupied than be obliged to remain for any lengthy period in a political atmosphere."

"I often wonder whether any cartoonist really feels funny," he said. "He sees politics with the frills off."

As a young man, Innes became a rancher near Calgary. He abandoned that career to operate the first telephone exchange in Calgary, submitting occasional cartoons around 1883 to *The Calgary Herald*. One of these cartoons sent the publisher of the newspaper to jail for contempt of court.

When war erupted in South Africa, Innes joined the Second Canadian Mounted Rifles, serving at the same time as a correspondent for Toronto's *Mail and Empire*. In 1907, he went to New York to become a newspaper illustrator. In his spare time, he directed the choir at a New York church.

He became a staff artist for the Hearst Sunday newspapers before returning to Vancouver in 1913. Already elected to membership in the Ontario Society of Artists in 1904, he held his first one-man show of paintings in

Innes/Vancouver/Sun

Vancouver in 1915 and eventually became known as "The Painter of the Canadian West."

Innes slowed down sufficiently toward the end of his remarkable life to write his curriculum vitae: "I have been a surveyor, horse wrangler, printer, telephone linesman, editor, cartoonist, government official, fiction writer, and special correspondent. Also I have fought for the Empire, been on the stage, taught Sunday-school, been a choirmaster, tended bar, written a hymn, and once was arrested for murder. Heigh-ho! It's a humdrum old world."

Less colourful than Innes but with a broader and more scholarly interest in historical illustration, C.W. Jefferys also started as a newspaper illustrator and cartoonist. Apprenticed to a Toronto lithographer at the age of eleven, he worked as an artist for The New York Herald for eight years before returning to Canada to join The Toronto Star as a staff artist in 1900. At this time he drew cartoons solely for The Moon.

This was toward the end of the newspaper artist's losing battle against the camera. During this period, Jefferys produced sketches of political meetings, murder trials and Royal tours.

Encouraged by the response to a series of historical sketches that he drew for The Star Weekly in Toronto, Jefferys became a freelance illustrator of the story of Canada's development. His major work was a three-volume Picture Gallery of Canadian History containing more than 1,800 drawings of early architecture, weapons, gar-

A Quiet Evening in a Canadian Home

Jefferys/The Moon/1901

ments and native implements with explanatory notes.

While Innes was settling down in Vancouver to paint the early days of the Canadian West and while Edwards was in its prime, Calgary produced its first great native-born car-

toonist, Stew Cameron. Born in 1912, Cameron spent the first part of his career working for the Walt Disney studios in Hollywood where he collaborated on the animation for "Snow White and the Seven Dwarfs." He became staff cartoonist for *The Calgary*

Herald in 1936 as William Aberhart and his Social Credit movement transformed Alberta politics. Cartooning against Premier Aberhart, who once referred to him at a public rally as "that moronic cartoonist," Cameron produced the best work of his career.

85

Political feelings ran so high that Cameron routinely entered and left his office in the *Herald* building by a fire escape in the rear. His home was once fire-bombed.

He joined the Canadian Army during the Second World War and served as a foot soldier while doing some cartooning for various military publications. In 1947, he went to *The Province* in Vancouver where he remained for three years, working by choice out of a flop house behind the newspaper building, just as, in Calgary, he had refused an office of his own and insisted on establishing himself in a large broom closet.

Cameron died in Calgary in 1970 and the Alberta government recently

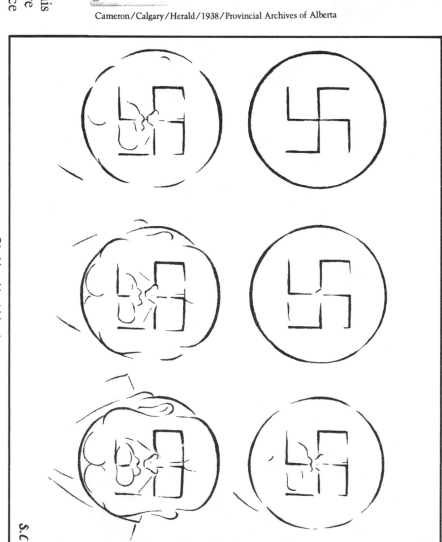

No Matter How Thin You Slice It—

Cameron/Calgary/Herald/1938/Provincial Archives of Alberta

Oh, You Nazi Man!

Cameron/Calgary/Herald/28 September 1938/Provincial Archives of Alberta

paid $50,000 for a collection of most of his cartoons.

Social Credit in the 1930s also provided the inspiration for many of the best cartoons by Arch Dale, in some respects the most typical cartoonist of the generation that followed Bengough and Julien. Dale was neither as eccentric as Innes and Cameron or as conventional as Racey. He didn't have Jefferys' sense of history or the artistic ambitions of a cartoonist like Owen Staples, but he was representative, in

the way he drew and the way he looked at the world, of many cartoonists of his period who worked for daily newspapers that were competitive and highly partisan.

One of Dale's most surprising traits, from the perspective of the 1970s, was his apparent lack of political commitment. He wasn't even interested in politics, according to some of the journalists who worked with him. When he first went to work at *The Winnipeg Free Press* in 1927, according to his

Dale/Winnipeg/Free Press

Dale's Tories

successor, cartoonist Peter Kuch, "Dale didn't known a politician from a leprechaun."

"It was probably one of the greatest mysteries of the Winnipeg newspaper world of those days," Kuch once wrote, "how an immigrant lad ... could cut through the issues of the day so clearly, and with such force, that political greats cringed before the acid of his pen."

The solution to the mystery was simple. Far from being an intuitive genius, Dale simply absorbed his editors' assessments and opinions. They created the cartoons within Dale's mind as routinely as they assigned editorial opinions to be expressed by their writers.

An editor who worked with Dale toward the end of his career once claimed that the cartoonist "didn't know anything about politics. To Archie, it was all crazy. He didn't care who was elected or what party was in, that didn't interest him at all."

He was a small stocky Scot, a "pixie of a man" in the recollection of *Winnipeg Tribune* cartoonist Jan Kamienski. For most of his twenty-seven years at *The Winnipeg Free Press*, he worked at an old desk in the corner of the newspaper's library, pen in one hand, cigarette in the other, squinting through the smoke beneath the traditional green eyeshade that he continued to use long after it had disappeared from the brows of most editors and reporters.

"Tobacco siftings littered the drawing-board, which was always an untidy mess," remembered Peter Kuch, "but

through the litter, the forms took shape ... the ideas took form, and another drawing was headed for the page."

As soon as the cartoon was on its way to the engraver, Archie "disappeared daily to gather new strength from the grass-roots for the day ahead."

"It would be unfair to suggest that the main attraction was beer," is Kuch's gentle analysis. "It was, rather, that the world of politics and social strata were unreal to him, and he had to return to the world he knew and understood, when he had freed his mind of his higher calling."

The attractions of the beer parlour were related directly to Dale's success and influence. There is no doubt that, as Kuch put it in 1963, Dale was "the pictorial spokesman of the West." If the opinions of his editors were myste-

rious at times to Dale, he probably excelled them all in understanding the newspaper's readers. They wanted cartoons that were comic but that also reflected their own cynicism about politicians, particularly during the bitter years of economic depression in western Canada. Dale provided this, with a distinctive touch that his audience recognized.

His Blimpish Tory, always muttering, "Gad, sir!" beneath its top hat and through its walrus moustache, ridiculed not only the Conservative party but, on a deeper level, the Anglo-Saxon elite that exerted decisive control over Canada's political and economic fortunes. The image survives today in the cartoons of Vancouver's Len Norris.

Dale was gently revolutionary in his attacks on the political system, in attitude if not in stated policy. Politically, he was expected to follow the editorials of the *Free Press* along a middle road between the reactionary elitism ascribed to the Conservatives and the dangerous radicalism that the newspaper perceived in the growth of the socialist Co-operative Commonwealth Federation. He did this job, in the words of one of his editors, "faithfully and well," but his attacks on the socialists revealed no greater love than for

the aristocrats of the political and business worlds. Dale criticized in the CCF the same dogmatic pretensions, the same political craziness that he perceived in the Conservatives.

As he portrayed Tories with walrus moustaches, he often drew the socialists wearing academic robes and mortar-boards. Other cartoonists of the period copied this and used it as a sym-

Dale's Socialists

Dale/Winnipeg/Free Press

bol of the CCF for the next twenty years.

Although the main themes of his cartoons might have been dictated by the editors, Dale often inserted himself in his drawings as his version of the common man, perpetually astonished, appalled or overwhelmed by the pomposity and perversity of his political leaders. Often he was accompanied by a little dog that expressed the comic-strip flavour of Dale's political world. It was the world of the hard-working, hard-drinking Scots immigrant who knew how difficult it was to establish a new life against the harsh climate and often rigid social and political systems of Canada.

Born in Scotland in 1882, Dale went to work at the age of seventeen for *The Dundee Courier*, switching later to *The Glasgow News*. In 1908, he decided to become a homesteader in Saskatchewan. According to an article in the *Free Press*, Dale "actually, so he says, did some manual work at the business end of a plow before deciding that there must be easier ways of making a living."

After a few months, he went to Winnipeg where his cartoons appeared briefly in *The Grain Growers' Guide* and in *The Grain Growers' Guide* and in the *Free Press*. His cartoons in the *Guide* were "a dynamic factor in the farmers' battles against freight rates, injustices in the grain trade, high interest rates, high tariffs, and all their other oppressions." Western farmers in those years were an organized and powerful radical force in Canadian politics and the young Arch Dale instinctively sided with them.

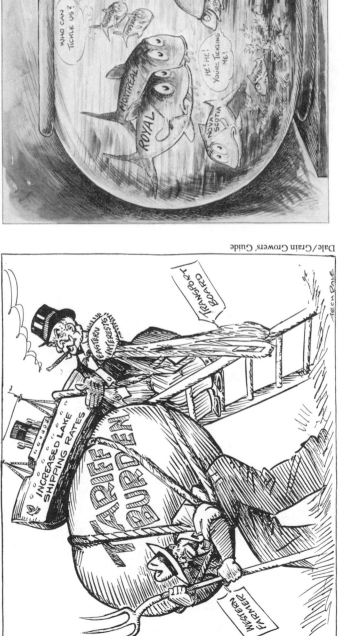

During the boom and bust cycles of those years in Winnipeg, Dale made enough money in real estate speculation to pay for a trip home. He stayed for three years, working at first on *The Manchester Dispatch* succeeding Poy, one of the best British cartoonists at that time, who had moved on to London. In 1913, he returned to Winnipeg and the *Guide.*

Like many Canadian cartoonists of his generation, Dale was excited and influenced by the work of cartoonists in the United States and the commercial possibilities created by the syndication of comic strips. He started to draw his *Doo Dads* strip for the *Guide* and, in 1921, Dale took it and himself to Chicago where the *Doo Dads* were syndicated by the Universal Feature

and Specialty Company.

The *Doo Dads* were bulbous little creatures who expressed Dale's own sense of gentle amusement at the inanities of life. At one time, they were familiar to the readers of fifty newspapers in the United States and Canada. In 1927, Dale returned to the *Free Press* where he remained until his retirement twenty-seven years later.

During this long period, Social Credit became an important political movement in Alberta under Premier William Aberhart, the Conservatives held power in Ottawa for a time under Prime Minister R.B. Bennett and the socialist movement took political form in the Co-operative Commonwealth Federation under such leaders as J.S. Woodsworth and M.J. Coldwell.

Dale's Social Crediters

89

The Grand Panjandrum Comes to Ottawa

Dale/Winnipeg/Free Press/29 July 1930

Following the editorial positions taken by the *Free Press*, Dale cartooned against these leaders. Bennett and Aberhart in particular, pompous and opinionated men in the eyes of many Canadians, were apt subjects for Dale's personal bias against all politicians.

In Dale's cartoons, Bennett became a symbol of political dogmatism and authoritarianism. By 1935, the cartoonist was comparing him with Hitler, Stalin and Mussolini. Bennett came close to being a comic-strip character in Dale's cartoons about *The Bennetts of Parliament Hill*. The Great Panjandrum, as Dale labelled him, still lives in these cartoons as a Canadian political type even as Bennett himself disappears almost entirely from living memory.

Decades of drawing political cartoons seemed to do nothing for Dale's political awareness. A preface to a collection of his cartoons published by the *Free Press* stated candidly but not unkindly that Dale "can draw anything and can spell nothing, so the staff helps out."

"One of my first chores in the morning was to think up ideas for Archie," related an editor who worked with him the last years of his career. "I thought of dozens and dozens of them and he would proceed to draw them, not always understanding the joke, I don't think, because Archie didn't take much interest in politics but he produced what we wanted."

He was still drawing for the *Free Press* in his seventies, although sometimes with difficulty. One of his edinal had been lost, Dale carefully redrew the cartoon for the Prime Minister.

The cartoonists of Dale's generation represented a middle stage in the development of Canadian cartooning and expressed the political opinions and social attitudes of a nation that was, from our vantage point, in a middle period of its national development.

Compared with the nation that existed in the first decades after Confederation, it was a relatively populous and confident country, optimistic about its future and slowly expanding its influence among the nations of the world. Its older rural areas could look back on generations of settlement. They had their own character. The older cities were large and prosperous enough to support a daily press that was more numerous and, in some respects, livelier than the newspapers of the second half of this century, and most of the major newspapers felt that it was essential to have a political cartoonist.

Proud of its achievements, Canada still had a long way to go. So did its cartoonists. The comparison with American models was continual, unfavourable and damaging.

Despite outbursts of patriotism, regionalism was often stronger than national sentiment. Federal politics often seemed dull. Political leadership during this period was exemplified by Mackenzie King, Prime Minister for twenty-one years and widely regarded as the dullest leader that the country had ever produced.

Cartoonists often had to label na-tionally prominent politicians. Provincial and local politics, on the other hand, were of consuming interest. The most effective cartoonists were often those who sacrificed a wider audience or more enduring subjects for a sharp but ephemeral impact on a local audience.

"The towns were smaller, the cartoonist was part of what you might call a family joke," recalled author, editor and political columnist Bruce Hutchison, who entered journalism as a reporter and sometime cartoonist in Victoria in the 1920s. "When a cartoonist drew something and said something, everybody understood what he was saying."

"They look to us now rather crude," he said of the cartoons of that era. "There's labels all over them; they're not too well drawn and the ideas are very obvious. Nothing subtle about them. But that was the nature of the society we lived in. My God, we were just on the edge of the wilderness!"

Toward the end of this period, in the 1950s, Canadian political cartooning generally had become so bland that some newspapers started to get along without cartoonists, sometimes using syndicated cartoons from American publications. No one suspected that dramatic political events lay just ahead and that they would coincide, not accidentally, with a golden age of Canadian cartooning.

Summer Styles, 1935

Dale/Winnipeg/Free Press/6 July 1935

tors discovered only after his death that younger staff artists often came to Archie's rescue.

"Archie, in the time I knew him, had developed a few idiosyncracies," recalled Peter Kuch, his successor at the Free Press. "He hated drawing girls ... and, whenever he had to include them in a cartoon, he would turn to me, or someone around, and have us pencil in our version of a pretty girl. At other times, he would protest that he could never draw George Drew. Invariably he would come to me to pencil in a caricature of Drew, but when he penned in the finished cartoon it was always his own figure."

"There was no ferocity in Archie," remembered Bruce Hutchison, author and former editor of the Free Press. "He loved everybody and everybody loved Archie, or so they should."

Even Bennett used to ask for Dale's original cartoons. Once, when an origi-

Filling in the Details

Between the two world wars, Canadians were preoccupied with their own problems. The nation now stretched from Atlantic to Pacific, wilderness regions were filling up rapidly with new arrivals, and the struggle for political influence within this circumscribed world seemed more relevant than the distant forces of revolution and imperialism at work in Europe and Asia.

Prime Minister Laurier had predicted that the twentieth century would belong to Canada, but he hadn't said which part of the country would get the lion's share. As the western provinces became more populous and prosperous, they began to compete for political and economic influence with the original provinces of Confederation. The Maritimes, doubtful all along about the benefits of union, were faced with new competitors in the West. The only aspect of national policy that most of these provinces could agree on was that the federal government was unduly influenced by demands from Ontario and Quebec. The pattern of regional rivalry expressed by strong provincial governments competing with Ottawa that was established during this period would remain a dominant feature of Canadian politics.

Canadians also started to look more critically at their own society. There were cartoons that illustrated both the racial prejudices of Canadians and the beginnings of bad conscience about

The Only Drawback

Uncle Sam (looking over Canadian West with Mr. Bull): "They say it's a fine lookin' country, John, but durn it all, you can't see it for the wheat."

Kyle / 1903

Real Encouragement

McRitchie / Halifax / Herald / 3 October 1925

Wooing the West

McRitchie / Halifax / Herald / 11 September 1925

The Heathen Chinee in British Columbia

Amor de Cosmos, i.e. The Love of the World
or the Lover of Mankind.

Heathen Chinee: "Why you send me offee?"
ADC: "Because you won't assimilate with us."
Heathen Chinee: "What is datee?"
ADC: "You won't drink whisky, and talk
politics and vote like us."

Unknown/Canadian Illustrated News/26 April 1879

Hyde/Vancouver/Sun/7 March 1912
British Columbia Archives

Bowser: "If the public knew what was in that book, they'd scuttle
this craft."

McBride: "Lucky thing we've got this weight to sink it."

Fin. Min. Ellison: "Bless your dear hearts, I don't know what's in the
precious book. I don't know nothink."

Jefferys/Moon/1901

Jack Canuck: "If that kid keeps on growing at that rate, I'll have to put him in long pants before
long."

Carr/Week/British Columbia Archives

The Cinderella of the Family

94

them. Particularly strong were feelings about the treatment of Oriental labour on the West Coast, a reflection of attitudes that were to have tragic consequences for Japanese Canadians during the Second World War.

The economic depression that started in 1929 brought a sharper awareness of the inequitable distribution of wealth among social classes. Many political formulas were devised to correct it. Taking root in Alberta, Social Credit preached reform of the monetary system as a cure-all. The Co-operative Commonwealth Federation came into

Hawkins/B.C. Saturday Sunset/13 July 1907

Miss B. Columbia: "Now, Mr. Bull, have you really any objections to my keeping these Japs out of my province to make room for your sons and daughters?"

John Bull: "Certainly not, my dear. I have no interest in the matter. Do as you please."

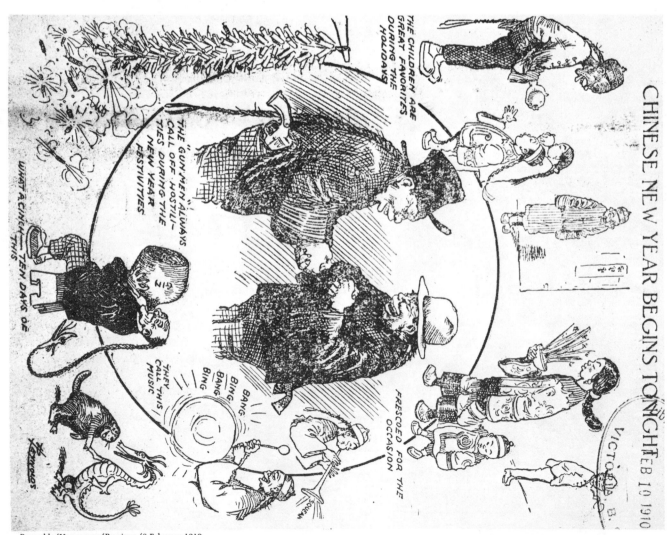

Reynolds/Vancouver/Province/8 February 1910

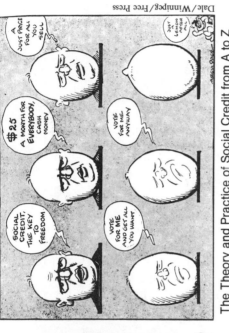

The Theory and Practice of Social Credit from A to Z

Dale/Winnipeg/Free Press

Bourgeois/Montreal/La Presse/1936

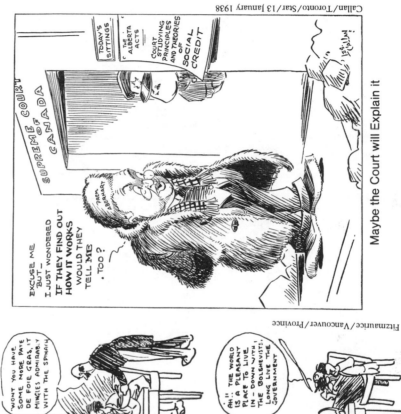

Maybe the Court will Explain it

Callan/Toronto/Star/13 January 1938

The Food Cure for Bolshevism

Fitzmaurice/Vancouver/Province

being in 1932-33, a partnership of discontented radical farmers from western Canada and intellectuals from the cities of central Canada influenced by the socialism of British Labour.

Even R.B. Bennett, the Conservative who was Prime Minister from 1930 to 1935 and who came to symbolize the capitalism of smug old Toryism for many cartoonists, tried to introduce "new deal" legislation strongly influenced by the socialism of his day. Unimpressed by this conversion, Canadians re-elected the pragmatic Mackenzie King who had summed up his

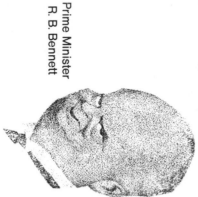

Prime Minister
R. B. Bennett

Glassco/Hamilton/Spectator

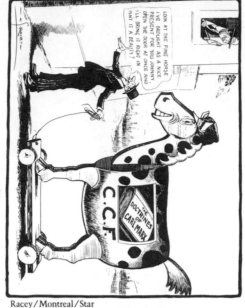

Racey/Montreal/Star

MY! MY! — I — I ¡

96

Dale/Winnipeg/Free Press/19 January 1931

"My Government"

Dale jumped at a peculiar phrase Mr. Bennett used in a speech. He referred to "My Government," a phrase usually reserved for the reigning monarch.

Dale/Winnipeg/Free Press

THE CAPTAIN'S GOING DOWN WITH HIS SHIP!

Grassick/Toronto/Star/3 July 1935

RBB: "Lucky for me I've got this life belt"

political philosophy, before his defeat in 1930, in his famous "not a five-cent piece to Tory provinces" speech, and who tried never again to say anything as straightforward.

The growing power of the provinces was reflected in the national reputations of a new generation of provincial leaders, in particular Quebec Premier Maurice Duplessis and Ontario's Mitchell Hepburn. Both men, from opposite positions, bedevilled the efforts of Mackenzie King to unite the nation for the greatest wartime effort in its history.

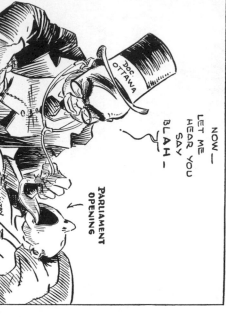
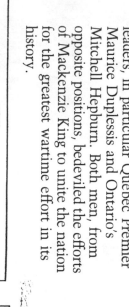

Careful Doc–It May Be a Long Story!

Callan/Toronto/Star/27 January 1938

Lezzall go out and get drunk!

Forrester/Calgary/Eye Opener Summer Annual/1922

Five-Cent Stinker

Hon. Ernest Lapointe: "It was a cheap thing fer you to put in your own mouth an' its evil odour will be impossible to git rid of."

Shields/Evening Telegram/July 1930

Hit and Run

Shields/Evening Telegram/July 1930

An Exchange of Seats

Hunter/Globe/10 December 1921

Mackenzie King's Political Poses Across Canada

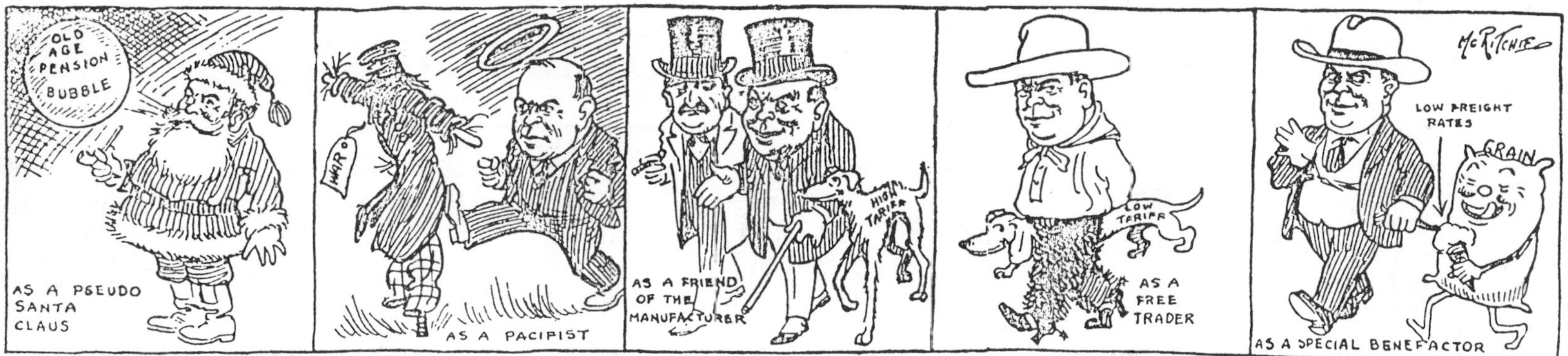
OLD AGE PENSION BUBBLE
AS A PSEUDO SANTA CLAUS
WAR
AS A PACIFIST
AS A FRIEND OF THE MANUFACTURER
HIGH TARIFF
LOW TARIFF
AS A FREE TRADER
McRitchie
LOW FREIGHT RATES
GRAIN
AS A SPECIAL BENEFACTOR

In the Maritimes | In Quebec | In Central Canada | On the Prairies | In British Columbia

McRitchie/Halifax/Herald/September 1926

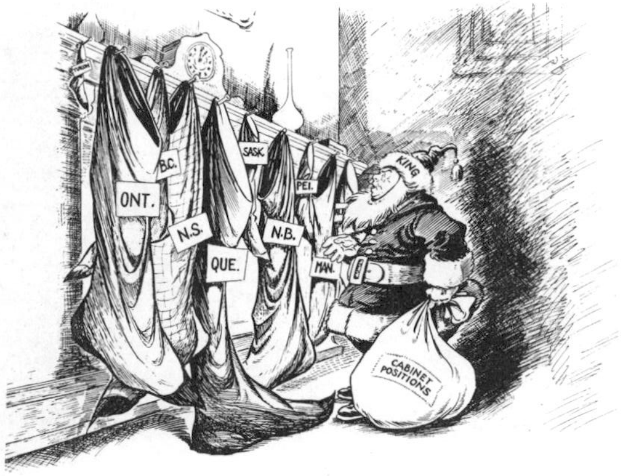
ONT.
B.C.
N.S.
QUE.
SASK.
P.E.I.
N.B.
MAN.
KING
CABINET POSITIONS

Racey/Montreal/Star

Ontario Premier
Mitchell Hepburn

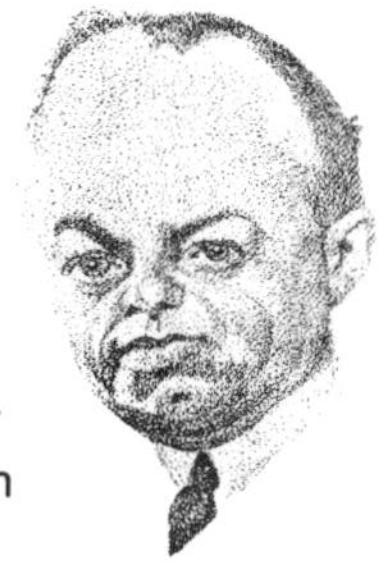

Glassco/Hamilton/Spectator

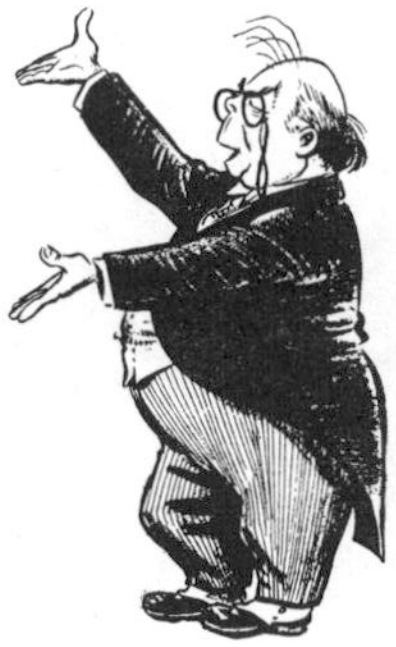

Jack Boothe/Globe and Mail

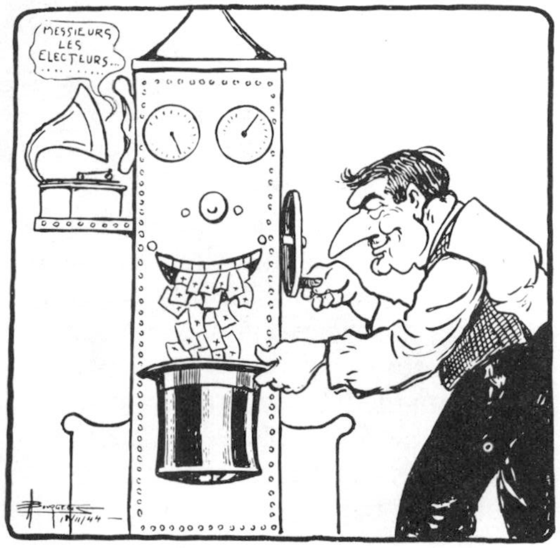
MESSIEURS LES ELECTEURS...

Bourgeois/Montreal/La Presse/18 November 1944

Union Nationale leader Maurice Duplessis

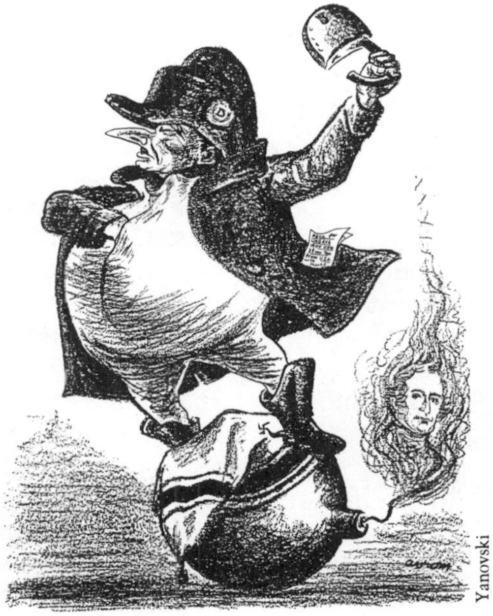

Yanovski

Spirit of Papineau?

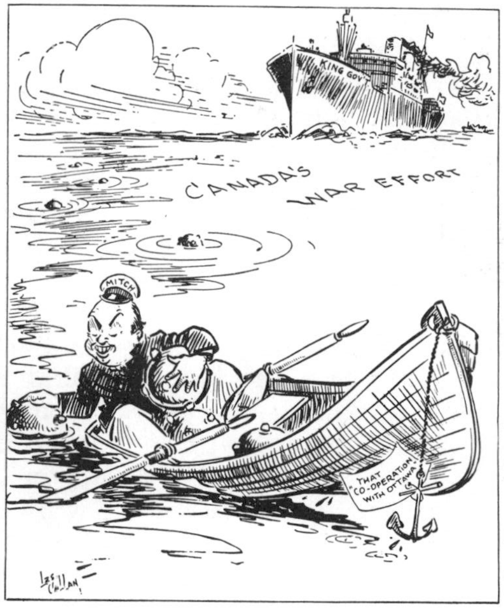
KING GOV'T
CANADA'S WAR EFFORT
MITCH
THAT CO-OPERATION WITH OTTAWA

Callan/Toronto/Star/25 November 1939

A Busy Little Minelayer

5: Robert LaPalme

LaPalme / May 1954

(Sob.) And to think I could be in Toronto tonight.

One evening in 1956, cartoonist Robert LaPalme was visited by a friend at his home in Montreal. The two men and their wives chatted sociably until the visitor, a lawyer and supporter of Quebec's Union Nationale government, said that he wanted to speak to LaPalme privately. They went upstairs to his studio where the lawyer said that he had been asked to transmit an offer to LaPalme. If he would do something publicly to support the Union Nationale in the forthcoming election—the exact nature of the service was never revealed—he would be given $50,000. This is the only reported attempt to bribe a contemporary Canadian cartoonist, as Boss Tweed had tried to buy out Thomas Nast in the previous century, and it provides a rough measure of LaPalme's importance at the time.

His cartoons electrified Quebeckers who had long forgotten the uninhibited political satire of Hector Berthelot's day. After Berthelot came the more formal cartooning of Henri Julien and the less accomplished work of Brodeur, Emile Vézina and Alonzo Ryan, who worked for various Montreal newspapers about the turn of the century.

For some of them, cartooning was only a part-time occupation. Joseph Charlebois, who started to contribute cartoons to Quebec magazines and newspapers in the first decade of this century, combined it with a career as an illuminator of manuscripts, used in those days as state gifts for visiting dignitaries. Charlebois was remembered toward the end of his career as the "most stylish and best-dressed man in Montreal," but his reputation as a cartoonist has been clouded by a number of his cartoons that were overly anti-semitic.

The most prominent Quebec newspaper cartoonist of the first half of this century was Albéric Bourgeois, who began his career with *The Boston Post* in 1902 after graduating from Montreal's Ecole des Beaux-Arts. He also painted frescoes for the Boston Opera before he returned to Montreal in 1903 to join *La Patrie* and then *La Presse* where, for more than fifty years, he drew a daily cartoon as well as a half-page cartoon for every Saturday edition accompanied by an article he wrote under the name of "Père Ladébauche." His most memorable creations were "Baptiste" and "Catherine" repre-

Patronage.

Baptiste: "You hear de news, Napoléon?"

Napolion: "What news is dat one?"

Baptiste: "De Queen Victoriaw, —he's dead."

Napolion: "Dat so. Who get his job?"

Baptiste: "De Prince of Wales,—I spose she get his job."

Napolion: "By gosh!—he must have big pull wit Laurier!"

Ryan/Caricature Politique

senting a traditional French-Canadian couple in rural Quebec who expressed Bourgeois' personal skepticism of current events.

Readers of Quebec newspapers in the 1930s who had become accustomed to the good-natured dialogues of "Baptiste et Catherine" were hardly prepared for Robert LaPalme's avant-garde drawings and slashing attacks on contemporary politicians.

Yet, for two decades, LaPalme was the leading cartoonist in French Canada and one of the few Canadian cartoonists with some reputation outside the country. In 1956, when the bribe was offered, he was working for *Le Devoir* to defeat a reactionary and corrupt Quebec government headed by Premier Maurice Duplessis.

Vezina/1912

Vezina's sketching trip to Africa, 1912

Broduer

Baptiste: "Oui, oui, on connaît ça! Ah, mais, par exemple, ça sera pas long avant que j'leur torde le cou!"

Quebec's Baptiste wants to wring the necks of Laurier's critics

Bourgeois/Montreal/La Presse

Catherine's Description of Rats after a Visit to the City

Charlebois

A French-Canadian attack on Irish-Catholic influence in Quebec

LaPalme's success in the 1940s and 1950s was an early sign of political changes in Quebec that would produce the "quiet revolution" of the following decade. It was significant that the Quebec public came to appreciate a cartoonist whose drawings were unconventional and whose political views were radical. More surprising was the fact that LaPalme was ready to play his part. The obstacles in his path at the outset of his career twenty years earlier would have seemed insurmountable to anyone else.

Like Julien, LaPalme spent part of his childhood and adolescence outside Quebec. In 1918, his father left a carpenter's job in Montreal and settled on a farm in Alberta where his two oldest sons, as farmers, would be protected from military conscription. The move was financially disastrous and the family returned to Montreal in 1925. Robert tried to enroll in Montreal's Ecole des Beaux-Arts, but he was rejected on the grounds that he lacked talent.

"My family were labourers and they knew nothing about what a career in art could be, so I felt that I was completely alone," he wrote in later life. "I was shooed out to get a job."

Moving from one job to another—theatre usher, crucifix maker, florist's helper, store clerk—LaPalme continued to sketch in his spare time. When one of his brothers, a barber, bought him a set of draughtsman's instruments, LaPalme used them to produce an unusual series of geometrical caricatures. He finished twelve drawings of Quebec politicians in this style and

they were published, in 1933, in a small journal devoted to Quebec nationalism, L'Almanach de la Langue Française. This was followed by a display of caricatures in a Montreal theatre, which helped LaPalme land his first job as a cartoonist with L'Ordre, a small political daily newspaper. For $17 a week, LaPalme produced a front-page cartoon every day.

He quickly became something of a local celebrity although he soon realized that his fame was a structure of imagination and talent without any formal education or training.

"One day, a fellow came here from Paris," LaPalme recalled. "He saw my drawings and he was happy to find someone in Montreal who—or so he thought—could speak at his level on contemporary art. So he invited me, and bought some beer, and there we sat. He began to talk to me about modern art, you know; Bracque, Picasso . . . I'd never heard of them! I sat there with my mouth open and I couldn't understand a word he said."

In 1934, a Paris newspaper repro-

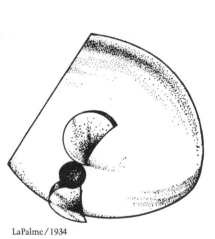

Prime Minister R. B. Bennett

LaPalme/1934

duced some of the Almanach caricatures. They drew favourable comment from a critic on another newspaper, L'Echo de Paris. A magazine in New York inquired about commissioning some drawings.

Encouraged by this early response from the critics and the public, LaPalme decided to try his luck in New York. He stayed there for two years, classifying himself as a student for US immigration purposes but working actively as a free-lance illustrator for such magazines as Stage, The Nation, Ringmaster of Chicago and a newspaper, The Philadelphia Ledger.
Jean-Louis Gagnon, a former news-

Prime Minister Mackenzie King

LaPalme/1937

LaPalme/Le Canada/1948

VAS-Y!

The Pimp
"Go with him!"

LaPalme/Le Canada/1948

tant Quebec politician in the federal cabinet, Ernest Lapointe, as a cracked chamber pot. Duplessis personally gave LaPalme $25 for the original drawing.

paper editor and old friend of LaPalme's, once wrote that the five-foot-nothing cartoonist turned to his new wife, Nanette, as they entered New York in 1935 and proclaimed, "This town is my size."

In 1937, he returned to Canada and worked briefly for *Le Droit* in Ottawa before moving to Quebec where he eventually became an assistant professor at Laval University "teaching things that I had never learned" while continuing to draw cartoons for newspapers.

In 1940, the commandant of a large army base near Quebec, a personal friend of LaPalme's, Adolphe Dansereau, commissioned the artist to prepare murals for the drill hall. LaPalme finished twenty cartoons for the murals, but Dansereau was replaced by another officer before he could order LaPalme to go ahead with his *History of War*. His replacement, Brigadier General Georges Vanier, later Governor General of Canada, took one look at the paintings and ordered LaPalme off the base.

"These drawings were a little bit crude in some details," LaPalme later admitted. "When I had to draw sex, I drew sex, and that was it. But it was all childish. There was nothing shocking."

"Vanier was a very austere man, very puritanical. I showed him my drawings, but he very coolly pushed me out the door. He was put off by them. He was a prude, remember that."

LaPalme took his colourful and elaborate paintings of ancient and modern warfare to a small gallery on 57th Street in New York.

"The newspapers came," he remembered, "and I had better reviews than some of the really great artists. It was crazy. They compared my work with that of David Low."

At home, editors and critics took notice. The paintings were given a six-week exhibition at the Montreal Museum of Fine Arts and at a Toronto gallery before being included in an exhibition of Canadian war paintings in Brazil. Eventually, the paintings were shown in Rome and Paris, where LaPalme's exhibition was opened by the Canadian ambassador, Georges Vanier.

"I knew that he didn't know what he was doing," LaPalme wrote later of the event. "He didn't connect this to that guy he had brushed off in Quebec. I saw him after but of course I never mentioned this."

By 1951, LaPalme was at *Le Devoir* and at his peak as a political cartoonist. His caricatures of Premier Maurice Duplessis became increasingly vicious. Quebeckers had never seen anything like them. They gasped in disbelief when the Premier was caricatured as a pimp selling the province to American businessmen or as a priest attended by his acolyte ministers.

LaPalme cartooned Duplessis and traditional Quebec institutions with all the vitriol of a disillusioned believer. Duplessis had come to power in 1936 on a reform platform and LaPalme had supported him enthusiastically at that time. He had also been flattered to receive a personal commission from the Premier to caricature the most impor-

LaPalme/Montreal/Le Devoir

LaPalme

LaPalme/Le Canada

LaPalme/Le Canada

"A long time after, I grew up," the cartoonist remembered. "The $25 that he gave me was the image that made me understand the way he played politics. He bought people. I did everything to downgrade that man."

For those familiar with Quebec gossip about the Premier's personal life, LaPalme's cartoons were filled with innuendo. When it was rumoured, for instance, that Duplessis kept a mistress in an apartment on Montreal's Van Horne Street, LaPalme would often insinuate the street sign into his cartoons for no apparent reason.

Nothing was sacred in LaPalme's eyes. When a priest attached to the Cardinal's staff in Montreal asked for a caricature of the great man, LaPalme exaggerated one of his favourite poses: standing on the steps of the dais leading to his throne with his robes flowing down the steps to make him look taller. In LaPalme's caricature, the Cardinal's shoes were plainly visible beneath the robe, far above its lower hem. The caricature was returned to the artist without having been shown to its subject.

In the 1950s, Quebec was emerging "from the seventeenth century," to use years, LaPalme lost not only an established newspaper outlet for his cartoons but his best subject. Duplessis died in 1959 and his party was defeated in 1960.

During the next few years, LaPalme felt that his career as newspaper cartoonist had ended. "Once you have a style, you can't get out of it," he has said. "It paralyzes you and you age with it."

He became deeply involved in organizing international cartoon exhibitions in Montreal. He was appointed director of the annual International Salon of Caricature and Cartoon, which attracted 1,200 entrants from sixty nations in 1963, its first year. The Salon soon became the largest competition of its kind in the world.

All this activity represented a new career for the cartoonist who perhaps suspected that he could never again match his achievements of the 1950s on *Le Devoir*.

LaPalme helped to create new freedoms for other Quebec cartoonists in the 1960s and 1970s. No one directly copied him, but the simplicity of his cartoons and his distinctive line influenced those who followed him in Quebec.

In the 1950s, Robert LaPalme was in the front lines of political conflict and his cartoons pointed the way toward political changes. In the following decade, Quebec politics underwent revolutionary changes and most Quebec cartoonists reverted to a more traditional role, observing from the sidelines and picking their targets from all parties.

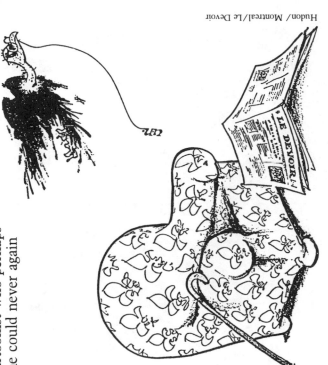

105

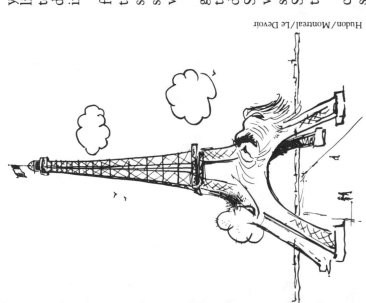

Obsession

LaPalme's phrase, and the cartoonist led the way along with such men as editor Gerald Filion of *Le Devoir*, journalist Pierre Laporte of *Le Devoir*, labour union leader Jean Marchand and labour lawyer and academic Pierre Trudeau. The tiny cartoonist also filled the new television screens of Quebec with his caricatures and his rapid-fire commentary.

In 1959, he joined Montreal's *La Presse*, Canada's largest French-language daily newspaper, but soon moved to the new *Le Nouveau Journal* to work with its editor, his old friend, Jean-Louis Gagnon. The newspaper was short-lived. In the space of a few

Waiting for Inspiration

The Second World War was a thin time for political cartoonists. Like other journalists, they became propagandists. Their cartoons are interesting today only because they recall the enthusiasm and hatred that animated Canadians as they left their comfortable homeland to fight overseas.

The Hun is at the Gate!

Chambers/Halifax/Chronicle-Herald/1942

The Approaching Storm

LaPalme/L'Action Catholique/1941

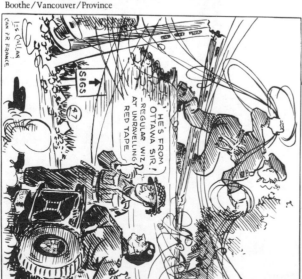

Boothe/Vancouver/Province

Callan/Maple Leaf

Monty and Johnny
by LES CALLAN

Callan/Maple Leaf

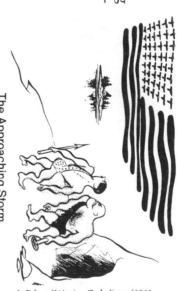

MEAN SCAMP-F
A humorous pictorial record of the war...

Hall/Toronto/Telegram/1941

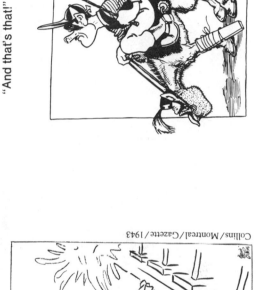

"And that's that!"

The Blushing Bridegroom

"She says here, 'The Victoria Day fireworks were simply marvellous. Too bad you missed it.'"

WHO SAID DEMOCRACY WAS "DECADENT"?

English and French in Canada approached the emergency from traditional positions. Conscription again became the most divisive issue of domestic politics. The veteran leader, Mackenzie King, slowly and carefully nursed the nation through the crisis at home while maintaining a full contribution to the war effort. King remained Prime Minister until 1948 when he picked his successor, Louis St. Laurent, who presided over the entry of Newfoundland into Confederation in 1949.

Glassco / 22 May 1940

Nervous One: "Will she weather this, captain?"
Skipper Churchill: "Weather what?"

Target Toyio!

Reidford / Montreal / Star / 16 February 1945

DON'T DISCUSS
INFORMATION
THAT MIGHT
BE VALUABLE
TO THE
ENEMY

DON'T GOSSIP

A WISE OLD OWL
SAT IN AN OAK.
THE MORE HE SAW
THE LESS HE SPOKE.
THE LESS HE SPOKE
THE MORE HE HEARD.
HE DIDN'T REPEAT A SINGLE WORD.
NO MATTER WHAT HE SAW OR HEARD
LET'S TRY TO IMITATE THIS BIRD !!

A Reminder for Us All

Boothe / Vancouver / Province / 1940s

The Hour Before the Dawn

Reidford / Montreal / Star / 14 August 1945

Hotting It Up!
Put Victory First—
Subscribe to the Sixth Victory Loan

Mozel / Winnipeg / Tribune / 1940s

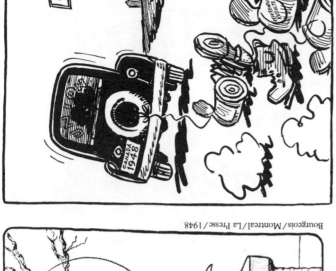

Collins/Montreal/Gazette/1948

Ready to Start the Honeymoon

Ting/London/Free Press/1949

"...and now we are ten!"

Bourgeois/Montreal/La Presse/1948

Collins/Montreal/Gazette/1946

A Dainty Dish to Set Before a King

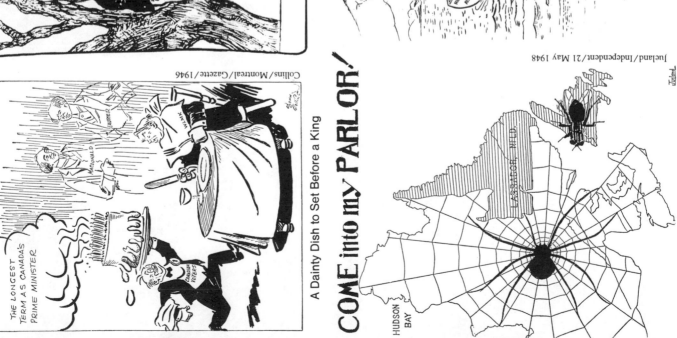

Boothe/The Confederate/31 May 1948

A Queer Fisherman!
For Confederation

Jueland/Independent/21 May 1948

Against Confederation

This was a relatively placid time in Canada's political development. The economy prospered. Because of its role during the war and its emergence from the war with an intact economy, Canada wielded greater international influence than at any time before or since. It was exerted at the United Nations by Lester B. Pearson, the first Canadian to launch a career as Prime Minister on the basis of a political reputation acquired outside the country.

Regional divisions continued to fuel domestic politics with occasional explosions sparked by such entertaining

Prime Minister Louis St. Laurent

LaPalme / Unpublished / 1950

They Know What They Want!

Chambers / Halifax / Herald / 1959

Boothe / Stand Up & Be Counted

"Them dang East'ners Want Us'n to Sell the Stuff."

Reidford / Globe and Mail / 31 August 1957

Callan / Toronto / Star / 1948

"Mind keeping that shadow on your side of the line?"

scandals as the discovery of horses on the military payroll at Ontario's Camp Petawawa.

During this prosperous period of Liberal government, Canadians became more aware of the importance of US capital in their economy and US military strength in their defence arrangements. The close and uncritical wartime alliance between the two countries developed into a vital economic association, each nation being the other's most important trading partner, but the political relationship became more difficult, at least on the Canadian side. Reliance on US money,

Ting / London / Free Press / 1952

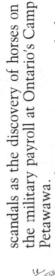

Reidford / Globe and Mail / 21 April 1953

How It All Happened

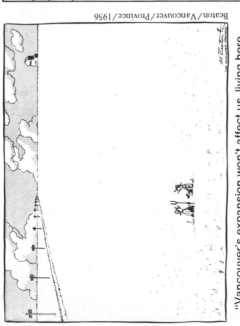

Beaton / Vancouver / Province / 1956

"Vancouver's expansion won't affect us, living here on the outskirts of metropolitan Toronto..."

Grassick / Maclean's / 15 January 1954

Norris / Vancouver / Sun / 17 December 1952

"Trust those politicians in Ottawa to make a big fuss about nothing..."

expertise, men, and equipment for the aerial defence of the northern half of the continent created concern about the effectiveness of Canadian sovereignty over the North. The virulent anti-Communism of the McCarthy era in the United States made Canadians appreciate some of the basic political differences between the two countries, and some of the virtues of their own system.

Not Exactly a 1949 Model
Defence Minister Brooke Claxton

Collins/Montreal/Gazette/1948

Progress

Collins/Montreal/Gazette/1946

Get in Line!

Grassick/Toronto/Telegram/3 October 1956

Yanovski

Time to Curb the Fearless Fosdick Committee

Collins/Montreal/Gazette/11 April 1957

A Position if Necessary, but..."
St. Laurent during the Suez Crisis

Reidford/Globe and Mail/2 November 1956

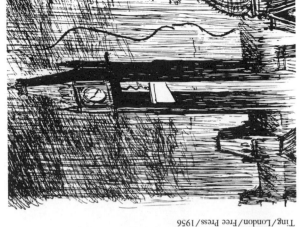

Closure

Reidford/Globe and Mail/1956

113

C. D. Howe

Collins/Montreal/Gazette/26 September 1956

Remote Control

Ting/London/Free Press/1956

"...Born? Where you going? For how long? ...Ever laugh at Charlie Chaplin?"

Norris/Vancouver/Sun/27 September 1952

This more sceptical attitude toward the United States was one element of the public response to the 1956 "pipeline debate" in Parliament. Canadians reacted negatively when the Liberal government of Prime Minister Louis St. Laurent and Trade Minister C.D. Howe used closure to force through legislation necessary for the construction of a trans-Canada gas pipeline financed largely by US capital.

Kuch/Winnipeg/Free Press/5 June 1956

Tuesday after closure vote—Howe and Lewis

Reidford

Pickersgill listening to Howe

Reidford

Reidford sketches the pipeline debate in the Commons

When the Conservatives late that year chose a new leader capable of eloquently expressing this sense of national concern and pride, the fate of the Liberal government was sealed.

John Diefenbaker's victory over the Liberals in 1957 and, three years later, the defeat of the Union Nationale government founded by Maurice Duplessis in Quebec, signalled the start of a more turbulent, absorbing, and creative period in Canada's political development.

114

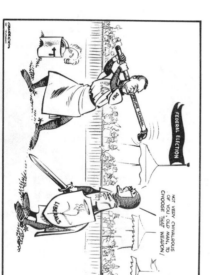

Choose Your Weapon

Grassick/Toronto/Telegram

Diefenbaker challenges St Laurent

Reidford

Starting to Roll

Reidford/Globe and Mail/22 June 1957

On TV It's Funny

Reidford/Globe and Mail/21 April 1953

Ting/London/Free Press/1957

"....I'm All Shook Up"

"And now—something for me!"

Grassick/Toronto/Telegram/11 December 1956

Collins/Montreal/Gazette/21 April 1958

Tulip Time in Ottawa

6: Len Norris

When Len Norris of *The Vancouver Sun* was awarded an honorary degree by the University of Windsor in 1973, the president of the university, Dr. John F. Leddy, described him "unhesitatingly, as the finest cartoonist not only in Canada but in North America."

For almost thirty years, Norris has been consistently the funniest cartoonist in the country and among the most popular. Since 1950, when he joined the *Sun*, his published collections of cartoons have been bought every year by about 30,000 Norris connoisseurs.

Norris also is a link between the men who worked during the middle period of Canadian cartooning, in the first half of this century, and the contemporary group heralded by the appearance of Robert LaPalme in Quebec and Duncan Macpherson in Ontario midway through the century. In 1979, when he moved into semi-retirement by reducing his output for the *Sun* to two cartoons a week, Norris was the dean of a generation of cartoonists that regarded itself, justifiably, as being the most productive, accomplished, inventive and influential in Canadian history. But when he joined the *Sun*, in 1950, cartoonists in Canada worked in isolation, as they had for decades, without the contemporary cartoonists' sense of belonging to a special group, playing a distinct role at a particularly

formative time in the history of the country.

Contemporary cartoonists, as a rule, have been trained in Canada and have spent their careers in this country, earning a degree of fame and financial

Len Norris by Roy Peterson

EGAD SIR! I TRUST THIS WON'T ALTER YOUR VIEWS ON LAW STUDENTS, LAWYERS, JUDGES, POLITICAL APPOINTEES, POLITICIANS, RED TAPE BUREAUCRATS...

"...or humour."

security that would have amazed their predecessors. Many of the cartoonists who worked during the middle period had to leave Canada to learn and, in some cases, to practise their profession. When they found a position with a Canadian newspaper, and a steady if modest salary, they tended to stay put for decades.

One of the most durable and typical cartoonists of this middle period is Robert Chambers of Halifax, whose career began in the United States in the 1920s when he worked as an animator for film cartoons and as an illustrator for the tabloid *New York Graphic*. When the depression made it difficult for a Canadian artist to find work in the United States, he returned to Nova Scotia where he drew cartoons for the daily newspapers in Halifax from 1933 until 1977.

The extraordinary length of Chambers' career spans all three periods of Canadian political cartooning. He sold his first cartoon in 1923, the year of Bengough's death. His first inspiration to become a cartoonist, as a sixteen-year-old student at the Acadia Seminary in Wolfville, N.S., was an original cartoon by A.G. Racey of *The Montreal Star*, given to him by a fellow student who was the daughter of a *Star* editor. When he started to work for *The Halifax Herald* in 1937, he succeeded Donald McRitchie, the cartoonist who had been "making people sizzle" at Port Arthur in 1906 and who had worked on Calgary's *Eye-Opener*.

Chambers' first job in Halifax, on his return from New York in 1933, was as a cartoonist for *The Halifax Chronicle*, attacking the provincial Conservatives. For $35 a week, he also acted as the newspaper's photographer.

The Liberals won the election but Chambers' job disappeared the day after. In 1937, *The Halifax Herald*, a Conservative newspaper, offered him $75 a week to draw cartoons attacking the Liberals in another election campaign. The strategy failed, perhaps because the *Chronicle* countered Chambers' work for the Conservatives by re-publishing many of his anti-Conservative cartoons from the previous campaign.

"I suppose I lost my credibility by switching politics," he recollected years later. "They were quite right, too. Offered me $75 a week ... I would have joined any party with that kind of deal."

His many years in a highly competitive field with its own share of star performers and self-promoters never affected Chambers' modest views about his own performance or about the importance of cartooning. When he first went to New York, he said much later, "I thought I was a genius and found out I wasn't." Since then, he stated, "I've known what the traffic will bear, and I've never tried to go beyond that."

"It's a pretty shaky job, cartooning," he testified. "You just want to do something that's going to please your boss. Anything that's going to upset him, you just don't do it, if you're smart."

In style and content, Chambers belonged to what he called "the old school." At the start, he simply copied American cartoonists. Only in the last decade of his career, influenced by a new generation of Canadian cartoonists, did he consciously start to improve his technique, despite the strain of drawing up to nine cartoons a week for various editions of the newspaper that was created by the merger of the *Chronicle* and *Herald* in 1948.

Chambers also described himself, toward the end of his career, as "completely a-political." His work became so reliable that, in his final years, his editors rarely saw his cartoons until they appeared in the newspaper.

"I've never done a cartoon that caused any controversy," he once stated.

In 1965, Chambers received an honorary degree from Nova Scotia's St. Francis Xavier University, a tribute to the visual political history of Nova Scotia and Canada that he had compiled over the years. Although he would continue to cartoon for more than a decade, Chambers by then was an anachronism–a cartoonist of the middle period preserved in Halifax by a combination of local conditions and his own tenacity.

While Chambers was working as a film animator in New York, another young Canadian, Les Callan, was studying at the Chicago Academy of Fine Arts. Callan had attempted to start his cartooning career in 1924 by walking into the offices of *The Free Press* in Winnipeg and asking to see George McManus, unaware that the creator of "Maggie and Jiggs" worked thousands of miles away in the United States. A kindly editor introduced him to a commercial artist in Winnipeg who advised him to study in Chicago.

Callan spent two years working for the Canadian Pacific Railway during the "grain rush" in the summer and autumn and studying in Chicago during the winter. Toward the end of the decade, he became the cartoonist for *The Sun* in Vancouver before he was hired by *The Toronto Star* in 1937. He worked for the *Star* until 1961 except for three years in the Canadian Army during the Second World War.

Callan was one of the most popular of the wartime cartoonists sketching for the army newspaper *The Maple Leaf*. He drew a series entitled "Monty and Johnny" which portrayed the hardships and predicaments of ordinary Canadian soldiers in France, Belgium, Holland and Germany. Many of them were published in 1946 in a book, *Normandy and On*.

In an unusual move for a cartoonist, Callan tried to join the ranks of his victims after his retirement from the *Star* by running for a seat in the Ontario legislature in 1963. After his defeat, he moved to British Columbia where he now lives quietly.

Another Canadian graduate of the Chicago Academy of Fine Arts, more famous in his time than Callan but not a better cartoonist, was Jack Boothe. He joined *The Vancouver Daily Province* in 1930, competing against Callan at the *Sun*. Some years later, he followed Callan to Toronto where he joined *The Globe and Mail* in 1943. By 1947, he was claiming to be the highest paid cartoonist in Canada with an annual salary of $7,000. In 1953, he was the first Canadian artist to cover the Korean conflict, on assignment for the Thomson newspapers.

James G. Reidford, editorial cartoonist for *The Montreal Star* from 1941 to 1951 and for *The Globe and Mail* of Toronto from 1951 until 1972,

Out–On a Double Play

Callan/Toronto/Star/6 May 1937

"is going through a renaissance period right now."

"Actually," he predicted, "it shouldn't be long before our work will rank with the best there is."

With the retirement of Robert Chambers in Halifax several years ago, John Collins of *The Gazette* in Montreal became the dean of editorial page cartoonists. Born in Washington, D.C., in 1917, he moved to Canada as a child with his family and sold his first freelance cartoon to *The Gazette* in 1937. He became the newspaper's first staff cartoonist in 1939. His wartime cartoons were published in many American newspapers. In the late 1940s, he invented his "Uno Who" figure to depict the average taxpayer and it has appeared in his cartoons ever since.

Despite the local popularity of many of these cartoonists, and the enduring quality of some of their work, none of them enjoyed the reputation that belonged to Len Norris almost as soon as he started to cartoon in Vancouver. Within a few months of his first appearance in *The Sun* in 1950, Norris

also studied and served part of his apprenticeship in the United States. After working as a commercial artist in Toronto and London, Ontario, he went to Los Angeles in 1938 and spent several years as an animator with the Walt Disney studios.

In a newspaper interview in 1958, Reidford said that Canadian cartooning

Collins/Montreal/Gazette/2 October 1953

Giving Them the Bird

Reidford/Globe and Mail/16 October 1965

Reidford/Globe and Mail/20 December 1957

Reidford's Pickersgill

Reidford/Globe and Mail/3 July 1954

Boothe/Stand Up & Be Counted

A Crisis Confronts Us

seemed to divine the secret of provoking laughter combined with rueful self-recognition among Canadians. The national traits that he caricatured, with an expertise and consistency unmatched by any of his predecessors, were evidently deep-rooted and lasting.

Although he presented himself as a social rather than political cartoonist, he dealt constantly if indirectly with Canadians' political attitudes. The response to his work indicated that his own political instincts represented those of many Canadians who inhabited, as Norris still does, the suburbs of Canada's larger cities.

At first glance, Norris appears to be a regional cartoonist dealing mainly with local topics. His cartoons are set on the West Coast and many of the peculiar characters in them find their natural habitat in British Columbia. Their favourite haunts are places such as the mythical Victoria Conservative Club, actually modelled by Norris on a military club in Toronto, and his elaborate version of the lobby of Victoria's Empress Hotel. Within its jungle of potted palms, survivors of Britain's colonial empire drink tea and bemoan the decline and fall of everything in the country, from the monarchy to the string trio that traditionally serenaded Empress guests at tea-time.

"I trust Mr. Stanfield didn't say anything during his BC visit to arouse political passions..."

Norris/Vancouver/Sun/11 May 1973

"We didn't have any of this tomfool nonsense before they changed it from Royal Mail to Postes Canada..."

Norris/Vancouver/Sun/21 August 1970

"...Don't be surprised if Harold Wilson offers us bookies, football pools, a nationalized steel industry and the right to drive on the wrong side of the street."

"All clear! The merger scare is confined to Burnaby, Vancouver, and the North Vancouvers..."

In Norris cartoons, Victoria is a maze of Elizabethan architecture, tea shoppes and fish and chip establishments advertising, "by appointment to Alfred the Great." The populace seems to have been recruited from among the eccentrics of village life in Britain, shipped to British Columbia to ripen in exile. It is a completely mythical place but every English-speaking Canadian recognizes it instantly as part of his own national landscape.

Norris was the first cartoonist in Canada to appropriate a distinctive regional culture as a vehicle to caricature and express underlying national atti-

tudes toward current events. Often, when he apparently is at his most parochial, he is dealing with old associations and new conflicts that are shared by all Canadians.

The village of Amblesnide and Tiddlycove is a caricature rendition of suburban Vancouver and, to some extent, of suburbs across the country. No matter that many of the quainter aspects of life in Amblesnide and Tiddlycove already were disappearing from the Vancouver scene when Norris arrived there in 1950. His version of suburbia continued to express the efforts of people everywhere to escape from the

uniform bleakness of suburban life. Rockbottom Creek, presumably somewhere in the interior of British Columbia, represents small-town Canada and expresses the conservatism and down-to-earth cynicism about modern life that is a notable feature of the Canadian outlook. Norris often uses Rockbottom Creek as well as the regional PGE railway to make fun of all the bureaucratic experts who never cease trying to engineer our lives for us.

The equivalent institution, for big business, is the Akme Pewter Tuning-Fork Company where the corporate elite is shown at its most asinine, and

121

"...and while $5.1 million to build a two-hole public comfort station was briefly questioned, we are pleased, gentlemen, to..."

Norris/Vancouver/Sun/27 November 1971

"It invariably takes Rodney a while to get over Les Canadiens winning Lord Stanley's cup..."

Norris/Vancouver/Sun/30 May 1978

"...I was just 'ammerin' up your sign on this 'ere tree...and bang...down she come..."

Norris/Vancouver/Sun/28 August 1956

"Your final demand...double or nothing...has intriguing aspects that management would like to study."

Norris/Vancouver/Sun/11 October 1974

"...found in possession of three Irish Sweep Tickets, one George Phelps, alias 'Fat Chance,' alias 'Lucky This Time,' alias 'Need You Now'..."

where labour–management relations are raised to a new level of absurdity.

All these settings are peopled frequently by a bizarre cast of familiar characters. One of the hardiest, and the character that Norris has identified as expressing something of his own personality, is Rodney. Many aspects of contemporary Canadian life infuriate Rodney, raging within the cluttered confines of his Victorian mansion, and his frustration is echoed in the living-rooms of condominiums across the nation.

"I know what I'd tell Quebec," he roared in 1970 in a typical outburst. "The Plains of Abraham are still there and I'll make it the best out of three."

The religious origins and evangelistic zeal of the Social Credit movement attracted the attention of Norris as soon as he arrived in Vancouver. At first, he drew the province's Social Credit politicians with haloes supported above their heads by thin rods emerging from the backs of their necks. Norris later concealed these haloes within the tall, rounded crowns of hats. The hats came to symbolize the Social Credit party in his cartoons long after many of his readers had forgotten about the haloes.

Norris' early debt to the British cartoonist Giles is expressed in his little old lady character, often used to voice the complaints of municipal taxpayers.

Not all Norris cartoons are located in Victoria or in Amblesnide and Tiddlycove. The setting is often a kitchen or living-room in the bleakest suburbs of Middle Canada.

The people who inhabit this world,

like George Phelps, Norris' average Canadian, are much closer in appearance to most Canadians than Rodney is. Often they are harrassed by their children, particularly by a little Frankenstein called Filbert Phelps that Norris created at the outset of his newspaper career. At other times, and with increasing frequency as Norris matured as a cartoonist, this suburban couple has been oppressed by external forces that are ordinary but overwhelming: high prices and taxes, remote political forces and threatening social changes.

"Before I bother getting up," says

the husband to his wife early one morning, "have a look, will you, and see if they've closed down the country."

Norris himself is an extremely conservative individual who once described himself, toward the start of his career as a cartoonist, as "an apathetic Tory." This has troubled many writers who have tried to portray him in print. The reality of his life doesn't fit stereotyped ideas of what a cartoonist should be.

"Most newspapermen tend to be irreverent, prickly and rumbustious,"

123

124

"Of course he's back, Miss Figsby....it's the law."

Norris/Vancouver/Sun/7 September 1960

"It's the Lafleurs...quick, turn on the French channel."

Norris/Vancouver/Sun/28 September 1976

"...not only that, but when I listen to OUR politicians, I feel anti-Canadian, too."

Norris/Vancouver/Sun/15 March 1963

wrote Norris' publisher, Stuart Keate, in 1971. "Cartoonists are no different. I know one who got so mad at a motorist who slipped into a parking space the cartoonist was trying to enter that he charged the offender like a maddened bull, and did $700 damage . . . In the midst of all this magnificent lunacy, Len Norris stands out as a wispy Pacific Coast beacon of sanity . . . a publisher's dream . . . a jewel. Conscientous. Unflappable. Loyal. A man of quiet dignity. A lousy putter."

"Norris is so sane, so steady, so balanced, so reliable," wrote Keate on another occasion, "that I have come to the conclusion that he doesn't really draw these cartoons at all. I suspect that his wife, Marg, secretly knits them."

The paradox is artificial. Norris is one of Canada's most effective cartoonists because he is what he cartoons, he knows what he is and he can laugh at himself without being apologetic. Other Canadians accept and understand his criticism because they sense that he is one of them, and because his talent is obvious.

Norris didn't have to wait long for his artistic abilities to be recognized, although fame as a cartoonist was a relatively late development in his career. Born in England in 1913, he came to Canada with his parents when he was thirteen years old. His father worked in a pulp mill in Port Arthur, Ontario, until he lost his job during the Depression. The family then moved to Toronto where Len found a job weighing coal at the harbour for $12.50 a week.

Len also worked on the telephone switchboard of the Elias Rogers Coal Company, doodling sketches in his spare time. Frank Dowsett, a member of the company's advertising department, saw the sketches and commissioned drawings for his brochures. He also introduced Len to members of the art department at *The Toronto Star* who showed him how they designed advertising layouts, retouched photos and performed other services for the newspaper.

At night, he attended classes at the Ontario College of Art before accepting a job with an advertising agency in Toronto. He was an art director with the agency for two years before he joined the army in 1940.

Military service, for Lieutenant Norris, was a continuation of his civilian career. He was posted to Ottawa where he spent the war years as editor of *Cam*, a magazine published by the Royal Canadian Electrical and Mechanical Engineers. It was a breezy publication filled with comics, cartoons, and easy-to-read material about preventive maintenance.

With an MBE for his wartime work, Norris returned to Toronto to become an art director for Maclean-Hunter, the largest Canadian magazine publisher. He worked as art director for *Canadian Homes and Gardens*, one of the more important members of the *Maclean's* fleet of publications, and freelanced in his spare time for some of the others including *Maclean's*.

"There was really just one drawback," Norris later recalled. "I didn't seem to be doing any living."

Author and television personality Pierre Berton, then managing editor of *Maclean's*, was responsible for the decisive change in Norris' career, from art director in Toronto to political cartoonist in Vancouver. A former feature writer for *The Vancouver Sun*, Berton was contacted by *Sun* publisher Don Cromie during a search for a cartoonist. Berton believed then that Norris was "one of the freshest and funniest Canadian artists" and Norris illustrated this by sending to Vancouver a drawing of Don Cromie and his brother reaching across the Rockies and beckoning a tiny, frightened cartoonist to come West.

Norris wanted to move to Vancouver, with its warmer climate and slower pace, but he was less confident about becoming a political cartoonist.

"I hardly knew who the Prime Minister was at that time," he recalled. "I turned down the first offer but after a year it was repeated, and it came with a dozen roses for my wife and a brolly which we had to figure out was a West Coast umbrella. They got me at a low ebb in the art-directing business and we decided to get into the car and come out here. It was a great move, one of the best things I ever did."

His immediate impact on Vancouver and *The Sun* was negligible. Cromie was away from Vancouver when Norris arrived and no one seemed to know what to do with the recruit from Toronto. He was assigned a cubby hole in the art department and asked to illustrate cheap novels that *The Sun* purchased from a syndicate in the United States. He also drew such routine illustrations for the news pages as diagrams of traffic accidents and bank robberies. After six months, he was discovered in the art department by Hal Straight, *The Sun's* managing editor.

This is Berton's version of the encounter: "Straight said, 'What are you doing here?' and Norris said, 'I am supposed to be doing political cartoons,' and Straight said, 'Well, for Christ's sake, draw a couple,' and Norris drew a couple and Straight was so enamoured that he put them on the front page immediately and Norris has never looked back."

As Norris remembers it, his development as a political cartoonist was slower and far more painful. At first, he tried to produce political cartoons "in the traditional way, as it was in Canada at that time: the use of symbolism in the classical editorial cartoon.'

"I was a dismal failure with this

"style," he recalled, "and apparently had no talent whatever for producing a symbolic cartoon, so things got a little desperate for a while."

Norris also discovered that he had only limited ability to create effective caricatures of politicians. In an interview, he once claimed that this flaw, which some cartoonists might have considered fatal, was the origin of his distinctive type of cartooning. From it, as a matter of necessity, came the idea "of relating the political events to ordinary people ... developing a series of characters who would represent ordinary people rather than doing the politician himself making the event."

Norris also was influenced by British cartoonists, particularly Giles of *The Express*, and had what he described as "an English lean in my feeling for the cartoon." His early career as a magazine illustrator helped to direct him toward exaggerated and often light-hearted illustrations of everyday activities rather than dramatic cartoons with sombre messages. Gradually he developed his cast of characters and his Victorian stage settings.

"Relate the thing to *character*," Norris once said, explaining his primary discovery. "I felt that my aim should be to *illustrate* social events.

"I just about went back to Toronto after six months. But I hung on, and after eighteen months, I began to feel comfortable. I seemed to know where I was going."

Occasionally, Norris experimented with other styles, usually when he wanted to convey a different kind of message. These cartoons stand apart in his annual collections as if they were the work of another cartoonist, the Mr. Hyde concealed within the bland Dr. Jekyll who handed his Amblenside and Tiddlycove cartoons to the editors of *The Sun* daily at 4.30 p.m.

In 1957, angered by communist-hunting in Washington, Norris showed members of the US Senate Sub-Committee on Internal Security brandishing banners labelled *Fear, Accusations, Innuendo* and *Suspicion*. In 1959, his usual Christmas fare—parents harassed by children demanding impossible toys and Santa Clauses tormented by Filbert Phelps—was interrupted by a cartoon without a caption showing a lonely old man sitting in his room, holding one end of a Christmas cracker and staring into space.

As political, social and racial tensions increased in Canada in the 1960s and 1970s, Norris' cartoon style often became simpler and his messages more serious. Yet while many Canadian journalists and cartoonists flirted with radical politics during these years, Norris remained true to his own temperament, his social background, and his audience. He expressed the strong conservatism of the middle class in English Canada, and in this role, he spoke with conviction.

Living for more than twenty-five years in suburban West Vancouver, Norris supporting a wife and two sons, Norris was in real life what he often portrayed

Norris/Vancouver/Sun/24 December 1959

Norris/Vancouver/Sun/25 October 1968

ACME
TV COMMERCIALS
PRODUCTIONS INC.

"our policy here is not to use Negroes in our commercials because
we don't have a racial problem in Canada."

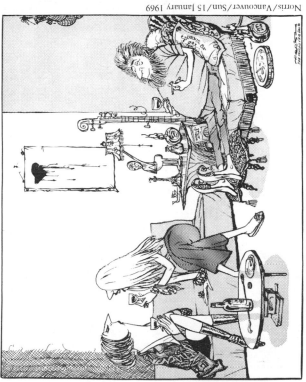

Norris/Vancouver/Sun/15 January 1969

"It's only vin du pays...we're a bit strapped as Cecil is
between Canada Council grants."

Norris/Vancouver/Sun/26 April 1962

NUCLEAR TESTS
START AGAIN
RUSSIA THREATENS
MORE A-BOMB TESTS
GENEVA DISARMAMENT
TALKS BOG DOWN
U.S. MOON SHOT FAILS

THE VANCOUVER SUN

"I suppose one simply must have faith in a country that produces the whitest wash,
the softest hands, the coolest smoke, the fastest relief from acid upset..."

Norris/Vancouver/Sun/5 December 1958

VOTE
BUTT

VOTE
BUTT

"First...let me say that I don't intend to bore you with
vital issues..."

in his cartoons and what he has de-scribed as "Mr. Average-everyday-reader." He purposely didn't attend editorial meetings at *The Sun* because he didn't seek to be a "political student . . . because if I'm much more in-formed than my readers are, there's a very good chance that only the politi-cal pundits are going to be getting any-thing out of my cartoons."

For a cartoonist, the Norris work routine was remarkably consistent, even humdrum. He confessed in an in-terview early in his career on *The Sun* that he had to "lash myself to a nine-to-five schedule or I'd never get any-thing done, except maybe reading the daily golf lesson."

By nine o'clock in the morning, he was usually at his drawing-board at *The Sun*, gazing into space. Norris has classified himself as a Starer as opposed to other cartoonists who may be Pacers or Match-Chewers. By noon, he usu-ally had three or four rough sketches ready for submission to the editor.

Norris is one of the few cartoonists who generates ideas according to a sys-tem and who has tried to describe that system.

"I call it my 'route map' system, and I start with a base subject—let's say the high price of beef.

"The base subject is home base and mentally, I draw a map. First of all, I picture what I call an obvious road, right down the middle, and it leads to gold, the mint, Fort Knox, etc. This is the idea route I try to avoid, so I go down side roads from that main road and try to relate everything down a side road to my base subject, and I

never turn back, no matter how silly things sound.

"For instance, I may go off on a side road to explore the butcher shop, the butcher's meal, the butcher's family, his steer chart. I might go down anoth-er road that has cannibals—I won't go too far down there—or onto one that takes me to the trapper and the hunter, the wife as a trapper, the cowboys, the cattle, people becoming rustlers, rus-tlers becoming hustlers, the farmers, and down another road that's into other foods and diets, and thin and fat, and Jack Spratt, and substitute foods, etc.

"I explore all these, roll them around and toss them about, and work

out ideas and scenes and settings for each one. This method so often does provide ideas, all in the form of little rough, quick thumbnail sketches . . . If this method doesn't produce anything, I discard the base subject and try an-other one."

After the editor selected the day's cartoon from the roughs presented to him, Norris returned to his drawing-board after lunch to ink in the final drawing. At this stage, he added the sec-ondary jokes that his readers learned to search for in his cartoons—quaint fish and chips signs in Victoria, crumbling antiques in Rodney's living-room and fiendish plots hatched by Filbert Phelps behind his mother's back.

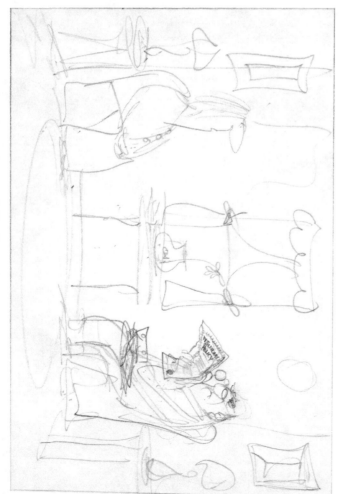

A Norris rough sketch

"Having been deprived lately of newspapers, mail, supermarkets, airplanes, citizenship rights and public transport...it's his centennial project."

"...he had just dropped in his income tax when along came the paper boy..."

...and the finished product.

"...why can't we have a retirement savings plan that doesn't require burning down the house?"

Norris also tried to express his characters' feelings through physical attitudes, not merely through facial expressions. He has described himself as "a great one for messing about with the position and stance of the body, and the knees, and legs, in achieving an effect. The basic idea of a cartoon should be apparent – bang – at first glance, but I like to put in the little gimmicks to give the reader something extra for his money."

By about four in the afternoon, Norris was ready to send his cartoon to the editor and head for home or the golf course.

When Pierre Berton described Norris as "quiet, retiring, rather shy ... but

I think, within that envelope, there is a pretty strong ego," he inadvertently gave a description of the national character. Part of Norris' popularity stems from the fact that he has represented Canada's "silent majority" at a time when it felt both ignored and cheated by the system and, subsequently, more aggressive about asserting its political power. As this occurred over the years, the middle-class characters in Norris cartoons lost something of their gentle fatalism.

In a 1971 cartoon, for example, a homeowner strides down his front walk in the suburbs carrying a placard: "Join the persecuted majority."

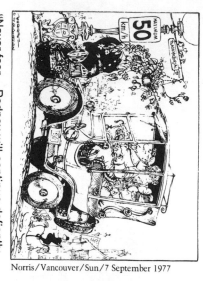

"Never fear ... Rodney will continue defiantly at 30 miles an hour."

Norris/Vancouver/Sun/7 September 1977

One of Norris' favourite cartoons of this type, drawn in 1971, shows an irate taxpayer with his arm caught in a mailbox, having tried to retrieve his income tax payment after reading a newspaper headline about higher salaries for Members of Parliament.

The same thinly concealed anger trembles under the surface of many of Norris' later cartoons about French-English problems. A French-Canadian civil servant is shown in Ottawa in 1972, in charge of paper clips. One of his colleagues whispers, "He may lack

"He may lack something in competence ... but his French is impeccable."

Norris/Vancouver/Sun/13 January 1972

something in competence ... but his French is impeccable." When a French-language television station is announced for Vancouver, Rodney's wife tries to calm him by saying, "But Rodney ... perhaps if they put it in the back of the box."

When Norris was once accused of playing on the bigotry of his audience, he said, "Sure, we are all little bigots. And I think we should be a little ashamed of ourselves without feeling too much guilt about it, because I think French-Canadians can be just as bigoted."

Norris' conservatism also is alarmed by the inroads made by government on his way of life and his income. "It makes me furious every time I think of it," he has said, "and I can do cartoons on that subject ... well, I can't resist them. I would do one every day, if I could."

They all express and contribute to something that Norris describes as "a general sense of outrage." As the revolt of the middle-class taxpayer became more apparent in the 1970s, it helped Norris cartoons to retain their vitality and validity.

In Pierre Berton's assessment, Norris gave Canada "a totally different kind of cartooning, which was not only new to this country—it was new to this continent." Within a few years of Norris' start on The Sun in 1950, many Canadian cartoonists were affected by the Norris style, particularly those who were social rather than political cartoonists, but Norris has remained unchallenged as Canada's most popular social cartoonist.

Caricaturing Ourselves

"We have just begun to fight."

Kuch/Winnipeg/Free Press/21 October 1960

Hour of Decision

Reidford/Globe and Mail/28 November 1961

Macpherson/Toronto/Star/1962

Prime Minister John Diefenbaker was a cartoonist's dream. The thousands of caricatures of Diefenbaker produced during his six years as Prime Minister, his four years as Opposition Leader, and his stormy retirement as Conservative leader said as much about Canadians as they did about the "Chief."

Diefenbaker's own excitement about politics communicated itself to a nation that had begun to perceive itself as politically boring toward the end of the long period of Liberal government in Ottawa. Diefenbaker rekindled the pioneering spirit of Canadians, directing the attention of the country to the

Macpherson/Toronto/Star

Laura Secord, 1963

McNally/Montreal/Star/29 March 1963

Macpherson/Toronto/Star

Blast Off

vast, unsettled territories of the North. He feuded with the United States, alternately delighting and appalling Canadians by his defiance of Washington. The internal politics of his government illuminated a well-concealed Machiavellian streak in the characters of Canadian public figures. Unlike the Liberals, who had a knack of muffling internal dissension, the Conservative cabinet seethed openly with plots and counter-plots as Diefenbaker's rule became increasingly autocratic.

Economic weaknesses became more apparent at the same time, symbolized by a decline in the international value

Macpherson/Toronto/Star/1962

"My friend and I would like to consolidate our debts."

of the Canadian dollar. The devalued "Diefenbuck" became a national joke and a symbol of mismanagement that seriously hurt the government.

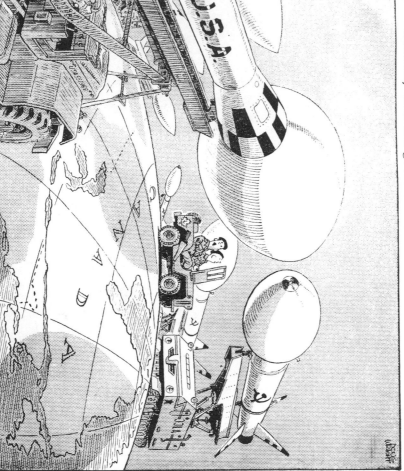

Drop in the Bucket

"Doesn't it seem kind of academic to be debating whether WE should have nuclear weapons?"

Wright/Hamilton/Spectator

Kuch/Winnipeg/Free Press/1962

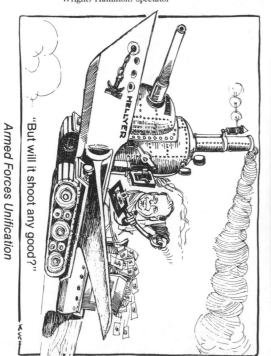

Armed Forces Unification

"But will it shoot any good?"

Kuch/Winnipeg/Free Press/13 November 1964

IT'S DEVASTATING!

Macpherson/Toronto/Star

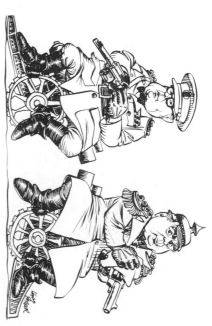

Parker/Maclean's

Macpherson/Toronto/Star

Macpherson/Toronto/Star/1962

Collins/Montreal/Gazette

Political Peanuts

Midway through the decade, under Pearson's leadership, Canadians became embroiled in a fierce conflict over the design of a new flag. Diefenbaker led the opposition to the removal

135

Kuch/Winnipeg/Free Press/22 April 1963

McNally/Montreal/Star

This was an age of classic political rivalries. Television magnified the role of the party leaders as the erratic Diefenbaker battled with an exasperated Lester Pearson. Inconclusive elections created minority governments that expanded the role of the elfin T.C. "Tommy" Douglas of the New Democratic Party.

Kamienski/Winnipeg/Tribune/1963

The balloteers

"Day after day, for sixty days, we stuck, nor breath, nor motion;

As idle as a painted ship upon a painted ocean."

of all symbols of Canada's British inheritance while Pearson insisted on introducing a completely new flag. The Liberals were accused of using the flag debate to distract attention from a series of scandals that linked the Mont-

"He's tugging at the covers!"

"Il tire la couverture!"

LaPalme/Montreal/La Presse

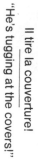

"Have I got it right?"

Kamienski/Winnipeg/Tribune

"You like it?"

Kamienski/Winnipeg/Tribune

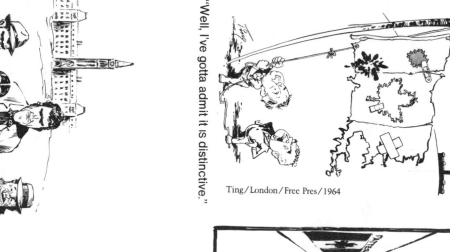

"Well, I've gotta admit it is distinctive."

Ting/London/Free Pres/1964

real underworld with Quebec members of the federal administration.

As the centenary of Confederation approached, the separatist movement in Quebec grew. Federal and provincial leaders made futile efforts to agree on a new constitution to replace the century-old British North America Act that still served as the legal foundation of the Canadian state. In western Canada, birthplace of political socialism,

"Ready, set, go!"

LaPalme/Montreal/La Presse

McNally/Montreal/Star/1965

Franklin/Toronto/Star

"But how can we Québecois identify with Canada when you're still
searching for a Canadian identity?"

137

Peterson/Vancouver/Sun/19 May 1964

"Stereo, anyone?"

Norris/Vancouver/Sun/30 June 1961

"What a nice neighbourly gesture...BC's keeping Dominion Day."

Hudon/Montreal/Le Devoir/1961

An early caricature of René Lévesque

Getting there the slow way

the Saskatchewan government began the first of a series of disputes with doctors over the introduction of state medicine that paved the way for national medicare under the Liberals.

Revelations about the liaison between a German beauty, Gerda Munsinger, and a Conservative associate minister of national defence meant that both Conservatives and Liberals were bespattered by scandal as Diefenbaker and Pearson headed into retire-

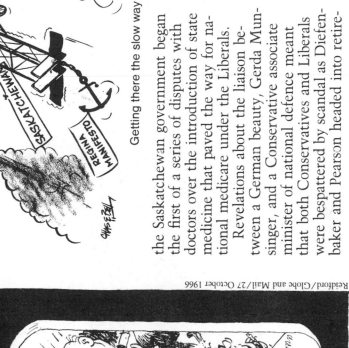

"Hold everything, boys–there's nothing over there but tourists, 'taters and Tories!"

12 November 1965: Conservatives take every Federal seat in Prince Edward Island

"Hello, fans, it's Dominion-Provincial Conference night in Canada."

140

Macpherson/Toronto/Star

"That's a heck of a way to run a railroad."

15 March 1966: The Munsinger Affair occupied Parliament to the exclusion of everything else

Chambers/Halifax/Herald/15 March 1966

"Have you any doctors in your car?"

YOU ARE NOW LEAVING SASKATCHEWAN

STOP

LLOYD

Sebestyen/Saskatoon/Star-Phoenix/14 March 1962

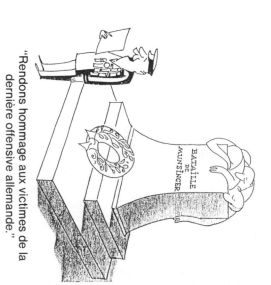

"Rendons hommage aux victimes de la dernière offensive allemande."

"Let us pay homage to those who fell in the last German offensive."

BATAILLE DE MUNSINGER

Berthio/Le Maclean/July 1966

Chambers/Halifax/Herald/20 July 1967

NATIONAL PC LEADERSHIP CONTEST

Blaine/Hamilton/Spectator

ment. The end of Diefenbaker's career as Conservative leader was as dramatic as its beginning. The party almost split as he forced the new leader, Robert Stanfield, to defeat him at a leadership

Gagnier/Montreal/Le Devoir/1966

CONTRE

"S'il en reste un, je serai celui-là—Victor Hugo

"If only one remains, I shall be that man!"

Macpherson/Toronto/Star/1967

TORY PARTY

Dalton Camp and Diefenbaker

142

With quarterback Mike Pearson's retirement from the game, many of the players were more intent on their own political aims than on the fortunes of the team.

convention. Pearson retired gracefully, to be succeeded by Pierre Trudeau, but not before the end of his term as Prime Minister and the centenary celebrations crowned by Expo 67 were marred by General Charles de Gaulle's cry of "Vive le Québec Libre!" from a balcony at Montreal's City Hall.

Kuch/Winnipeg/Free Press/18 January 1968

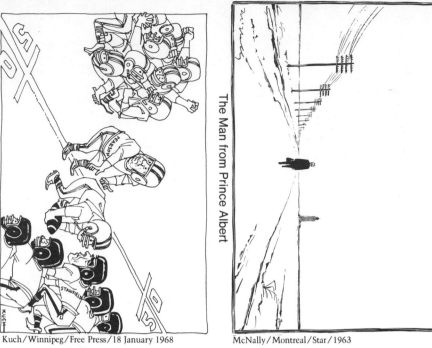

The Man from Prince Albert

McNally/Montreal/Star/1963

Berthio/Montreal/Le Devoir

Peterson/Frog Fables/1973

"Of course I wouldn't mind...but how do we catch one...?"

Bierman/Victoria/Times/1 May 1968

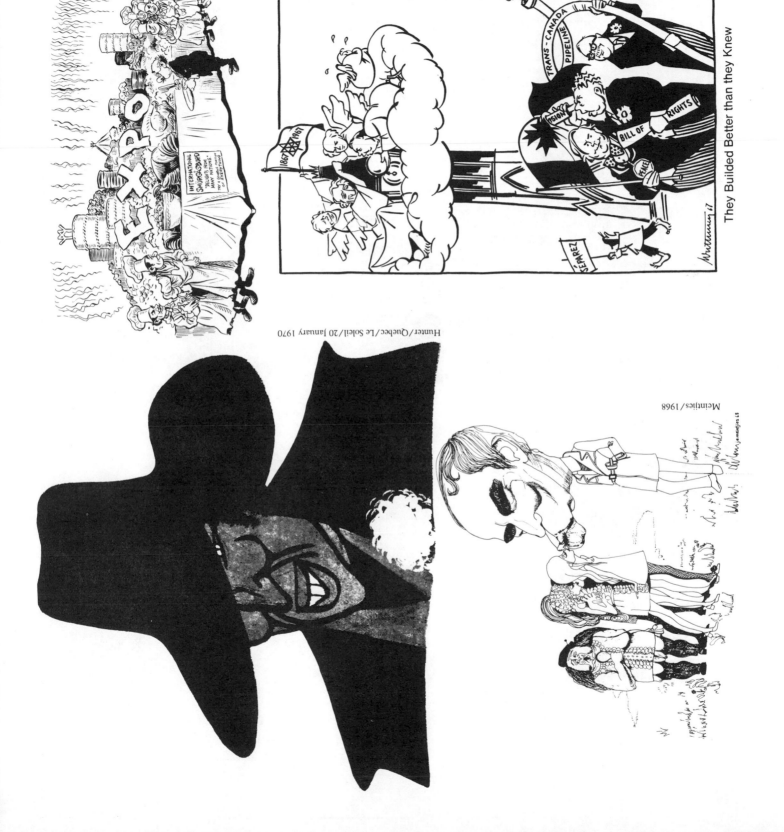

Chambers/Halifax/Herald/1 May 1967

Werthman/Fredericton/Gleaner/1967

They Builded Better than they Knew

Hunter/Quebec/Le Soleil/20 January 1970

MacInnes/1968

Pièce de Résistence

Macpherson/Toronto/Star/1967

The party's over

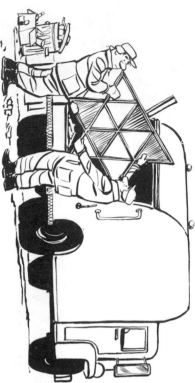

McNally/Montreal/Star/2 January 1968

Donato/Toronto/Telegram/29 November 1967

Célébrons-là à mort!
The Last Dance

Berthio/Le Maclean/January 1967

The 1960s, a time of rapid change in social conventions and political upheaval in Canada, saw a renaissance of Canadian cartooning. Something of the partisan savagery and painstaking draughtsmanship of the finest cartooning of the nineteenth century reappeared. The best group of cartoonists ever to work in this country developed the talents that would find full inspiration in the dramatic events and sharply defined conflicts between leaders in the next decade.

Aislin/Le Maclean/1977

Franklin/Globe and Mail/14 October 1970

Tweedle dee and Tweedle dum

7: Duncan Macpherson

Duncan Macpherson by Lewis Parker

Parker/Maclean's

Duncan Macpherson is the best political cartoonist that Canada has produced and he ranks among the best in the world, "head and shoulders above anybody else in North America," according to Len Norris.

In his *An American's Notes on Canadian Culture*, critic Edmund Wilson wrote that Macpherson's cartoons were the only ones, in English Canada,

to contain "a high level of political satire." Wilson stated that Macpherson's work, which he compared with James Gillray's, has the power to be "fascinating quite independently of our interest in or knowledge of the happenings it commemorates."

Writing in *The New Yorker* in 1964, Wilson credited Macpherson with creating "a phantasmagoria for which the mediocre subjects themselves sometimes seem hardly adequate."

His ideas are almost always original and provocative; his technique is openly admired by other cartoonists. "He draws so bloody well," said Andy Donato of *The Toronto Sun*. "He can draw a guy, and you know exactly who it is, even if it doesn't look like the guy at all."

"He has a magnificent eye," according to Sid Barron, whose cartoons also appear in the *Star*. "The eye is not a reliable instrument until it's trained, and his eye is trained. He learned to draw."

Macpherson himself is now "past the point of being critical of the technical side" of cartoons. Cartoons succeed or fail, in his opinion, according to "how well they get the point across."

He has been making his point, in a variety of styles but always with a recognizable touch, since he joined *The Toronto Star* in 1958. Within a few months of joining the *Star*, he pro-

duced a caricature of Prime Minister John Diefenbaker as Marie Antoinette that was regarded instantly as a classic. It has probably been reproduced more often than any other Canadian caricature.

Macpherson's virtuosity has developed over the past two decades, but his satirical approach to politics, his angry insight, and his genius for caricature were evident at the outset. Despite that, he had to be cajoled into becoming a political cartoonist.

"He was very unsure of himself," recalled Pierre Berton, who brought Macpherson to the *Star*, just as, eight years earlier, he had arranged the marriage of Len Norris and *The Van-*

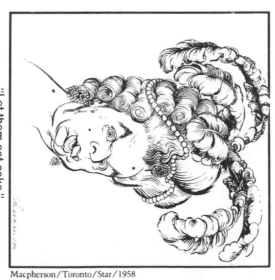

"Let them eat cake."

Macpherson/Toronto/Star/1958

couver Sun. "He was a disciple of Gillray and Rowlandson and he had a real respect for the profession. He didn't think he was good enough."

Macpherson had admired cartoonists for almost as long as he had wanted to draw. Born in Toronto in 1924, the only son of Scots parents, he once covered the walls and ceiling of his room with cartoons when left at home with orders to paint it.

Discouraged by his parents from attending art classes because they wanted him to enter the family textile business, Macpherson dropped out of school when he was seventeen to enlist in the Royal Canadian Air Force. He served in England in the lower ranks, packing bombs and waging a characteristic war against military discipline, including a short time in confinement for damaging cutlery during a typical outburst of temper.

The war also gave him an opportunity to take art courses in London. He remembers spending hours studying the cartoons of David Low that were hung on the walls of a room used by military personnel in the *Express* building on Fleet Street, where Low worked. Before the war ended, he had won a prize in an RCAF poster contest for drawing a stick of bombs coming out of a bomb bay.

After the war, he used his veterans' credits to help finance study at the Boston Museum of Fine Art. When his father died in 1947, he tried to run the family business but soon abandoned this to continue his artistic training at the Ontario College of Art.

He was still at the college when he

Macpherson/Toronto/Star/1962

Small Comfort.

was given a freelance contract by the weekly *Montreal Standard* to replace the late Jimmy Frise as illustrator of the stories of Gregory Clark. Macpherson was hired by Dick Hersey, art director for the *Standard* and its successor, *Weekend*, who had seen some of Macpherson's wartime drawings in a collection in Ottawa and who had persuaded J.W. McConnell, the publisher of the *Standard*, to subsidize part of Macpherson's art studies in Boston.

The illustrations for the Clark stories caught the eye of Pierre Berton, then managing editor of *Maclean's*. Berton hired him to illustrate the humorous stories of Robert Thomas Allen and Macpherson developed a caricature of Allen, without having seen the writer, that Allen always disliked. Eventually it became the prototype of the ragged little figure who represents the average Canadian in Macpherson's newspaper cartoons.

147

A frustrated cartoonist himself, Berton recognized the gift in Macpherson. "For years on *Maclean's*, I thought he was brilliant and I was terrified that some newspaper would find him and steal him. After I joined the *Star*, I went back to him with a proposal."

Macpherson's uncertainty about taking the job was balanced by the lure of the $11,000 annual salary offered by *Star* publisher Beland Honderich. It would make Macpherson, at the start of his career, possibly the highest paid cartoonist in the country at that time.

Toward the end of his first year on the *Star*, Macpherson walked into Honderich's office and handed him a box of cigars. When the publisher asked what the occasion was, Macpherson told him that he was celebrating his departure from the *Star* for a new job with *Maclean's*.

"I was away on my first holiday and I came back and there was no Macpherson cartoon in the paper," said Berton. "So I called Honderich and said, 'What's happened to Macpherson—is he sick?' And he said, 'No—he quit.'

"I said, 'What do you mean he quit? He is the hottest thing you've got at this point.'"

Macpherson had asked the *Star* to reduce his assignment from five cartoons a week to three and to allow him to travel, specifically to Cuba to draw sketches for the newspaper. Honderich had told him, according to Berton's recollection, that "he couldn't have everything."

"And I said—why not? If he does three cartoons a week, it's still better than no cartoons a week."

The *Star* met Macpherson's demands and the cartoonist returned to the newspaper. The incident illustrated Macpherson's stature and spirit at the very beginning of his career, but there was more than pride involved in his behaviour. There was fear. When he had first joined the *Star*, the newspaper's treatment of Les Callan, the cartoonist already on staff, had left a deep impression on Macpherson.

"They just pretended that he didn't exist any longer ... after twenty-five years," he said. "That's why I've never joined the staff of the paper to this day. It's a pretty cold-blooded business."

Despite some initial misgivings, the *Star* soon appreciated Macpherson's quality.

"The first reaction to Macpherson's cartoons was that they were cruel," Honderich later recalled. "People had never seen this type of cartooning in Canada. They weren't prepared for it."

If so, they soon developed an appetite for it and Macpherson used his popularity to bargain for a greater degree of independence than any previous newspaper cartoonist had achieved in Canada.

Cartoonist Terry Mosher, "Aislin" of *The Gazette* in Montreal, declared years later that "Macpherson established a new ground rule for all political cartoonists to follow: Never give an editor an even break."

Before Macpherson, most cartoonists were part of an editorial-page team, attending meetings of the editorial board and frequently illustrating ideas suggested by others. Macpherson refused to attend editorial meetings. He succeeded in having himself recognized not merely as an illustrator of the newspaper's editorials but as a contributor to the editorial page with a measure of independence.

He claimed for himself at least the freedom enjoyed by columnists who signed their own names to their articles. This was a new approach and it has influenced many Canadian cartoonists since.

Macpherson's independence probably had as much to do with temperament as with his professional ability. *Star* columnist Gary Lautens has described Macpherson as a "combination of Mary Poppins, Mark Twain, and Attila the Hun." Many of the Macpherson stories that illustrate the progressive development of this combination start with a few drinks at the Toronto Press Club, an institution that has frequently banned him for life. In his cups, the burly Macpherson is subject to unpredictable fits of enthusiasm and rage. He may decide to prove that he is strong enough to raise the bar single-handedly, only to succeed in tearing the top from it. One of his favourite Press Club tricks, according to legend, was seeing how far he could toss a heavy armchair with one hand.

When a policeman once tried to arrest him on the street outside the Club, Macpherson dragged him into the premises and staged a donnybrook in the lobby, escaping minutes before the riot squad arrived. Another episode that started in the Press Club ended several days later when Macpherson and a *Star* journalist were thrown off an Air Canada flight in Ottawa for disorderly behaviour.

Roy Shields, the journalist who was with Macpherson on the abortive flight, once claimed in an interview that he had never seen the cartoonist drunk enough to be irrational.

"He doesn't do the irrational things of a drunk," he said. "When he's drinking heavily, he'll break a bar, or steal a potted plant, or sit on somebody, but all the time he's doing this, in his black way, he's releasing terrible tensions. He's a very tormented man."

Making light of these conflicting aspects of his personality, Macpherson usually tries to protect himself from attempts to analyze his character and relate it to his work.

"There has to be a connection between the nature of a cartoonist and what he does," he once admitted, "and I defy any cartoonist to define it."

Some of the connections aren't as obscure as he pretends. A description by Pierre Berton of Macpherson after "a few over the eight" applies to the cartoons as aptly as to the man: "…Wild, expansive, sometimes bitterly sarcastic, often wicked and totally unpredictable."

Whenever he is accused of cartooning viciously, Macpherson becomes defensive. "I don't think that I ever intended a cartoon to be vicious in the sense of taking a vengeful attitude personally," he has said, "but if the only way to make a point is through a pretty tough delivery … well, the point's going to be made."

The point will be made even if, on the surface, it appears to violate the cartoonist's own political opinion. Talking about the famous Marie Antoinette caricature of Diefenbaker, Macpherson once said that, in fact, he had agreed with the political decision that inspired the cartoon: Prime Minister Diefenbaker's decision to scrap Canada's Arrow military jet and 1,500 jobs in favour of buying US aircraft.

"Even though he was correct, his attitude was wrong," Macpherson explained. "If a man is correct but his attitude is wrong, pick on his attitude."

Macpherson's initial approach to a political event is instinctive rather than intellectual, and aggressively critical. "You're a heckler, basically," he has said. "It's the same as the old political meetings when you'd hire a couple of fellows to go into the hall and raise hell."

A former classmate at the Ontario College of Art claimed years later that Macpherson's early drawings betrayed "a great dislike of the human race." Macpherson has described his critical attitude as being "against the wrongness in public life." As the Diefenbaker cartoon showed, "wrongness" isn't necessarily a moral quality. It can consist purely of Macpherson's gut reaction to a personality or situation.

Recalling his hesitation in 1958 about becoming a political cartoonist, Macpherson once said, "I had no great social conscience then, and I don't now. Anything I had to say was just a personal beef."

"I don't think Macpherson has any politics except the politics of the iconoclast," Pierre Berton has stated. "He reacts, and I think he reacts from the gut, and that's the best thing for a political cartoonist to do if he's not a political scientist, and Macpherson doesn't pretend to be."

"You react to a situation," Macpherson said, "not because you're a moralist or anything like that. It's because you're a contrary sort of person, a cynic."

Macpherson often has said that he addresses himself in his cartoons to the average drinker in a Toronto tavern. In his early years on the Star, when editors objected to a cartoon, he would wander through the Star building showing the drawing to anyone that he could find, as if to demonstrate that the opinions of copy boys, pressmen and elevator operators carried as much weight as those of his editors.

Sweeping generalizations about Macpherson cartoons are risky because his work varies in style, mood and intent. Despite his professed lack of social conscience, for instance, he has produced, from time to time, moralistic cartoons on such issues as the war in Vietnam, poverty, racial discrimination, the threat of nuclear warfare, Watergate and political terrorism. These cartoons are often drawn white-on-black, the reverse of his usual technique, using a scratchboard to produce a woodcut effect. Macpherson also uses the same technique, or a heavy black line, to produce obituary portraits of public figures whom he wants to honour: Pope John XXIII, former Prime Minister Lester B. Pearson, and Martin Luther King.

Travelling for the Star in Cuba, Germany, Russia and other countries, sketching in the Press Gallery of the House of Commons, Macpherson on occasion has returned to his original vocation as an illustrator of articles written by journalists. In 1969, carrying this a step further, the *Star* published a book entitled *Macpherson's Canada*, a selection of sketches and notes recorded in all parts of the country. It was a popular success but, despite his efforts every summer in the studio he has built at Lake Simcoe north of Toronto, Macpherson has yet to achieve critical recognition as an artist. His national reputation is based primarily on his cartoons.

Macpherson has never been funnier than when he caricatured John Diefenbaker in his prime. Diefenbaker became Prime Minister in 1958, the year of Macpherson's start on the *Star*. As John A. Macdonald helped to launch Bengough as a cartoonist in the nineteenth century, Diefenbaker gave Macpherson a flying start.

"I had more fun with Diefenbaker than anybody," he said. "Absolutely no restraints at all. I had him going as a wild man in my imagination and that's the way he turned out."

Although the Marie Antoinette cartoon became the symbol of Macpherson's treatment of the Prime Minister, it was followed by an increasingly manic series of caricatures. The Prime Minister paraded across the editorial pages of the *Star* in a bewildering variety of preposterous disguises: Charles I, Nero, the Cheshire cat, Captain Ahab, the Red Queen, and Batman. At other times, the Prime Minister was a ship's captain, a Greek god, a tattered showman reminiscent of Bengough's John A. Macdonald and even something re-

sembling the Deity walking on a sea entitled *Election Swim*, to the astonishment of a pair of boaters: "Migawd, there he goes again."

In 1959, Macpherson was quoted in the *Star* as saying, "I've been watching Diefenbaker on TV for a long time and he has always given me the feeling of a Billy Sunday, a circus barker, and a third-rate actor, all put together."

Diefenbaker often saw himself as the central figure in a great national drama; Macpherson saw him as the crazy ringleader of a national circus. In his cartoons, over the years, the front teeth grew more prominent, the eyes wilder and the antics more berserk. Years after he had been defeated as Prime Minister, Diefenbaker contin-

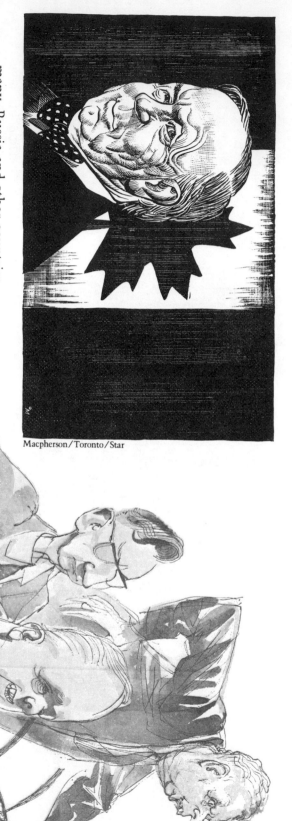

Macpherson / Toronto / Star

Macpherson/Toronto/Star/1966

Macpherson/Toronto/Star

MIGAWD, THERE HE GOES AGAIN.

ELECTION SWIM

Macpherson/Toronto/Star

"Charge!"

ued to appear in Macpherson's cartoons, ultimately becoming a shawled pensioner with a needlepoint Union Jack in his lap telling the new Conservative leader, Joe Clark, to "run along and play."

Macpherson's fame rests, in part, on his ability as a caricaturist but his work shows that, occasionally, it has taken him a long time to achieve a stable caricature of a politician. On the eve of Diefenbaker's defeat as Prime Minister, Macpherson confessed that he was afraid that "if Pearson got in, I'd be lost."

"He doesn't have a good face," he

Macpherson/Toronto/Star

152

said, "no excesses that a cartoonist can take apart."

Pearson's baby-face was never a natural vehicle for Macpherson's zaniness but eventually he captured the rumpled and befuddled character that the Prime Minister presented to an affectionate if sometimes exasperated public. One of his typical cartoons about Pearson (and one of the few embodying another person's ideas—in this case, journalist John Brehl of the *Star*) showed Pearson as a pianist in a bordello being raided by the police. The caption: "I always wondered what they did upstairs."

With Diefenbaker's successor, Robert Stanfield, Macpherson was again

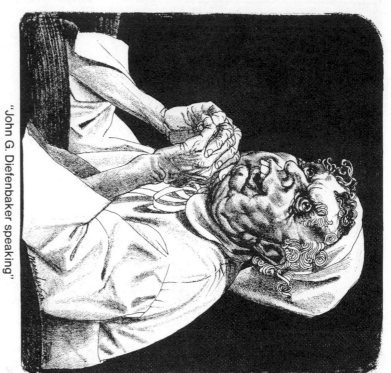

"John G. Diefenbaker speaking"

Macpherson/Toronto/Star

"Looks like it's going to be another one of those days."

Macpherson/Toronto/Star/1970

"I always wondered what they did upstairs."

Macpherson/Toronto/Star

Le Grand Dan Johnson

Macpherson/Toronto/Star/1967

Macpherson/Toronto/Star/1970

"The problem in tendering my resignation
is . . . I might not accept it."

working with a congenial subject.
Stanfield stumbled through years of
Macpherson cartoons as an emaciated
Ichabod Crane character who could
never get anything right.

Among international figures, Macpherson was at his best with de Gaulle,
whom he obviously disliked. In a 1970
cartoon, he showed de Gaulle in a typical haughty pose: "The problem with
tendering my resignation is . . . I might
not accept it." Presidents Lyndon
Johnson and Richard Nixon were
often given harsh treatment, Nixon
from the moment of his election.

Macpherson was less certain about
Pierre Trudeau at the outset. In 1967,
he drew him as a hippie-style Minister
of Justice without achieving a good
caricature. The following year, after
Trudeau became Prime Minister,
Macpherson was still obviously strug-

Macpherson/Toronto/Star/1973

"Are you really a power-hungry obstructionist, Daddy?"

Macpherson/Toronto/Star/1971

Question Period

Macpherson/Toronto/Star

"Tomorrow pistols at dawn"

153

gling to focus on him. Gradually he adopted a variation of the de Gaulle treatment but rarely with the same animosity. Caricatures of Trudeau as Napoleon, Nero, Oliver Cromwell and even as the first Emperor of Canada seemed to lack both the exasperation and the grudging admiration that had animated his caricatures of Diefenbaker.

Macpherson's treatment of René Lévesque showed a similar uncertainty at the start, until Lévesque's political objectives became more apparent. Eventually, Macpherson adopted the device of dressing him up as a member of the 1837 Paris Commune. His supporters also were given battered top hats, tricolour rosettes and wooden clogs. Although the historical reference probably was lost on some members of Macpherson's audience, the

Macpherson/Toronto/Star/1976

Macpherson/Toronto/Star/24 June 1978

Macpherson/Toronto/Star/1977

THE OCTOBER CRISIS

Macpherson/Toronto/Star/1970

Rarely has Macpherson drawn with such apparent hatred as when he caricatured the terrorists of the 1970 October Crisis as sub-humans. Later he confessed that he was "emotionally upset" by events in Quebec at this time, not only by the terrorism but by the response of the Trudeau government. It seemed to Macpherson that implementing the War Measures Act and "calling out the troops" was a "disgusting thing." He said that it was a "Latin" response to the situation: "Trudeau is a Latin, and he called out the troops."

Racial differences of temperament may explain why Macpherson has never caricatured Trudeau with the same gleeful confidence that he showed with Diefenbaker. Diefenbaker as Marie Antoinette was hilarious; Macpherson's caricature of

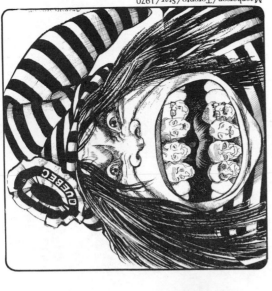

Macpherson/Toronto/Star/1976

A little self-restraint, s'il vous plaît.

costume exactly expressed his feeling that separatism was a ridiculously antiquated and somewhat seedy expression of Gallic radicalism.

Racial animosity in Canada is expressed almost as clearly in some of Macpherson's cartoons as it was in the work of nineteenth-century cartoonists in Canada. His caricatures of

Lévesque as a Parisian revolutionary even smack of the spirit that animated Gillray in the eighteenth century. As Gillray expressed the horror and incomprehension of England at the excesses of the French Revolution, Macpherson showed the puzzlement and indignation of English Canada in the face of Quebec separatism.

Trudeau as the Emperor of Canada is ominous as well as funny.

Trudeau came to power ten years after Diefenbaker was elected Prime Minister, and after Macpherson had spent ten years in his "gut-rending" job. Even a cartoonist of Macpherson's originality and skill periodically shows signs of exhaustion. At the beginning of his career, Macpherson had confidently described himself as belonging to the "elbow smash school of journalism." By 1974, he was saying that he was "at the stage now where I'm not a boat-rocker anymore."

Macpherson also showed the effects, as the years passed, of working for Canada's largest and most successful newspaper at a time when Canadian newspapers were prosperous, relatively uncompetitive and increasingly conservative in their social and political views. On most occasions, when Macpherson's viewpoint was at odds with the *Star's* editorials, the paper was big enough, morally and financially, to tolerate the contradiction, but there have been times when the *Star* has refused to publish his cartoons. When the newspaper itself was hit by a labour dispute, for instance, it rejected a Macpherson cartoon that was sympathetic to the strikers.

Restless within the confines of newspaper cartooning, Macpherson experimented with cartooning for television in the 1960s. Like many cartoonists, he believed for a time that the small screen should be a more compatible outlet for the graphic work of cartoonists than the editorial page of a newspaper largely devoted to print.

Working with the CTV network in Toronto, he patented a process for drawing cartoons for television but the attempt came to nothing.

In one respect, however, television has been a great help to Macpherson and other cartoonists. "In the standard man's news photo," he said, "you get the know how he walks. He's frozen. You don't know what his mannerisms are like ... There is an attitude in every person, a dumb attitude, which is very helpful in caricature. Even though you are not going to use the whole body, if you understand how the person moves, it's a big help.

"And of course, television helps. Not so much pictorially, but you get the man's attitude verbally which provides another insight."

Caricature is the starting-point and foundation of most Macpherson cartoons. Even a static situation can be enlivened. He once said, "if you get the proper expression on the man's face—you read the sort of anti-thought or pro-thought."

Macpherson's cartoons often are also literary compositions which, in the opinion of some critics, reveal "an extraordinary ear for the comic properties of spoken and written English." He has used quotations from Swift, Burns, Lewis Carroll, William S. Gilbert, Robert W. Service and many others in his cartoons, sometimes in deformed versions to suit his purposes.

"Even more revealing," according to an essay about Macpherson in the magazine *Canadian Dimension*, "is the way he searches in offbeat literary and historical byways, always with an ear cocked for antique words and expressions. Books of magic, military manuals of yore, court proceedings, Edwin C. Guillet's books on travelling circuses—such are the curiosa he likes to ransack for verbal odds and ends.

"In this, he is a throw-back. The great comic artists of the past (and particularly Gillray and Nast) had to be literary men as well as artists ..."

The elaborate vocabulary of many Macpherson cartoons reflects and complements the abundant graphic detail in his drawings. His cartoons are lavishly theatrical. The characters in a typical Macpherson cartoon enact plots and sub-plots from carefully determined stage positions and with precise gestures and facial expressions. The entire production is costumed and designed to express the correct historical period and emotional atmosphere. This theatrical quality, with its attention to detail and almost histrionic display of the cartoonist's virtuosity, recalls cartooning of the nineteenth century. In savagery, inventiveness and painstaking elaboration of a distinctive style of cartooning, Macpherson is closer to Bengough than to most of his immediate predecessors.

His technique also relates him to the careful draughtsmanship of that other master cartoonist of the nineteenth century in Canada, Henri Julien. Bengough lacked the artistic skill of Julien; Julien didn't possess Bengough's genius for humorous invention. If the abilities of these two men had been combined in one person, he would have been the Duncan Macpherson of his time.

Adding the Final Touches

The 1970s opened ominously with the October Crisis. Quebec terrorists kidnapped a British diplomat in Montreal and abducted and murdered a Quebec cabinet minister. The federal government resurrected the War Measures Act to deal with the emergency. Hundreds of Quebeckers were arrested and jailed without trial. In English-speaking Canada, the events of October 1970, were greeted with horror; cartoonists in these provinces reflected this in drawings filled with heavy symbolism. Quebec cartoonists, closer to the situation, tended to ridicule the authorities for over-reacting to the terrorist threat.

Uluschak/Edmonton/Journal/October 1970

Dupras/1971

Rusins/Ottawa/Citizen/1971

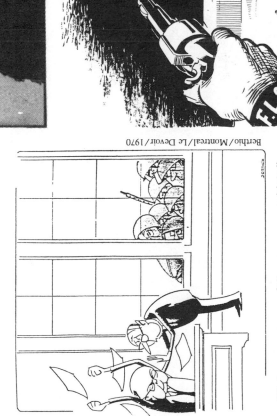

Berthio/Montreal/Le Devoir/1970

"Calmez-vous, vous faites peur aux soldats."

"Calm down, you're scaring the soldiers."

"Is that one of the FLQ's demands?"

Girerd/Montreal/La Presse/1970

"Some day, son, all this will be yours."

Innes/Calgary/Herald/18 September 1972

Although it was a milestone in the development of Quebec nationalism, the October Crisis marked the end of almost a decade of terrorism rather than the beginning of anarchy in Quebec. With his leadership proven under fire, Prime Minister Trudeau directed his efforts toward strengthening the unity of Canada, mainly through language policies and constitutional changes to reflect the demands of Quebec and the growing economic and political power of the western provinces. At the same time, he recognized that unity depended on a strong national economy capable of maintaining a high level of employment and an acceptable rate of inflation.

Franklin/Globe and Mail

159

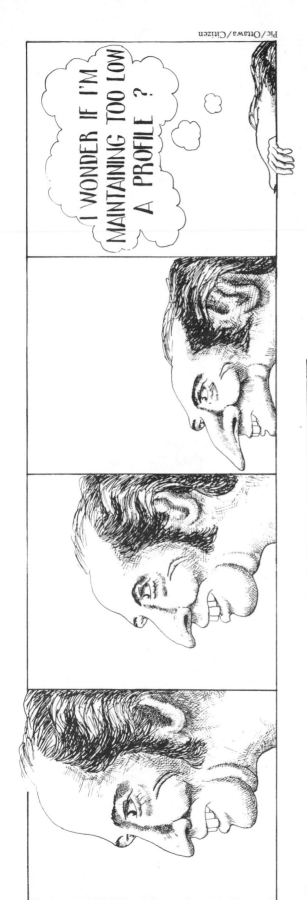

I WONDER IF I'M MAINTAINING TOO LOW A PROFILE?

"...AND IF IT GETS ENOUGH RAIN, AND SUN, AND IF IT ISN'T KILLED BY HAIL, AND IF IT ISN'T DAMAGED BY FROST, AND IF WE CAN GET IT OFF BEFORE IT'S COVERED BY SNOW, AND IF WE GET IT TO THE ELEVATORS, AND IF THE TRAINS ARE RUNNING, AND IF THE GRAIN HANDLERS AREN'T ON STRIKE, AND IF..."

Vaughn-James/Toronto/Star/6 May 1972

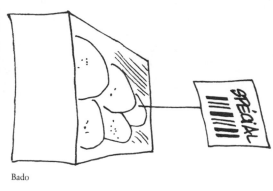

Bado

BEN WICKS

"The only way to create more jobs is to fire a few people."

Wicks/1977

Cummings/Maclean's/1978

Pier/Journal de Montréal

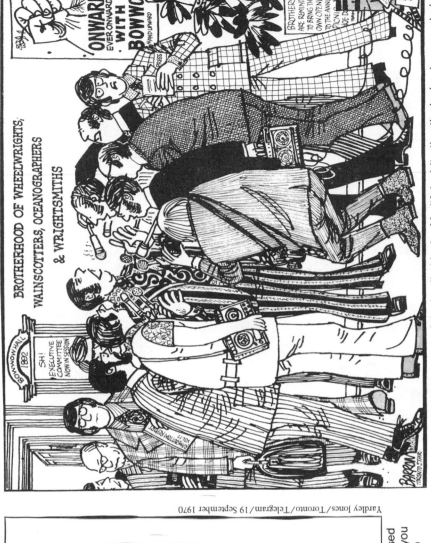

BROTHERHOOD OF WHEELWRIGHTS, WAINSCOTTERS, OCEANOGRAPHERS & WRIGHTSMITHS

"...no....you see, because of the implied lack of fruitful arbitration the lockout aggravated our industry-wide bargaining stance while the Minister's flagrant intervention in the negotiating committee caused our rank and file to rescind in good faith their declaration in a binding vote on reasonable proposals with a return-to-work pact on calling for a work-to-rule proposal contrary to the management negotiating team's position on intervention and to establish ground rules ironing out labour incentives and a basic residual two-year contract with retroactivity accruing acceleration benefits...the split occured when the implicit kiss-off inter ..."

Barron/Toronto/Star/1973

Many established institutions came under scrutiny in this decade. For the first time since the nineteenth century, when it proudly brought law and order to western Canada, the Royal Canadian Mounted Police was brought into disrepute when an official inquiry re-

161

Carless/CUPE Journal/1973

Yardley Jones/Toronto/Telegram/19 September 1970

"Regardless of the more democratic structure endorsed by the World Congress on the Future of the Church—you will desist in referring to me as the Reverend Shop Steward..."

162

vealed that it had used illegal methods to combat terrorism and subversive activity in Quebec. Other inquiries raised basic questions about government: Was public spending out of control? Had bureaucracy grown into a costly drag on the economy? Should government workers in the post office and other public services have the right to treat their fellow taxpayers as adversaries in contract disputes by depriving them of essential government services?

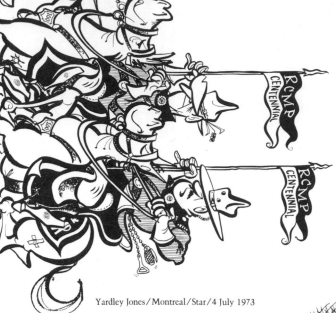

"Well sure we've progressed—Have you any idea how many phones we bugged in 1873?"

Yardley Jones/Montreal/Star/4 July 1973

Royal Commissions

"Can't help that, men…besides your pistol, funny little pouch, belt, lanyard, spear, spurs…now we have to find a spot to carry this steam kettle."

Norris/Vancouver/Sun/28 January 1978

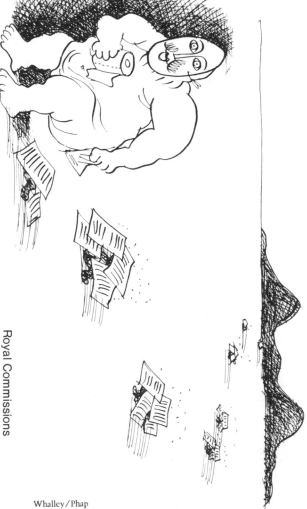

Whalley/Phap

REDUCTIONS
GOVERNMENT SPENDING

"Political Crating"

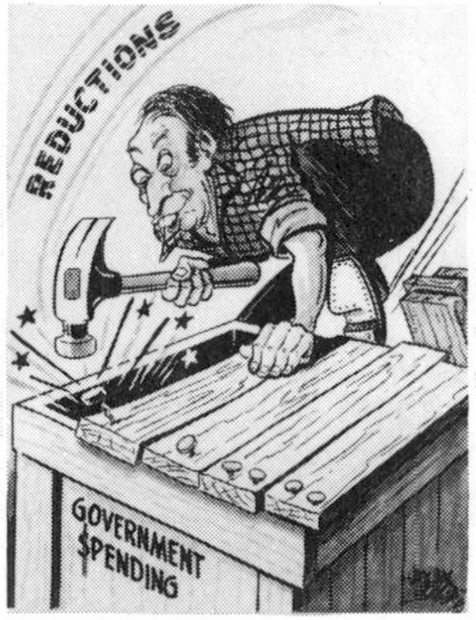

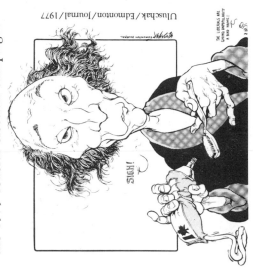

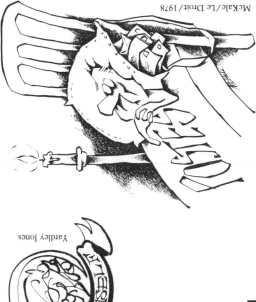

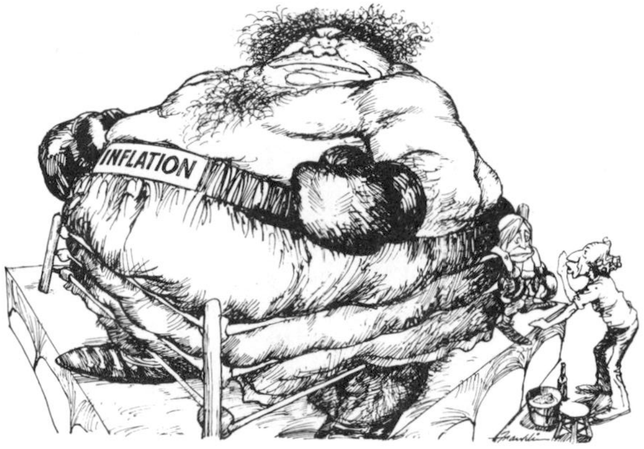

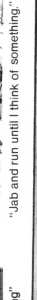

MacMellon/Moncton/Times and Transcript

INFLATION

"Jab and run until I think of something."

Franklin/Globe and Mail
4 October 1973

HIMSELF

Yardley Jones

POSTES

McKale/Le Droit/1978

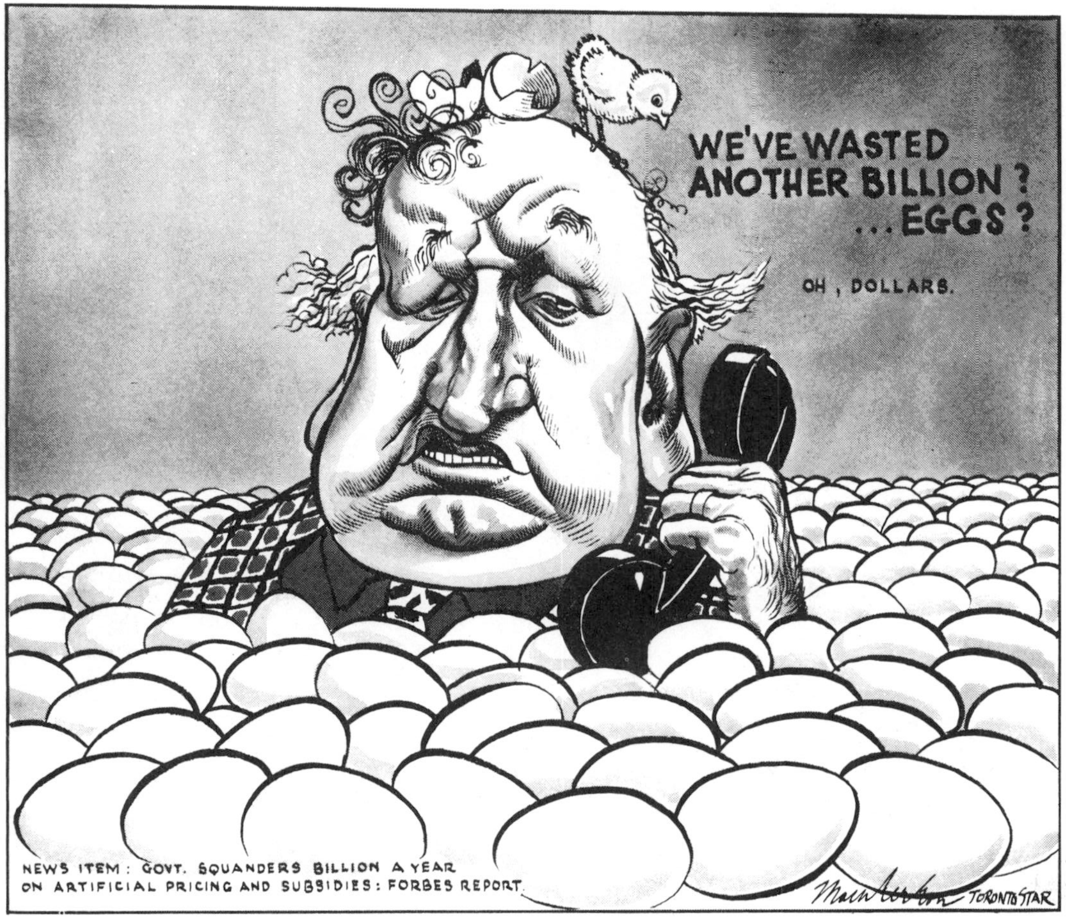

WE'VE WASTED ANOTHER BILLION ? ... EGGS ?
OH , DOLLARS.
NEWS ITEM : GOVT. SQUANDERS BILLION A YEAR ON ARTIFICIAL PRICING AND SUBSIDIES : FORBES REPORT.
TORONTO STAR

The Yolk's on Us

Macpherson/Toronto/Star/1975

Slowly, internal disputes wore down the federal cabinet and eroded Trudeau's credibility as leader. The Prime Minister's personal life clouded his political image. At first, the fairytale marriage of Pierre Trudeau and Margaret Sinclair seemed too good to be true, with children arriving just in time for Christmas. Then it became grotesque as Margaret left home and wrote an intimate autobiography published during the 1979 federal election campaign.

SIGH!
THE LIBERALS ARE GIVING UNPOPULARITY A BAD NAME!

Uluschak/Edmonton/Journal/1977

April Showers

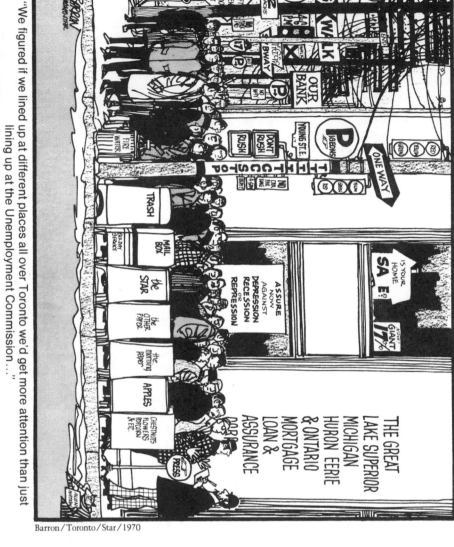

"We figured if we lined up at different places all over Toronto we'd get more attention than just lining up at the Unemployment Commission..."

Barron/Toronto/Star/1970

Peterson/Vancouver/Sun/9 April 1975

Pilsworth/Saturday Night/April 1973

Trudeau wrestles inflation to the ground

Chapleau /Montreal-Matin/1975

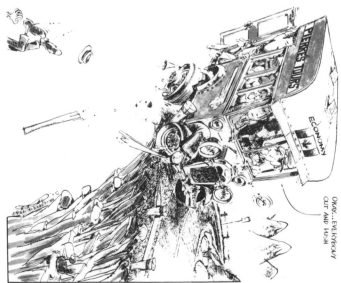

Larter/Lethbridge/Herald/1976

Remeche / Fiddle Diddle

THE CONTINUING ADVENTURES OF......

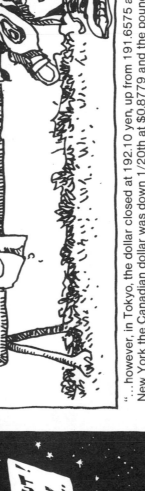

Biermann / Victoria / Times / 25 August 1978

"... however, in Tokyo, the dollar closed at 192.10 yen, up from 191.6575 at Tuesday's close, while in New York the Canadian dollar was down 1/20th at $0.8779 and the pound sterling was down 3/4 at $192.45..."

Yardley Jones / Canada Wide

Great! I'll call ya when she sells the movie rights

The MARGARET TRUDEAU Book

Pier / Journal de Montreal

HÉ! LÀ-HAUT! 2 À 1!...

After Trudeau's second child is born on Christmas day

Macpherson/Toronto/Star

"A bundle of toys he had slung on his back..."

Kamienski/Winnipeg/Tribune/5 December 1975

In the midst of continuing affluence, cartoonists reminded Canadians that the vast wealth of their country was inequitably shared. Native cartoonist Everett Soop criticized not only government agencies but the weaknesses of his own Indian people. Women's rights were both defended and ridiculed by cartoonists –always, in this country, male cartoonists.

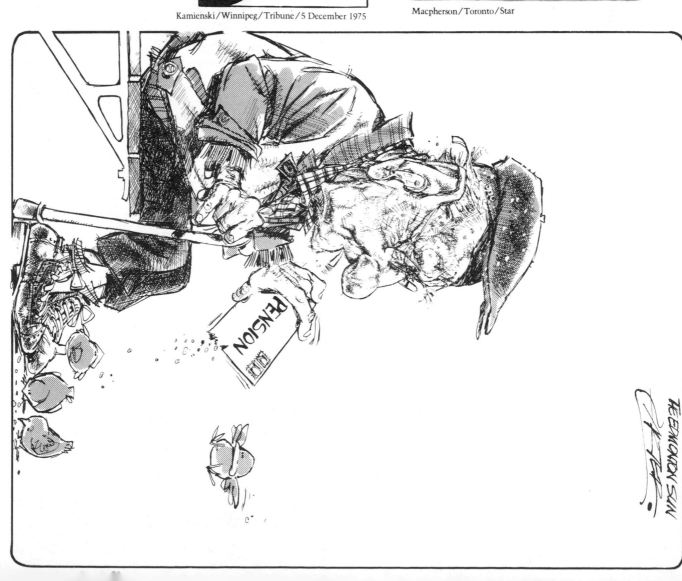

THE EDMONTON SUN

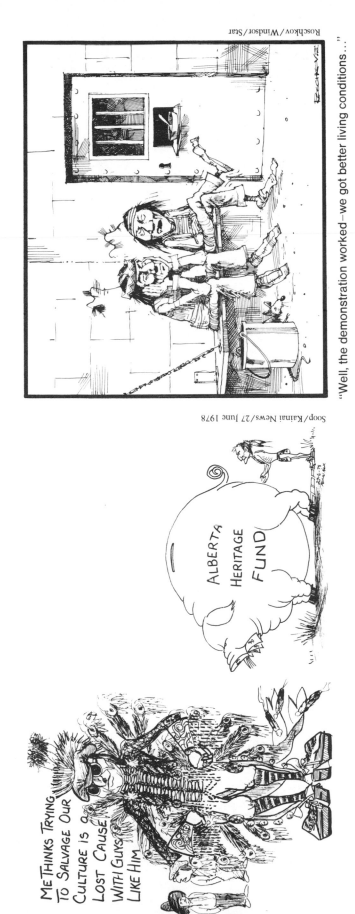

Roschkov/Windsor/Star

"Well, the demonstration worked—we got better living conditions..."

Soop/Kainai News/27 June 1978

ALBERTA HERITAGE FUND

MeThinks Trying To Salvage Our Culture is a Lost Cause With Guys Like Him

Constable/Union Art Service/1979

"THE ONLY GOOD NATIVE PERSON IS A DEAD ONE."

WE HAVE BEEN GUIDED BY ENLIGHTENED POLICIES, WE SAY...

HERE AT THE DEPT WE HAVE NEVER SAID "THE ONLY GOOD INDIAN IS A DEAD ONE"

168

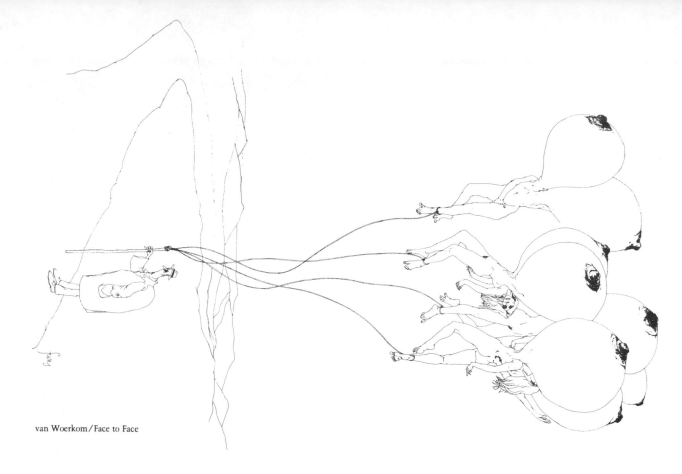

van Woerkom/Face to Face

" ...all right, now hear THIS...I'm the new woman of
1970...I'm not your loving, spoiling mother and chore lady
any more...now let's get this kitchen cleaned up
QUICK...come on, MOVE..."

Barron/Toronto/Star/1971

"Mother's getting a fix."

Norris/Vancouver/Sun/24 July 1971

"....atta boy, Martha...."

The Group of Eleven

Rusins/Ottawa/Citizen

Berthio/Le Jour

Barbecue...Western style

Innes/Calgary/Herald/6 May 1976

Ability

Whalley

While the government took steps to expand the Canadian content of popular culture, Canada's "macho" self-image suffered at international hockey tournaments, despite our efforts to win by substituting skull-bashing for skill. The decline in the calibre of professional hockey as leagues expanded into the United States prompted a healthy examination of the structure of sports in Canada.

Barron/Toronto/Star/1973

"...Dad, I want you to meet Harold...he's back-up organist at Maple Leaf Gardens..."

Ting/London/Free Press/1970

"Stay with the Leafs. We gotta get our 60% Canadian content."

Martin/Toronto/Sun/1975

"Do you have an American edition of *Maclean's?*"

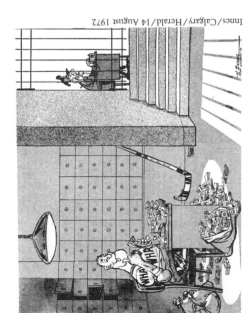

Innes/Calgary/Herald/14 August 1972

"He can't be disturbed at the moment...he's in training."

Aislin/Montreal/Gazette/1977

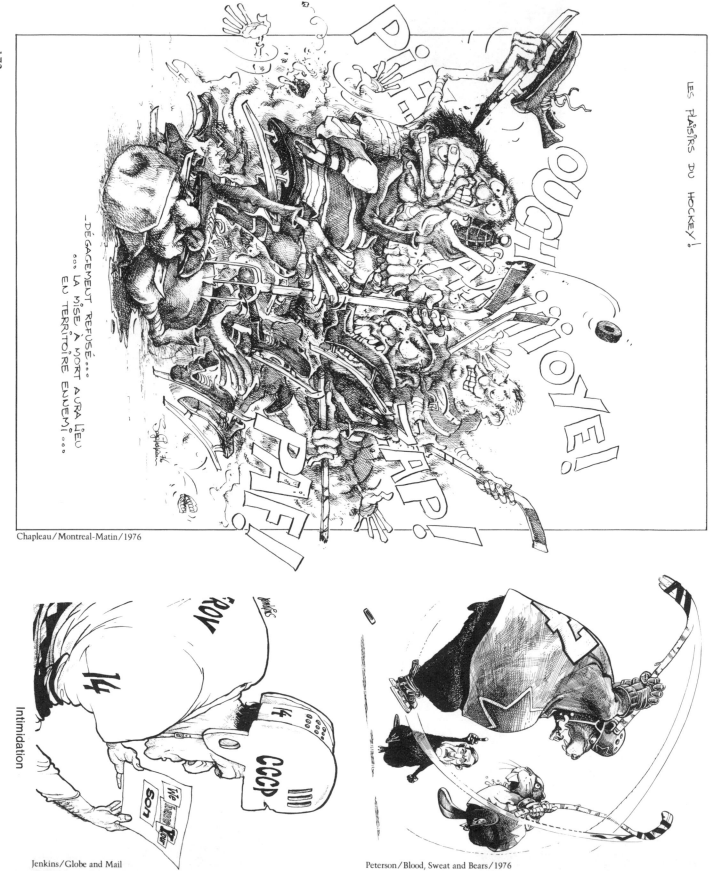

LES PLAISIRS DU HOCKEY!

—DÉGAGEMENT REFUSÉ...
...LA MISE À MORT AURA LIEU
EN TERRITOIRE ENNEMI...

Chapleau/Montreal-Matin/1976

Intimidation

Jenkins/Globe and Mail

Peterson/Blood, Sweat and Bears/1976

Aislin/Montreal/Gazette

'ELLO, MORGENTALER?

"The Olympics can no more have a deficit than a man can have a baby." Jean Drapeau, 29 January 1973

Chapeau/Montreal-Matin/1976

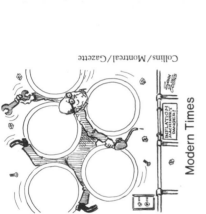

Collins/Montreal/Gazette

Modern Times

INFLATION DANGER!

The 1976 Olympics also promoted sport, but failed to do as much for Montreal as Mayor Jean Drapeau had hoped. While the unfinished Olympic Stadium became a popular cartoon symbol for Montreal, the Toronto equivalent was the CN Tower, the highest free-standing structure in the world. It was a sign of the city's pre-dominance that cartoonists found irre-sistibly preposterous.

EN CE QUI CONCERNE LE VILLAGE OLYMPIQUE J'AI UNE IDÉE !

NON ?!

DU CALME !

LES FEMMES D'ABORD.

ET POURQUOI ÇA ?

Girerd/Montreal/La Presse

Mayor Drapeau has yet another idea....

174

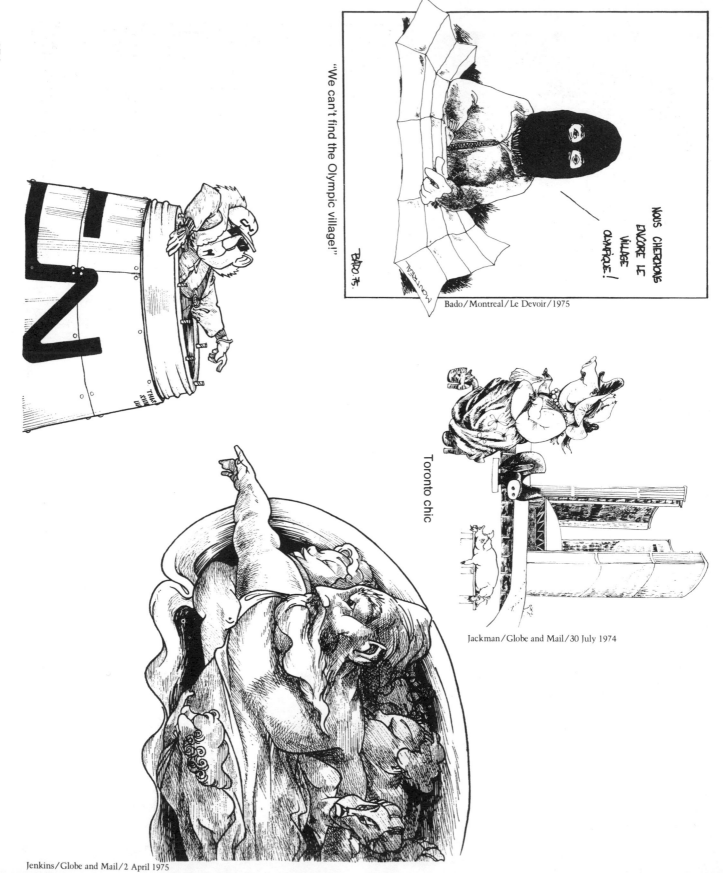

"We can't find the Olympic village!"

NOUS CHERCHONS
ENCORE LE
VILLAGE
OLYMPIQUE!

Bado/Montreal/Le Devoir/1975

Toronto chic

Jackman/Globe and Mail/30 July 1974

Jenkins/Globe and Mail/2 April 1975

Thirsty or Hungry?

175

"But what possible retaliatory measures could the Americans take?"

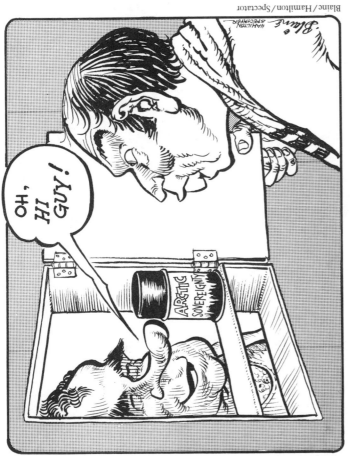

OH, HI GUY!

ARCTIC SOVEREIGNTY

"Hi, there...we're taking over your resources...know of any in this area which have been overlooked...?"

Barron/Toronto/Star/1972

8: The Golden Age

"... there's an editorial cartoon showing a chap in the same position as myself looking at an editorial cartoon and saying to his wife, 'There's an editorial cartoon showing a chap in the same position as myself looking at an editorial cartoon and saying to his wife, "There's an ..."'

In Canada, at the present time, there are about twenty-five cartoonists who support themselves by working for newspapers. Perhaps the number of cartoonists was larger in the early decades of this century, when the principal Canadian cities had many more daily newspapers, but never have there been more good cartoonists at work.

Unlike the illustrators of a previous generation who often drifted from one newspaper to another, as restless as crime reporters, poorer than many of their editors, contemporary cartoonists have started to occupy a distinctive place in the world of Canadian journalism. The best of them now enjoy the editorial independence, the salaries and the fame of the most successful newspaper columnists.

Cartoonists today are conscious of this. Because of Canadian involvement in the American Association of Cartoonists and in the various international competitions such as the one organized in Montreal every year by Robert LaPalme, they now form a cohesive if informal group. They see one another regularly, exchange information about working conditions, and develop an awareness of the work done by others.

There is now a consensus within this group that rapid political and social changes in Canada and the existence of a stable and prosperous newspaper industry have created unprecedented and even unparalleled opportunities for cartoonists in this country. As a result, the standard of cartooning has never been higher.

Despite the popularity of published collections of the work of individual cartoonists, Canadians have been slow to appreciate the excellence of their own cartoonists and the close relationship between cartooning and their own national development.

"Perhaps not far in the future,"

Barron/Toronto/Star/1971

178

wrote critic Doug Fetherling in 1976, "is the realization that the editorial cartoon is the quintessential Canadian art form . . . Not only do such cartoons sum up our obsession with politics," he continued, "but they also put the famous documentary bias of Canadian culture to its best use."

The full flowering of this relatively modern intermarriage of art and journalism has come in our own time. In terms of style, the most influential cartoonist has been Len Norris. Over a period of almost three decades, every social cartoonist in Canada has had to develop his own style in a world dominated by Norris' success.

This is particularly true of cartoonists working in western Canada and perhaps explains why the West has produced a disproportionately large number of good cartoonists during Norris' career.

Sid Barron is the best example of a cartoonist stimulated into excellence by the existence of Norris. Born in Toronto in 1917, Barron belongs to the same generation as Norris but he started newspaper cartooning only after Norris was firmly established on the West Coast.

From 1937, when he studied alongside Pierre Berton in art classes in Victoria, to 1959, when he joined The Victoria Times, Barron wandered across the country through a series of jobs as a commercial artist and illustrator. He lettered window display cards in Victoria and painted billboards in Toronto. In 1942, he was part of the short-lived Canadian comic book industry that flourished during the Sec-

ond World War. By 1944, he was in Toronto illustrating romantic stories for The Star Weekly until the magazine started to purchase cheaper illustrations that already had appeared in US publications.

Before he surfaced on The Victoria Times in 1959, Barron migrated periodically between Toronto and the West Coast, living a somewhat bohemian life and picking up illustrating

jobs wherever he could. During this period, it later became apparent, he developed a caustic assessment of the manners and moral values of his compatriots who populated the newer suburbs of Canada's expanding cities.

Norris was firmly established in Vancouver when Barron started to work the same regional and social territory in 1959. The influence was apparent in his early cartoons. In 1961, mundane, and his dialogue (not to mention his little slogans, signs, book titles, assorted graffiti) catches perfectly the tone of 1970s Toronto.

"If Macpherson tells us about the people who do things, Barron tells us about the people to whom things are done."

Like Macpherson and Norris, Barron often fills his cartoons with secondary jokes: paintings with ridiculous titles hang on the walls, inane books fill the shelves and newspapers casually display lunatic headlines. Like Yardley Jones of *The Montreal Star,* Barron uses a cat as a kind of trademark in his cartoons. Aircraft almost always fly through the sky trailing slogans that vary according to the locale. "Come home, Cynthia," was the message in Barron's Victoria cartoons; in Calgary, it was, "Aren't the mountains pretty today?"; and in "Dawn Mills" in the suburbs of Toronto, the motto in the sky is always, "Mild, isn't it?"

After a lifetime of wandering across Canada, with sporadic detours to paint in Spain or Morocco, Barron apparently has settled down at last in a small cottage in Victoria where he distils his gentle radicalism into cartoons that are sometimes a jeremiad and always a blessed relief for readers trapped in the suburbs of Toronto thousands of miles to the east.

Barron is perhaps one of the best examples of a contemporary cartoonist who has absorbed and developed a style of cartooning into something identifiably different and completely his own.

In a more direct way, Norris was an

Barron/Toronto Star/1969

"...hi...I'm looking for something in a six-cent stamp...light warmish blue with perhaps one stark historical figure in a simple design...no birds, maps, scientists, flags or leaves...it's to go on a plain, small darkish peach envelope..."

with Pierre Berton again acting as the go-between, Barron joined *The Toronto Star* and started to develop his own style and technique. In 1962, he moved to Calgary to become the cartoonist for *The Albertan* but he continued to produce several cartoons a week for *The Toronto Star.* His *Star* cartoons from Calgary and later from Victoria, where he eventually came to rest, continued to illustrate life in To-ronto, and Barron is today unique as the only "Toronto cartoonist" living on the West Coast.

"Barronland," wrote Robert Fulford, "is a place that is simultaneously baffling and comforting, as baffling and comforting as the real world of Toronto suburbia which Barronland reflects.

"Barron brings to this world not scorn but poetry. He's the poet of the important early influence on Roy Peterson, the most skilled caricaturist now at work in Canada. Peterson was still in high school when he went to see Norris at *The Sun* in Vancouver. He received what he still remembers as an unusually straightforward de- scription of cartooning as a career.

"Len is very down-to-earth," he re- called. "He says that most people who want to become cartoonists want an easy life. They want to dash off a few lines, a little bit of humour, and that's it. In actual fact, it is a hard grind, as any cartoonist will tell you. And he really is blunt about this: that it is a hard grind and that you'll probably never make it."

After graduating from high school, Peterson worked for seven years in the advertising departments of Wood- ward's and Eaton's, taking art courses at night and on weekends. In 1956, he started cartooning in his spare time for

". . . don't turn the box around that way, Ricky . . . you know your father can't stand all that French in the morning . . ."

Barron / Toronto / Star / 1967

a small British Columbia newspaper, the *South Cariboo Advertiser*. In 1962, he left Eaton's, drew briefly for *The Vancouver Province* as a freelance cartoonist and then became a regular cartoonist for *The Sun* as Norris' col- league and eventually as heir apparent.

Peterson's strength is in caricature, where Norris is weakest. In 1973, he won the $5,000 grand prize in the an- nual international cartoon competition at Montreal's *Man and His World* for a drawing of French President Georges Pompidou as *Le Sommelier Grotesque* about to uncork a blast of "Mururoa '72 – A full bodied Pacific vintage with a strong bouquet of Strontium 90 . . ."

Peterson is one of the most versatile contemporary cartoonists. He has designed many book jackets and in recent years, has collaborated with author Stanley Burke in producing a series of books that began with *Frog Fables and Beaver Tales*, illustrated with brilliant caricatures of Canadian public figures as animals.

Peterson has Macpherson's techni- cal skill and something of his savagery but his sense of fun is reminiscent of Bengough. He often disguised the former Mayor of Vancouver, Tom Campbell, in the carnival motley that Bengough used for John A. Macdon- ald, and his cartoons were adorned with messages that might have been scripted by Bengough: "Live on this Stage, Tom Terrific's Freeway Follies! Starring Tom Terrific, Local Radio and TV Personality! Plus Oriental Jugglers, Drama, Comedy, Suspense, Egghead Revue! Itza Riot!"

"Tom Terrific" became an unusual

Peterson/Vancouver/Sun/27 March 1976

... and Son

Peterson/Vancouver/Sun

Father...

example of a caricature that assumed a political life of its own. Several years after Peterson invented "Tom Terrific," Mayor Campbell adopted the title as an effective campaign slogan.

"His PR men just latched onto it and said: Tom is Terrific," Peterson recalled. "They ran an entire campaign on this theme, and he got back in."

"It rather demolished me. I didn't want to draw him after that point, as this character, for fear that I was playing him up. He outfoxed me but, in the long run, he is still a figment of my imagination."

Peterson's images of local BC politicians reached the ultimate goal of caricature, in that they looked more like the politicians than the politicians themselves. This was particularly true of his drawings of the former Premier of British Columbia, W.A.C. Bennett, that perfectly captured the rollicking spirit of Bennett's political showmanship. He is one of the few cartoonists to successfully caricature the almost sinister efficiency of Bennett's son, Bill,

the current Premier of British Columbia. On the national scene, Peterson has produced brilliant caricatures of Pierre Trudeau that rank alongside the famous early caricatures of John Diefenbaker by Macpherson.

The influence of Len Norris dominated not only the West Coast in recent decades but affected younger cartoonists in the neighbouring province of Alberta. Ed Uluschak of Edmonton was recognizably of the Norris school when he started cartooning for *The Journal* in 1968. After winning a

National Newspaper Award a year later, Uluschak confidently developed his own style, as Peterson had, but in another direction. His drawing became firmer and his cartoons tougher and more radical.

The son of Polish immigrants, Uluschak grew up on a "homestead on a rockpile" near the small northern Alberta town of Prosperity. The family lived for a long time in a log cabin and four of his six brothers and sisters died in infancy or childhood. When he was ten years old, his family moved into a

Peterson/Vancouver/Sun

tough immigrants' district in Edmonton where Uluschak, in his own words, "freelanced as a thug."

His cartoons about racial or social discrimination have all the subtlety of a mugging. Middle-class cartoonists dealing with the same subjects often take refuge in heavy symbolism. Uluschak uses a bare-fisted approach inspired by a gut reaction rather than a political or moral position, reinforced by his continuing development as a caricaturist.

Despite the radicalism of some of his cartoons, Uluschak is typically Albertan in his pride at his success as a syndicated cartoonist and the lifestyle that it brings to him. Despite the fact that his political views, by Alberta standards, are "sometimes to the left of Mao-Tse-Tung," western Canadians respond to the rugged individuality of his preference for cartoons that he once described as "hard-hitting, satirical, kick-them-in-the-you-know-where kind of stuff."

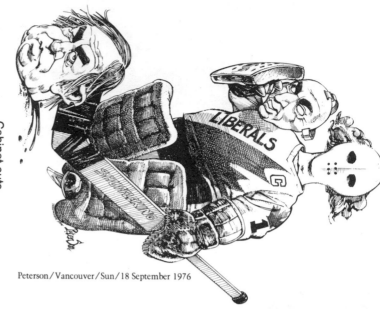

Cabinet cuts

Peterson/Vancouver/Sun/18 September 1976

Out of sight–out of mind

Uluschak/Edmonton/Journal/1975

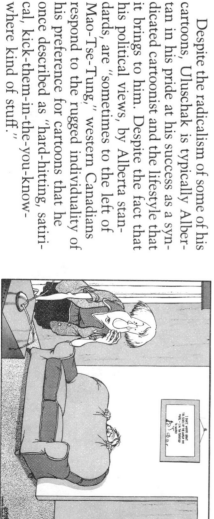

"Here goes –I'm turning on the news!"

Uluschak/Edmonton/Journal/1978

In western Canada, for the past two decades, the work of Jan Kamienski for *The Tribune* in Winnipeg has been marked by a distinctive sophistication, in style and content. Born in Poland and trained in Europe, Kamienski worked as a commercial artist in Winnipeg before he joined *The Tribune* in 1958. He is also the newspaper's art critic, a rare example of a cartoonist with a continuing academic interest in art and the literary ability to express it.

In addition to Duncan Macpherson, Ontario now has three cartoonists who are among the most popular in Can-

ada: Ed Franklin of *The Globe and Mail* and Andy Donato of *The Sun* in Toronto, and Blaine of *The Spectator* in Hamilton.

One of Franklin's distinctions is that he came to Canada when he was thirty-eight years old and was in his forties before he established himself as a newspaper cartoonist in Toronto. Most cartoonists in Canada have grown up in the society they caricature, and many of them, by the time they reach middle age, are concerned about maintaining their freshness and originality. Franklin's relatively late

Uluschak/Edmonton/Journal/1975

"Shine, mister?"

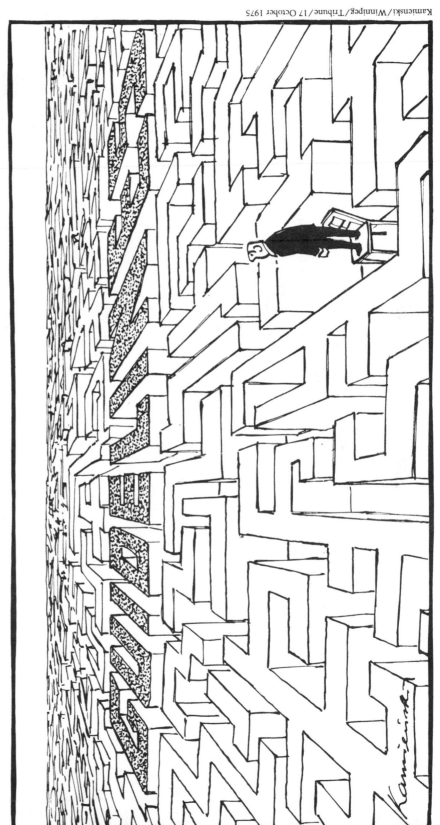

start as a political cartoonist in Canada perhaps accounts for his distinctive way of looking at Canadian politics.

His caricatures always illuminate public figures with harsh clarity but his ideas are often as labyrinthine as his drawings and sometimes remain tantalizingly obscure for a large part of his audience.

Like Macpherson, Norris and Peterson, Franklin spent much of his early career as an illustrator. Born in Texas, he started as an advertising artist for local newspapers before moving to New York, where he freelanced as a commercial artist and illustrator for four years. In 1959, he almost decided

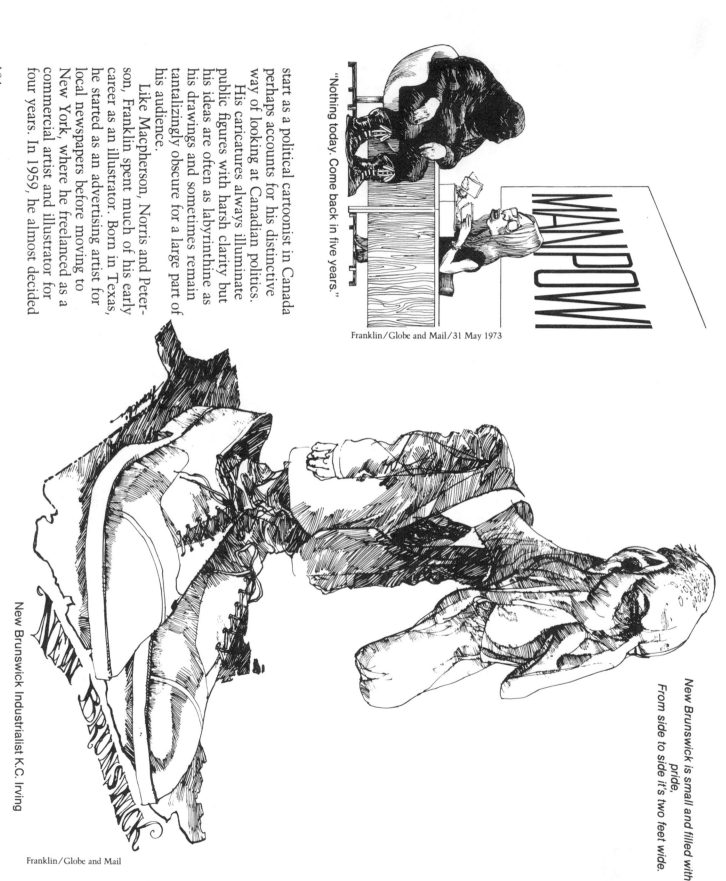

"Nothing today. Come back in five years."

Franklin/Globe and Mail/31 May 1973

New Brunswick Industrialist K.C. Irving

Franklin/Globe and Mail

New Brunswick is small and filled with pride,
From side to side it's two feet wide.

to return to Texas but emigrated instead to Toronto where he continued to work as a commercial artist.

In the mid-1960s, he began to draw for the *Globe* as a freelancer, at a time when almost every cartoonist in the country was working in Duncan Macpherson's shadow and every editor seemed to want cartoons that looked like Macpherson's. Franklin worked for eighteen months as a *Star* cartoonist, supplying cartoons on the days when Macpherson wasn't scheduled to produce, before joining the *Globe* as a full-time cartoonist in 1968.

In an unusual free-verse description of his cartooning, written for his own newspaper, Franklin listed "invention" as the essential element in a cartoon. His description of his purpose accurately described his cartoons:

"... occasionally a peculiar humour solemn and frothed with bitterness more rarely a gut laugh but always to draw well with vitality and taste ..."

In the 1970s, as the new tabloid *Sun* flourished in Toronto, cartoonist Andy Donato expressed the newspaper's irreverent and aggressive pos-

ture, particularly in opposition to the Trudeau government. The son of a Toronto grocer, he worked as an artist and art director for *The Telegram* in Toronto before it folded. Donato has chipped away at developing his style over the years, sometimes borrowing heavily from Macpherson and others. For him, technique is plainly a means to an end. He has said that "the idea is the thing" and his obvious enjoyment at making a strong editorial point has made him one of the more widely syndicated cartoonists.

Donato's admirers have learned to

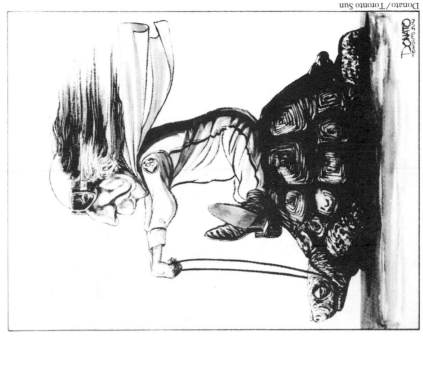

Donato/Toronto Sun

Economic recovery

Franklin/Globe and Mail

185

look for secondary references in his cartoons. For instance, caricatures of Pierre Trudeau often contained miniature drawings of Michael Pitfield, the influential Clerk of the Privy Council in the Liberal government who was also one of Trudeau's personal friends.

In Hamilton, Blaine has been drawing for *The Spectator* since 1961, after working for several years for *The Cape Breton Post* in his native Nova Scotia and for a few months, as a substitute cartoonist, for *The Globe and Mail*. An intense individual, both about himself and his work, Blaine is regarded by his contemporaries as being a master of brush technique. He also has his black belt in karate, a distinction that prompted a journalist on *The Spectator* to remark that "Blaine might just be the only cartoonist anywhere who can

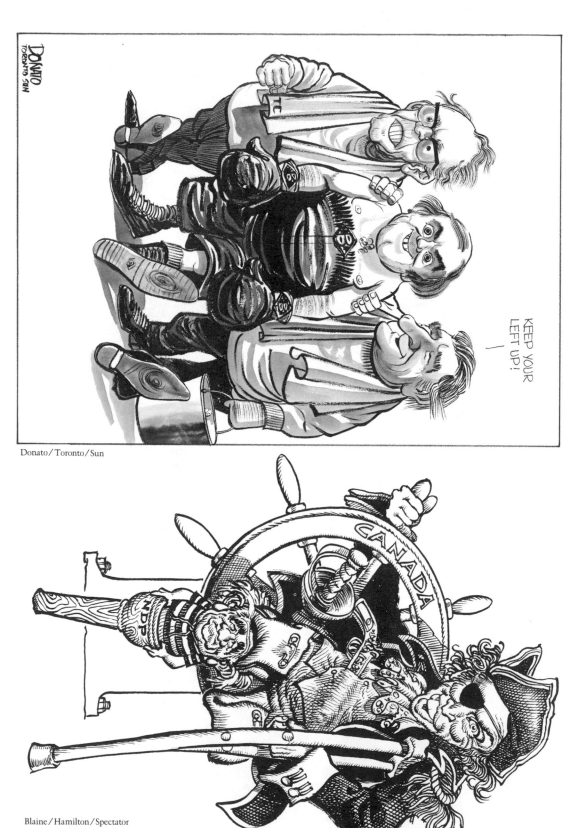

Donato / Toronto / Sun

KEEP YOUR LEFT UP!

Blaine / Hamilton / Spectator

MENU
TRUDEAU
TRANCHÉ

La rareté des aliments
Food Shortage

Berthio/Montreal/Le Devoir

"She'll be the death of us yet!"

Berthio/ Le Jour

I GOTTA BE ME...
I GOTTA BE WEEE

Blaine/Hamilton/Spectator

not only tickle your funnybone but also break it, if you don't laugh."

In 1970, Blaine won the prestigious Reuben award in the United States, named after the cartoonist Rube Goldberg, for being "the outstanding cartoonist of the year."

In French-speaking Quebec, the most popular cartoonist of the past few years has been Roland Berthiaume, who succeeded Normand Hudon at *Le Devoir* in 1965. "Berthio," as he signs himself, drew for *Le Devoir* for more than ten years. Toward the end of this

time, his separatist views created irreconcilable differences between himself and the federalist editor of the newspaper, Claude Ryan, and he left *Le Devoir* to become the cartoonist of the separatist daily newspaper *Le Jour* during its short life.

Like all Quebec cartoonists, Berthio regards his work as being different from the productions of cartoonists in English Canada: "Our pictures are simpler, more linear, more spontaneous."

Quebec cartoonists often simply place their main characters in the foreground of their cartoons where they deliver their punch lines against sketchy backgrounds. Many cartoonists in English Canada, in contrast, produce detailed cartoons that often contain minor characters, furniture, posters — all the paraphernalia of a stage set — as well as secondary jokes.

The simpler Quebec style also seems to suit cartoonists who have come to the province in recent years from French-speaking countries overseas: Roland Pier of *Le Journal de Montréal* who came to Canada from France in 1960 and lived in western and northern Canada for five years before settling in Montreal; and Jean-Pierre Girerd of *La Presse* who left Algeria in 1961 and lived in the United States before arriving in Montreal in 1964. "I don't care about the details in the drawings," Girerd has said. "I think that the most important thing is to give a strong idea, and rapidly. The readers of a newspaper are always in a hurry."

In Algeria, Girerd was cartoonist for *Le Journal d'Alger*, a newspaper supported by the French government. There, he was expected to follow the editorial line. Cartoons critical of de Gaulle, for instance, would often be rejected without any explanation. Girerd discovered more freedom in Quebec in the 1960s although the pressure to conform politically in Quebec often came from other journalists as well as from editors and newspaper owners. During the October Crisis of 1970, when he was critical of terrorism in Quebec, Girerd found that his independent political attitude and his personal bias against violence placed him in opposition to many journalists and other Quebec intellectuals.

"If they send in the army we will 'Be Prepared'"

Pier/Journal de Montréal

English language tests for immigrant children in Montreal

Girerd/Montreal/La Presse

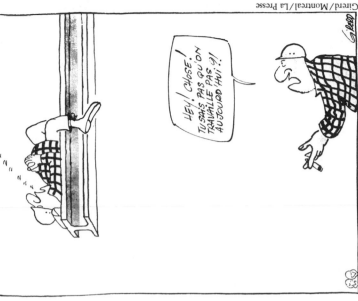

"Hey, you! Don't you know we're off today?"

Hunter/Québec/Le Soleil/11 December 1978

Queen Elizabeth: "And what do you want for Christmas, René, dear?"

Premier Lévesque: "EVERYTHING!"

189

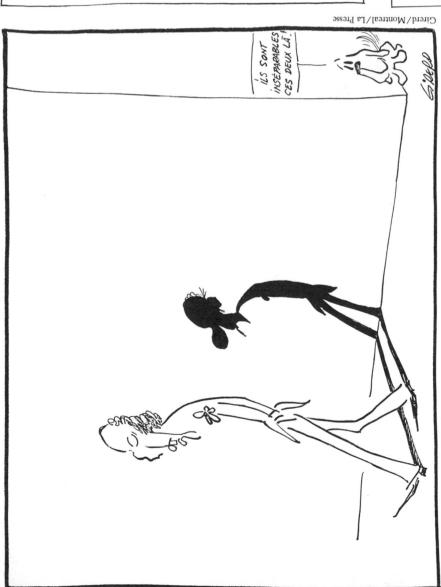

Girerd/Montreal/La Presse

"Those two are inseparable!"

Raoul Hunter, cartoonist for Quebec's *Le Soleil* since 1969, also ran afoul of his newspaper colleagues during the October Crisis for his criticism of terrorist actions. An art teacher as well as a cartoonist who has said that his job is to "make jokes, not war," Hunter was publicly condemned, along with his editor, by members of the journalists' union at *Le Soleil* in 1970. He maintained his right to make an independent judgement of events and continued to produce cartoons.

Girerd believes that cartoonists who have committed themselves politically are "prisoners of their own nationalism." At the same time, he believes that cartooning has a serious political purpose.

"A cartoonist is charged with making people laugh," he has stated, "but more than that, to make them reflect on certain things."

Because they have worked in a society undergoing revolutionary social and political changes while still being conscious of its own weaknesses, Quebec cartoonists of the 1960s and 1970s perhaps have been more protective about their community than have many cartoonists in English Canada. Nor have they caricatured the politicians and lampooned the shortcomings of English Canada with as much spirit as the cartoonists of English Canada have employed against separatist leaders and what they see as the excesses of Quebec nationalism.

Among younger cartoonists in English Canada, Terry Mosher, working under the name "Aislin" at *The Gazette* in Montreal, has achieved a national reputation that rivals the fame of Macpherson or Norris. This is based partly on his cartoons and partly on his ability, unusual among cartoonists, to talk forcefully and knowledgeably in public about the development of Canadian cartooning and its place in Canadian journalism.

Mosher has been drawing since he was expelled from high school in 1963. For two years, he hitchhiked across North America, supporting himself most of the time by sketching people in bars and taverns. In 1965, he enrolled in Quebec's Ecole des Beaux-Arts. During the summer, he was among the young artists who congregated on the Rue du Trésor near the Château Frontenac to sell sketches and paintings to tourists. This is where Mosher started to caricature for profit and where he did his first political cartoon—a drawing of President Lyndon Johnson produced on order for a tourist from Boston. Mosher signed his daughter's name, Aislin, to the carica-

tures, apparently because he wanted at that time to save his own name for his serious drawing and painting.

In 1969, after freelancing for various student and underground publications in Montreal, Mosher was hired by *The Montreal Star*. His cross-hatched caricatures, all plagued by clouds of dandruff, immediately attracted attention and created controversy. Many of his cartoons became so closely identified with the political events they commemorated that Canadians could hardly recall the incidents without thinking of the cartoons.

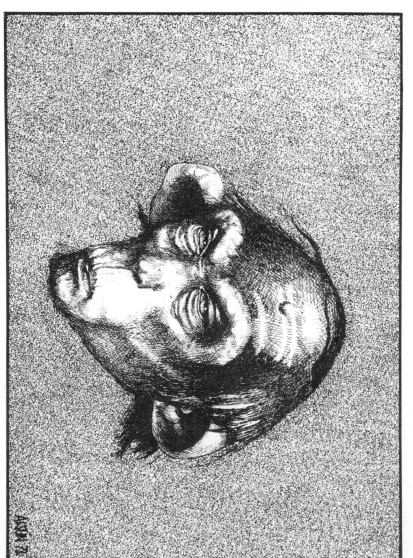

The Swinger

The October Crisis of 1970, for example, was symbolized by Mosher's caricature of Jean Marchand, a member of the Trudeau cabinet, clasping the telephone directories of Montreal, Quebec, Sherbrooke and Hull: "We now have a list of FLQ suspects."

The election of a separatist government in Quebec on November 15, 1976, was depicted unforgettably by a cartoon of Premier-elect René Lévesque telling everyone to "take a Valium." Mosher's image of Pierre Trudeau as a hard-eyed simian swinger is the most savage caricature ever pub-

Aislin/Last Post/1971

Jean Marchand: "We now have a list of FLQ suspects!"

Jean Drapeau promises to back the PQ on certain issues

Aislin/Le Maclean/1970

Aislin/Montreal/Gazette/1977

lished of the former Prime Minister and seems likely to haunt his reputation forever.

Doug Fetherling wrote in 1976 that "Aislin is, in traditional terms, the best artist now working for Canadian newspapers." Noting his debt to American cartoonist David Levine, Fetherling described Mosher as "the spokesman for the present generation of educated radicals now so prominent in Canadian media, publishing and art . . ."

In his relationship to newspapers, in particular *The Gazette* of Montreal since 1972, Mosher has continued and elaborated the progress achieved by Duncan Macpherson.

"A lot of writers and editors figure that a drawing is something to illustrate their copy," he said. "My attitude is, I have a point of view like a columnist and you're damn well going to treat me that way or I'm not going to work for you."

Mosher's early cartoons dealing with such subjects as the monarchy and religion outraged and delighted many Canadians. In those years, the cartoonist himself was often a fairly outrageous character on the Montreal scene.

Much of the exuberance still remains, but it has been tempered by financial success and the heavy demands on Mosher's time and talents. His research work on the National Film Board's documentary about Canadian cartooning and his subsequent collaboration on this book have made him an authority on the development of cartooning in this country and brought him into contact with almost every cartoonist now at work.

In 1978, when cartoonist Bob Bierman of *The Victoria Times* was sued for libel by a member of the British

Columbia cabinet, Municipal Affairs Minister Bill Vander Zalm, Mosher was flown from Montreal to Vancouver as a witness for the defence.

Vander Zalm's legal action was unusual in Canada and the decision, handed down by Mr. Justice Craig Munroe in British Columbia's Supreme Court in January 1979, was an important event in Canadian journalism. Judge Munroe awarded Vander Zalm $3,500 and costs after finding that the cartoon "was not, objectively,

The Quebec Nationalist

Aislin/Unpublished/1977

a fair comment upon facts."

The captionless drawing, published in *The Victoria Times* on June 22, 1978, showed Vander Zalm gleefully and diabolically pulling the wings from flies. Bierman intended the cartoon as a comment upon the minister's conduct when he held the portfolio of Human Resources. The judge decided that "literally, upon its face, the cartoon depicts the plaintiff as a person with a love of cruelty who enjoys causing suffering to defenceless creatures,"

In the judge's opinion, Vander Zalm's conduct in office "could not fairly lead an ordinary person to conclude that the plaintiff acted in a cruel, sadistic or thoughtless manner when performing his duties." He also ruled that "freedom of the press and of political cartoonists is a freedom governed by law and is not a freedom to make untrue defamatory statements" and that "the political cartoonist has no special immunity from the application of general laws."

This space is reserved for Bierman's cartoon of Bill Vander Zalm, which will appear in future editions, if the appeal of Bierman's libel conviction is successful.

Bierman/Victoria/Times

Rodewalt / Calgary / Albertan / 1979

"Boy, you're really asking for it!"

Donato / Unpublished / 1979

Uluschak / Edmonton Journal / 2 February 1979

"It's a fun thing, don't you see!"

In his judgement, now under appeal, Judge Munroe went beyond the question of libel to make an aesthetic decision on the cartoon.

"That the cartoon would interest a reader is possible," he wrote. "Amusing it was not."

The conviction of Bierman and his newspaper shocked cartoonists across the country and provoked a number of cartoons that almost pleaded for legal prosecution. Almost simultaneously, Mosher in Montreal and Uluschak in Edmonton drew cartoons of Vander Zalm pulling the legs off frogs, referring to a more recent controversy when the same politician had used the term "frogs" to refer to French-speaking Quebeckers. Girerd in Montreal went so far as to caricature the judge in his cartoon on the verdict. Cartoonists feared that the Munroe ruling might encourage other politicians to sue cartoonists. More fundamentally, the Bierman case in British Columbia illustrated the importance, vitality and courage of Canadian politi-cal cartooning in our own time.

It showed that the editorial-page hecklers of modern Canadian journal-ism have not become tame jesters in the courts of our political and financial establishments. They are exploring the territory between fair and outrageous comment where great cartoonists have always precariously existed.

Bado/Unpublished/1979

Bill Vander Zalm pulls the wings off Bob Bierman

Girerd/Montreal/La Presse/19 January 1979

Sketches for Tomorrow

Robert Stanfield's failure to defeat Prime Minister Trudeau in three elections and his lugubrious manner in public endeared him to cartoonists.

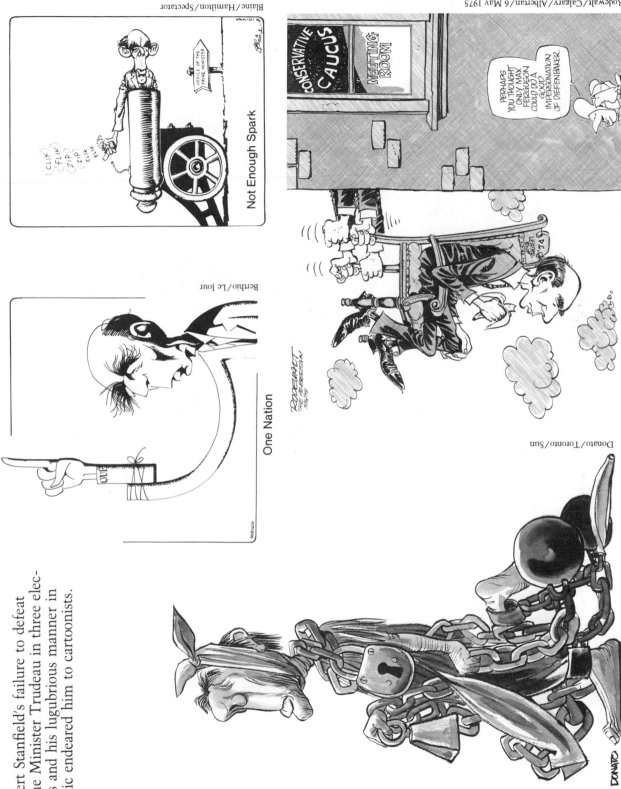

Blaine/Hamilton/Spectator

Not Enough Spark

Berthio/Le Jour

One Nation

PERHAPS YOU THOUGHT ONLY MAX FERGUSON COULD DO A GOOD IMPERSONATION OF DIEFENBAKER.

CONSERVATIVE CAUCUS MEETING ROOM

Donato/Toronto/Sun

When the Conservatives ignored more promising candidates and elected a young Albertan to succeed Stanfield, cartoonists and their readers found it hard to take Joe Clark seriously. A world tour early in 1979, when Clark lost his luggage and seemed bewildered by international politics, confirmed the impression that here was another Stanfield in embryo.

Aislin/Maclean's/1973

Peterson/Vancouver/Sun/7 February 1976

The Firing Squad

Macpherson/Toronto/Star/1976

"You can't take this with you...it's passed on from leader to leader."

Kuch/Winnipeg/Free Press/6 July 1976

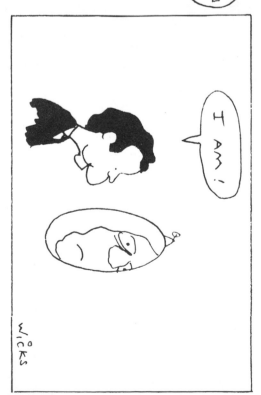

Wicks

Roschkov/Toronto/Star

"Ah...C'mon in Jack."

"Too bad, his French was really improving."

But events were undermining the leadership of Prime Minister Trudeau as Clark was learning his trade. A dispute over the language of air traffic control became a symbolic test of English Canada's commitment to bilin-

CLARK KENT

TOUTES LES DEMI-HEURES IL NOUS COMPTE POUR VOIR S'IL EN MANQUE...

"Ever since Jack Horner left, every half hour he counts the ranks."

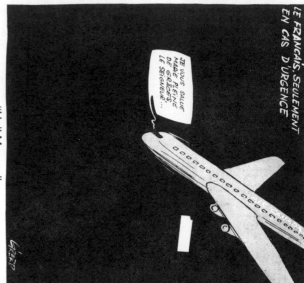

"Hail Mary…"

Girerd/Montreal/La Presse

French in emergency
situations only

gualism. Concluding that it wasn't very deep, many Quebecois supported the efforts of the Quebec government to strengthen the position of French in Quebec, sometimes at the expense of English. The drift of Quebec toward unilingualism undermined the Prime Minister's efforts to promote bilingualism in other provinces.

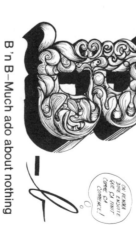

B 'n B—Much ado about nothing

Hunter/Quebec/Le Soleil
29 March 1971

Bilingualism in Ottawa

Daigneault/Le Droit

"We have ways of making you talk French…"

Norris/Vancouver/Sun/21 January 1972

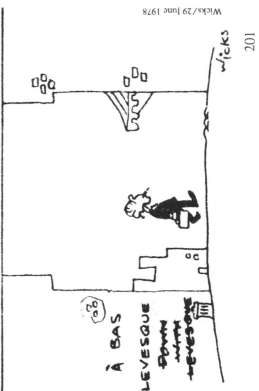

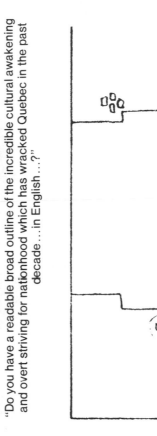

"Do you have a readable broad outline of the incredible cultural awakening and overt striving for nationhood which has wracked Quebec in the past decade . . . in English . . . ?"

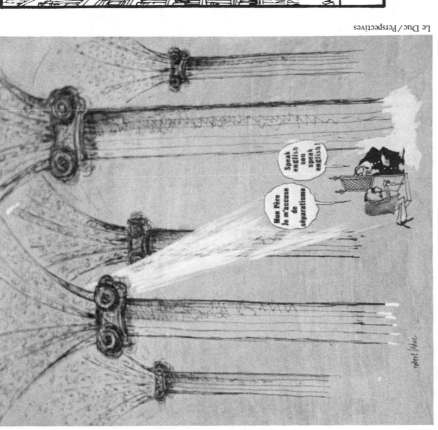

When the Parti Québécois won the Quebec election of November 1976, and René Lévesque became Premier with the intention of moving Quebec toward political sovereignty, it confirmed the popular impression that Trudeau's efforts to unify Canadians were no longer productive.

Roschkov/Toronto/Star

The Ugly Duckling

Rusins/Ottawa/Citizen
14 July 1977

Aislin/Montreal/Gazette/1976

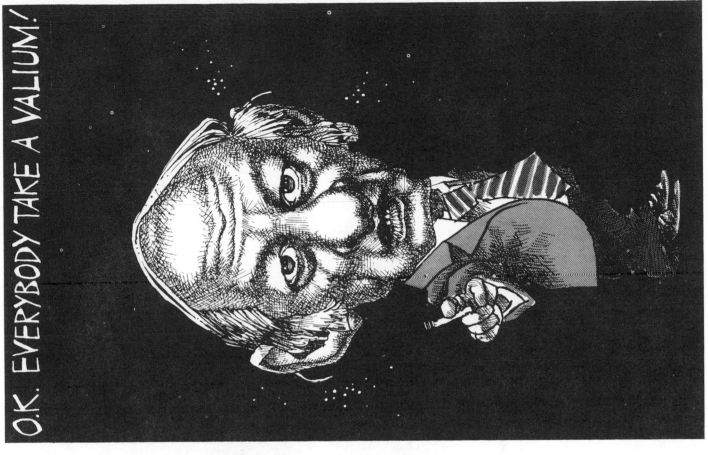

O.K. EVERYBODY TAKE A VALIUM!

Chapleau/Montreal-Matin/1976

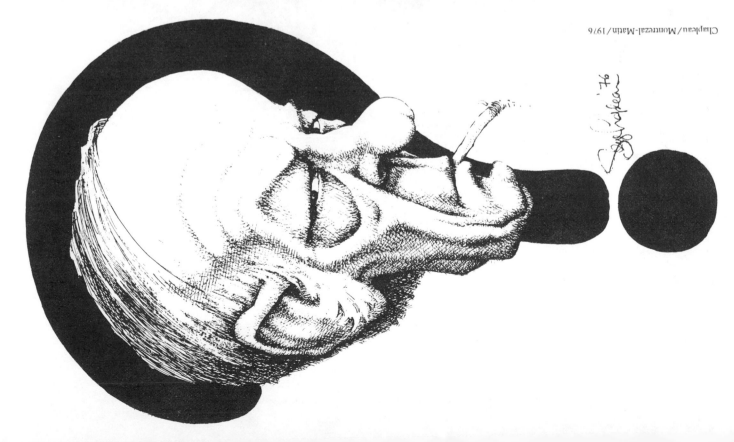

Kamienski/Winnipeg/Tribune/17 November 1976

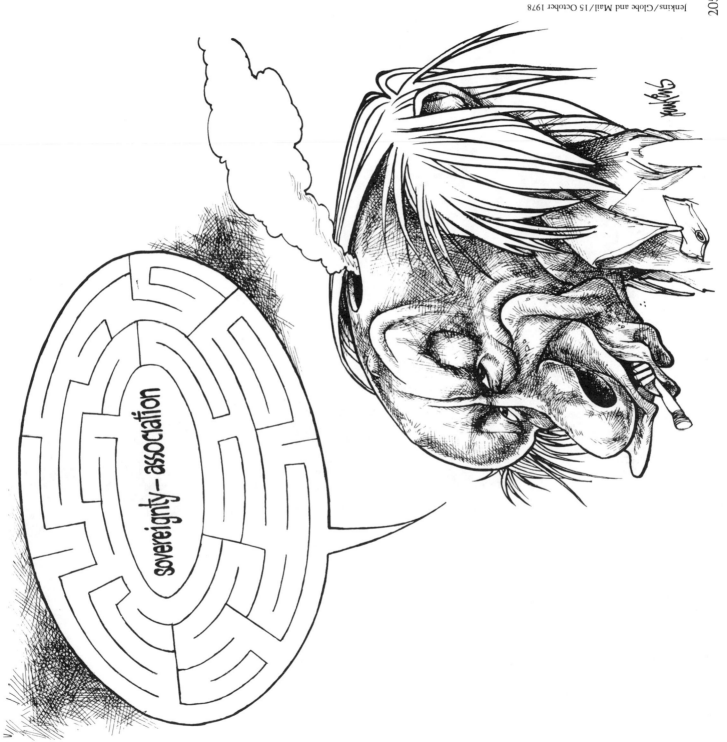

"We'll eliminate English from Quebec if it takes the rest of the 18th century..."

Hunter / Victoria / Colonist

Speak Softly

Yardley Jones / Montreal / Star / 23 October 1978

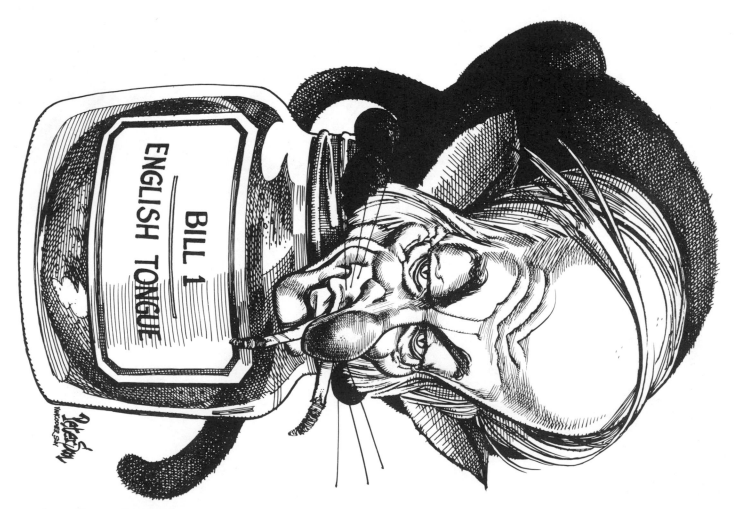

Peterson / Vancouver / Sun / 7 February 1976

"Who's afraid of flats?"

Hunter/Quebec/Le Soleil/28 June 1977

Girerd/Montreal/La Presse

"It's unfortunate that we need a law to teach Quebeckers to speak the language of the majority!"

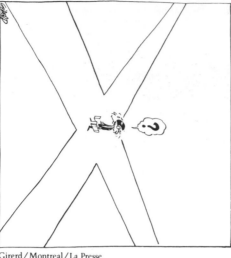

Girerd / Montreal / La Presse

The defeated Quebec Premier, Robert Bourassa, was replaced as leader of the Quebec Liberals by Claude Ryan who, as editor of *Le Devoir*, had established a strong personal following in Quebec and across the country. Ryan's spirited opposition to the Parti Québécois further weakened Trudeau's claim in the 1979 federal election campaign to be the only public figure capable of dealing with Quebec during the period of its referendum on sovereignty-association.

HOT-BOB

Aislin/Montreal/Gazette/1978

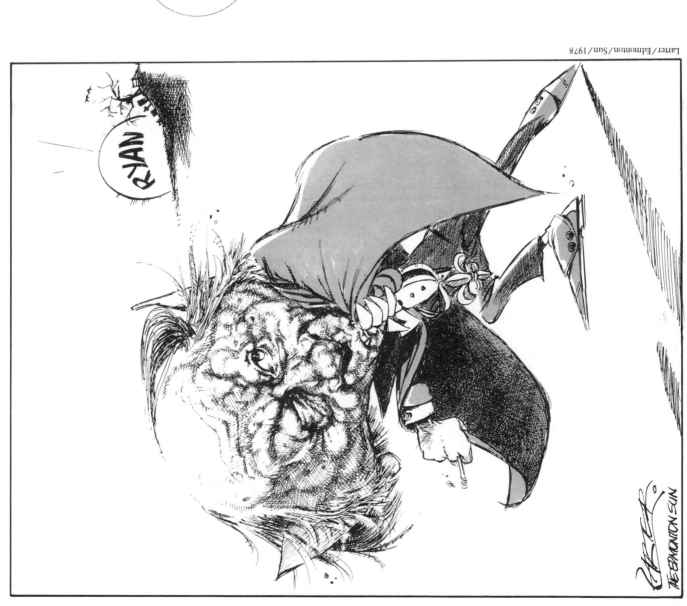

Larter/Edmonton/Sun/1978

With more than a million Canadians unemployed and inflation rising, the Trudeau government's economic management also came into question.

Uluschak/Edmonton/Journal /1977

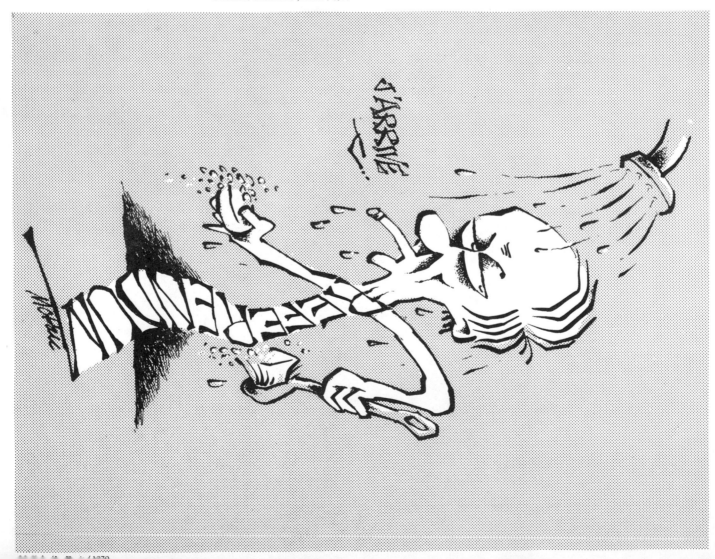

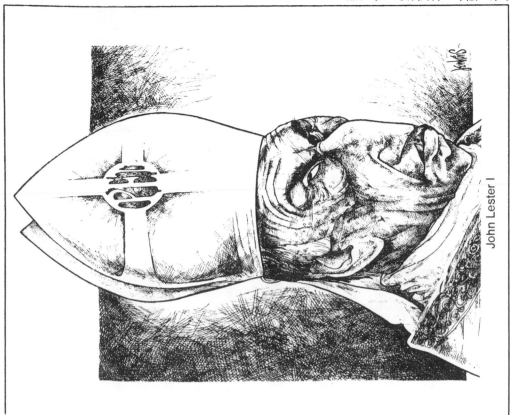

John Lester I

Although Trudeau continued to impress Canadians as a leader according to public opinion polls taken during the campaign, voters everywhere but in Quebec turned against the Liberals in the spring of 1979 and elected a Conservative minority under Prime Minister Joe Clark.

Waghorn

Innes/Calgary/Herald

Waghorn/1979

McKale/Le Droit/1979

The nation's cartoonists were confronted once again by a changing cast of political leaders, but the issues remained remarkably the same as those they had dealt with for more than a century.

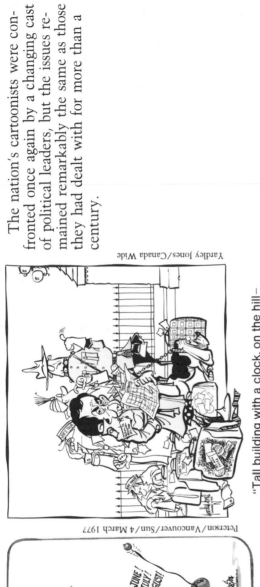

Peterson/Vancouver/Sun/4 March 1977

The Baby Sitter

Yardley Jones/Canada Wide

"Tall building with a clock, on the hill—can't miss it."

Franklin/Globe and Mail/16 September 1978

"And with a little luck we can peak over the winter."

214

Old Mother Hubbard went to the cupboard …

Rodewalt / Calgary / Albertan

"The Liberals don't have anything to offer …"

McKale / Le Droit / 1978

Sneyd / Scoops

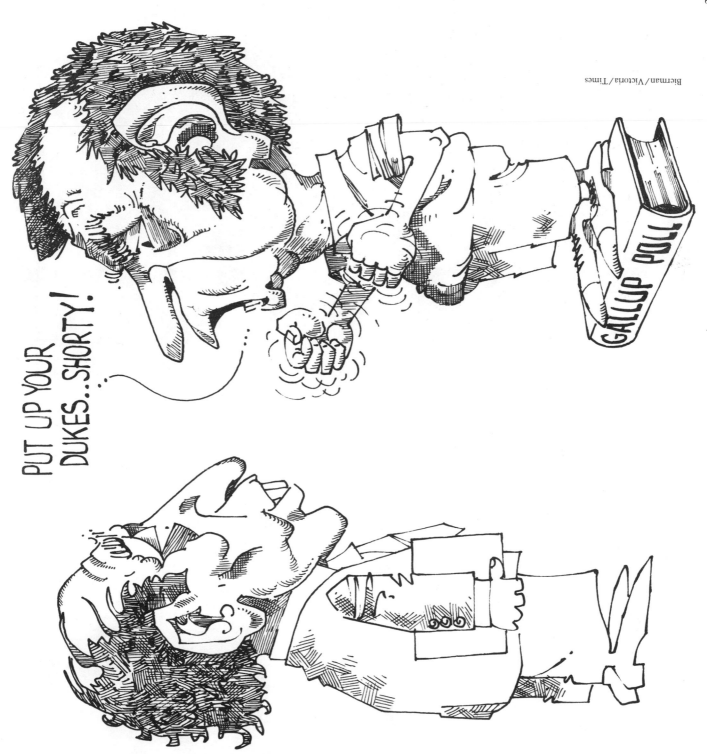

Bierman/Victoria/Times

216

Hudon

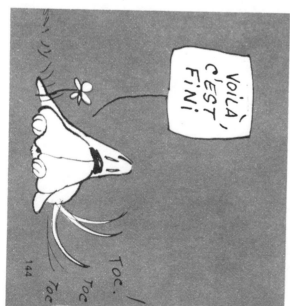

Girerd / Montreal / La Presse

Peterson / Vancouver / Sun / 4 June 1977

NNA

The Canadian National Newspaper Award for Political Cartooning

This award is granted annually by the Toronto Press Club for what it judges to be the best political cartoon of the year. It is the only award of its kind in Canada, and is considered to be the equivalent of the American Pulitzer Prize for cartooning. The award has been granted annually since 1949.

The NNA recipients are:

1949 Jack Boothe
1950 Jim Reidford
1951 Len Norris
1952 Robert LaPalme
1953 Robert Chambers
1954 John Collins
1955 Ting
1956 Jim Reidford
1957 Jim Reidford
1958 Raoul Hunter
1959 Duncan Macpherson
1960 Duncan Macpherson
1961 Ed McNally
1962 Duncan Macpherson
1963 Jan Kamienski
1964 Ed McNally
1965 Duncan Macpherson
1966 Robert Chambers
1967 Raoul Hunter
1968 Roy Peterson
1969 Edd Uluschak
1970 Duncan Macpherson
1971 Yardley Jones
1972 Duncan Macpherson
1973 John Collins
1974 Blaine
1975 Roy Peterson
1976 Andy Donato
1977 Aislin
1978 Aislin

Boothe/Globe and Mail/1949

Futility

217

Canada's Undefended Border

Norris/Vancouver/Sun/12 December 1951

One World

Reidford/Globe and Mail/31 May 1950

Different countries—different customs

Chambers/Halifax/Chronicle-Herald/1953

Finance Minister Abbott's sleight of hand

LaPalme/Montreal/Le Devoir/1952

Ting / London / Free Press / 29 January 1955

Hands Across the Border

NEWS ITEM —

MACKENZIE KING SPEAKS TO NEWSMAN ON A BENCH AT KINGSMERE

KINGSMERE RUINS

I'M GETTING TO BE SORT OF A RUIN TOO

A QUARREL FROM QUEBEC

QUEBEC OTTAWA FEUD

St Laurent seeks the source of Mackenzie King's political inspiration.

Collins / Montreal / Gazette / 1954

"Have you anything to say to me?"

EGERTON HERBERT NORMAN (1909-1957)

Norman was the Canadian ambassador to Egypt when he committed suicide in 1957. He was repeatedly harrassed by the American Senate Sub-committee on Security, although the Canadian authorities had cleared his name several times. The American accusations were never proved.

Reidford / Globe and Mail / 1957

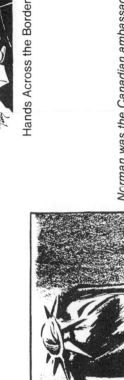

Reidford / Globe and Mail / 1956

Closure

"Smile"

Macpherson / Toronto / Star / 1960

Hunter / Quebec / Le Soleil / 3 April 1958

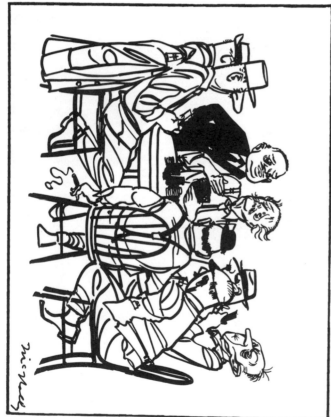

"What'cha got there, Mac?"

McNally / Montreal / Star / 1961

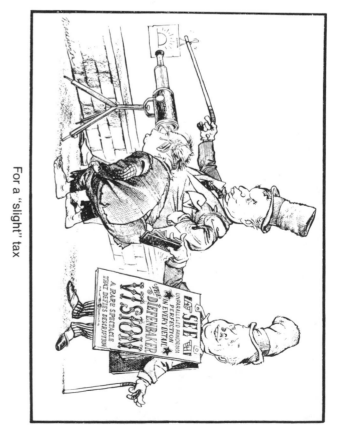

For a "slight" tax

Macpherson / Toronto / Star / 1959

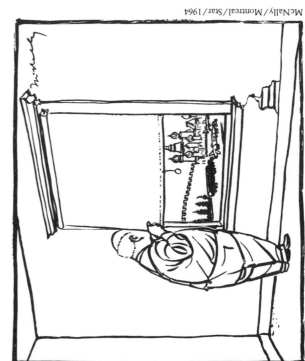

Kamienski/Winnipeg/Tribune/1963

"One for none, none for all!"

MacPherson/Toronto/Star/1962

"Take it or leave it, no special rates for kiddies."

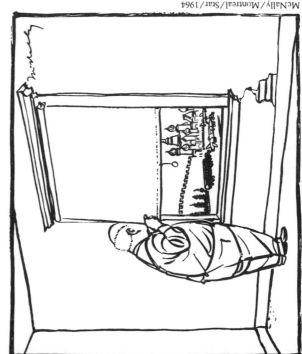

McNally/Montreal/Star/1964

Deposed Nikita Kruschev watches a parade on Red Square.

Chambers/Halifax/Herald/27 September 1966

An albatross keeps Pearson from winning a majority government in November 1965.

Macpherson/Toronto/Star/1965

Chambers/Halifax/Herald/3 October 1966

Johnson: "Comme dirait Churchill, ça commence a peser...."
Daniel Johnson: As Churchill would say, it's becoming a burden...."

Hunter/Quebec/Le Soleil
30 November 1967

Tomorrow's Guerillas

223

"Our boy's on DRUGS!—Where have we failed?"

"Dad! ... Son!"

"I wish they'd stop moaning—I can't concentrate."

Blaine / Hamilton / Spectator / 1974

"Of course I've been a good boy."

Collins / Montreal / Gazette / 1973

Sing-a-long with Alice

Macpherson / Toronto / Star / 1972

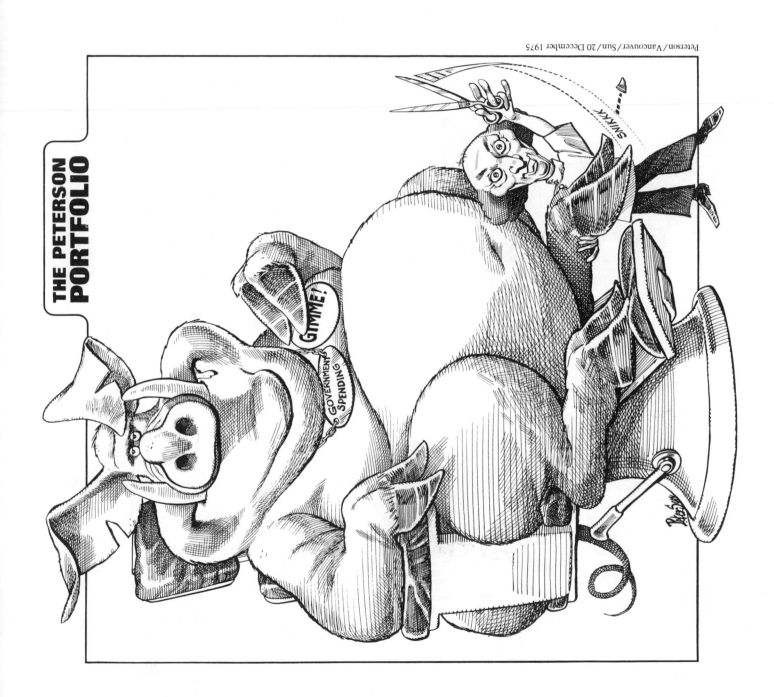

Peterson/Vancouver/Sun/20 December 1975

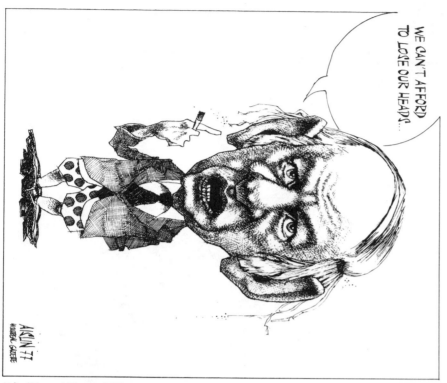

Aislin/Montreal/Gazette/1977

Donato/Toronto/Sun/1976

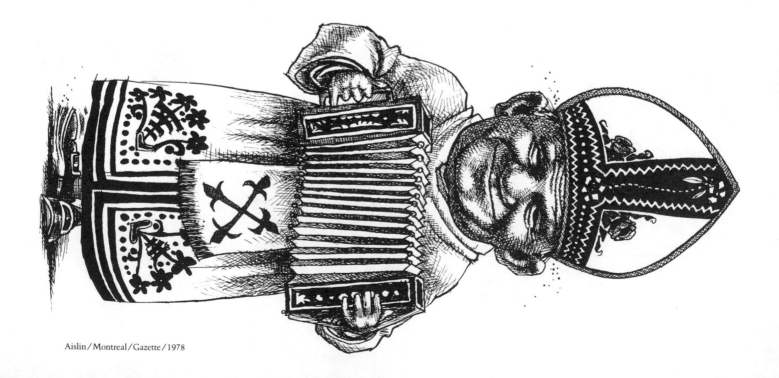

Aislin/Montreal/Gazette/1978

Biographies

Aislin

This is the pen-name used by *Montreal Gazette* cartoonist Terry Mosher. Born in Ottawa in 1942, he studied art at Toronto's Central Technical School, The Ontario College of Art and l'Ecole des Beaux-Arts in Quebec. After graduating, he free-lanced for several publications and became a staff cartoonist for *The Montreal Star* in 1969. Moving to *The Gazette* in 1972, he alternates with fellow cartoonist John Collins on the editorial page. Aislin

cartoons are known for the clouds of dandruff that emanate from the caricatured personalities. The cartoonist considers this to be a common leveller – bringing the high and mighty back down to earth. During the last decade he has also drawn free-lance for many of Canada's major publications and other periodicals abroad including *Punch*, *The Atlantic Monthly*, *Harper's*, *The National Lampoon*, *Time*, *The Washington Star*, and *The New York Times*. Awarded first prize for political cartooning at the 1970 International Salon of Caricature and Cartoon, Mosher also was the recipient of The Canadian National Newspaper Award in 1977 and 1978. Syndicated to many Canadian newspapers, he has published five collections of his cartoons to date.

"A political cartoon diagnoses the disease. It should not presume to prescribe the cure."

Arem

This is a pen-name sometimes used by Bob Bierman of *The Victoria Times*. It is derived from the initials of the cartoonist's first two names, Robert and Maximillian.

Arsenault

Sylvain Arsenault was born in Rogersville, NB, in 1931. Having worked as a surveyor and in forestry, he took correspondence courses in art. As a layout artist for the Acadian publication, *L'Evangeline*, he regularly contributes editorial cartoons to this newspaper.

Atkinson

In the late 1890s, occasional political cartoons appeared in the Hamilton *Spectator* that dealt with Canadian subject matter. These cartoons were signed Atkinson but, as in the case of many of the cartoonists of that era, no biographical information on the cartoonist was found.

Avrom

This was the pen-name used by Avrom Yanovsky. Born in the Ukraine in 1911, his family came to Winnipeg two years later. His parents were both involved in the 1919 Winnipeg general strike, which was to have a profound effect on his career. He began cartooning for various labour-union newspapers in the 1920s. He studied briefly at The Winnipeg School of Art in 1928, The Ontario College of Art in 1933, and at The American Artists' School in New York in 1938-39. In addition to drawing political cartoons, Avrom designed posters and murals, and gave occasional lectures or "chalk talks" for numerous labour and

ethnic groups in Toronto. He was editorial cartoonist for *The Clarion* and later, *The Canadian Tribune*. Although not well known to the general public in Canada, his work was reproduced in numerous socialist publications throughout the world during the last forty years. Yanovsky died in Toronto early in 1979.

"Perhaps more than any other art form, the cartoon reflects our own personal prejudices as victim."

Bado

The pen-name used by Guy Badeaux, a Montreal-based cartoonist born in 1949. Bado studied art at L'Ecole des Arts Appliqués and free-lanced as a cartoonist and caricaturist, also trying his hand at animation and comic strips. His work appeared in *Mainmise*, *The Gazette*, *La Presse*, *Le Devoir*, *Baloune* and several

other local publications. In 1977, he was the staff cartoonist for the weekly *La Jour* until it folded. Since then, he has contributed editorial-page cartoons to *Le Devoir*. A collection of his political cartoons and comic strips was published in 1979 entitled *Tout Bado... Ou Presque*.

"Political cartooning is thought for food."

Barré

Raoul Barré was a caricaturist active in Montreal before the First World War. His interest in comic strips took him to New York where he changed his name to Raoul Barry. There he worked with the established comic-strip cartoonist Pat Sullivan and experimented with animation.

Barron

Born in Toronto in 1917, Sid Barron moved to Victoria with his family as a very young child. Like most cartoonists, his studies in art were minimal, but he did take some classes in Victoria in 1937. Shortly afterwards he began wandering back and forth across the country picking up usually art-related jobs here and there: a $15-a-week job hand-lettering window cards, painting outdoor displays and billboards. In Toronto he did some illustrations for *The Star Weekly* until the paper discovered that for pennies it could buy cratefulls of illustrations that appeared originally in various American publications. After the war, Barron studied art briefly in Detroit. For the next ten years or so, he wandered back and forth between Toronto and Vancouver, picking up ad work and illustrations where he could.

In 1959 he took a crack at drawing editorial-page cartoons for *The Victoria Times*. Barron produced two annuals while at *The Times*. In 1961 he started doing cartoons for *The Toronto Star* where he was hired on by Pierre Berton. Barron has had an on-and-off working relationship with *The Toronto Star* ever since. He moved to Calgary in 1962 and began doing some work for *The Albertan* while continuing to do work for the *Star*. In 1964 he also began to appear in *Maclean's*. Robert Fulford dubbed Barron as "the poet of the mundane." Although he creates tremendous reflections of suburbia (*Dawn Mills*), he has never been a part of it himself and lives very quietly in Victoria, BC.

"Cartooning is just too much goddamn work."

Batsford

Ben Batsford worked for the *Manitoba Free Press*, now the *Winnipeg Free Press*, during the period of the First World War.

Beaton

Al Beaton was born in Vancouver in 1923. Serving overseas with the RCAF during the Second World War, he attended the Vancouver School of Fine Art. After graduating, he wandered around Mexico with a sketchbook until faced with the reality of making a living. He ended up working as a clerk for a construction company in Kitimat, BC. Always doodling, he produced some cartoons for the company that were seen by an editor at the Vancouver *Province*. Len Norris had become extremely popular in the competing Vancouver *Sun* and the *Province* countered by hiring Beaton in 1953. Beaton began including a mouse, his symbol for the little man in all his cartoons. Finding working conditions at the *Province* extremely restrictive, he joined the Toronto *Telegram* when a job was offered in 1961. However, Beaton found the *Tely* just as difficult to work for under the strict control of John Bassett: He was required to produce five rough ideas daily and six editorial-page cartoons a week. In addition, he was competing against Duncan Macpherson at *The Toronto Star*, by then the most popular cartoonist in the country. Beaton died at age forty-four in 1967.

"All my best ideas ended up in John Bassett's wastepaper basket."

Bell

Charles Edward Bell was born in Portage la Prairie, Saskatchewan. After serving in the Canadian navy during the Second World War, he joined the staff of the *Regina Leader-Post* in 1948 as a reporter. Always interested in cartooning, he began producing cartoons for his paper in the 1950s, and eventually became their daily editorial cartoonist. He is remembered particularly for his cartoons critical of Saskatchewan's CCF government. Several of these were collected in a popular booklet entitled *Pie in the Sky*. Eventually, Bell stopped cartooning and became a senior editor at the *Leader-Post*.

Bengough

John Wilson Bengough was born in Whitby, Ontario in 1851. He is considered to be the first important cartoonist that Canada produced. His working career paralleled that of our first Prime Minister, Sir John A. Macdonald. The cartoons that Bengough produced on the subject of Macdonald and his political activities are regarded today as a document of that turbulent period. What Bengough lacked in technical ability he made up for with clout. He was a great admirer of his contemporary, Thomas Nast, the brilliant American cartoonist. Indeed, we see today that many ideas Bengough applied to Canadian politics in his cartoons were taken directly from Nast's cartoons in *Harper's Weekly*.

Bengough started as a reporter for *The Whitby Gazette*. In 1872, he established a weekly humour publication in Toronto called *Grip*, named after the raven in Charles Dickens' *Barnaby Rudge*. *Grip* rode to success on the back of Sir John A. and the Canadian Pacific Railway scandal of 1873. A life-long Liberal, Bengough drew a weekly cartoon in addition to editing and writing articles for *Grip* for the next twenty years. In 1892, he left *Grip*, which folded shortly thereafter. Bengough then worked at different times for the *Montreal Star*, *The Globe*, *The Canadian Courier*, *The Moon*, and other Canadian publications. In addition to being a cartoonist, Bengough was a gifted speaker, and travelled throughout Canada giving a series of illustrated lectures which came to be known as "chalk talks." He also published two volumes of poetry. He died in Toronto in 1923.

Berneche

Stan Berneche is a cartoonist who was involved in the short-lived humour publication *Fuddle Duddle*. Produced in Ottawa in the early 1970s, the magazine's name was derived from remarks made by Prime Minister Trudeau in the House of Commons. The magazine's content touched on activity on Parliament Hill and printed the work of numerous cartoonists. Unfortunately, the magazine's lifetime was a short one.

Berthelot

Born in Trois-Rivières in 1842, Hector Berthelot was referred to in his time as "The Prince of Canadian Humourists." During the 1860s he lived in Quebec City for five years, then Ottawa, and finally settled in Montreal in 1870. Fraternizing with the intellectual elite of the period, Berthelot eventually turned his notorious wit to good use by producing his first humour publication, *Le Canard*, in 1877, serving as both editor and cartoonist. An impatient man, he was to establish many other publications of a similar nature including *Le Grognard* and *Le Violon* over the next few years. In all, Berthelot collaborated on sixteen different publications in his lifetime. Berthelot worked at various other vocations including translator, professor, reviewer, and photographer. But he always found time for his true calling as a humourist and caricaturist. He died in Montreal in 1895, leaving $10 in his will so his friends could have one last party in his memory.

Berthio

Berthio is the pen-name used by Roland Berthiaume, whose work has best expressed the growing nationalism in Quebec over the last fifteen years. Born in Montreal in 1927, Berthio's spontaneous style is easily recognizable, starkly simple and incisive in the European tradition.

Working for numerous newspapers in Montreal including *La Patrie*, *Le Nouveau Journal* and *La Presse*, he began working for *Le Devoir* in 1968 as the daily editorial-page cartoonist under Claude Ryan. Berthio established a large following while at *Le Devoir*, something that the influential newspaper has not been able to duplicate since his departure. He moved on to the separatist publication *Le Jour* when it was founded in the early 1970s and took his public with him, creating some memorable caricatures of Robert Bourassa and Pierre Trudeau. After the demise of *Le Jour*, Berthio worked for Montreal *Matin* and several other newspapers and publications. Presently, Berthio works for the television program *Hebdo-Samedi*, producing caricatures that are integrated with topical news items and features.

In 1973, Berthio received the prestigious Olivar-Asselin Award for Journalism presented by La Societé Saint-Jean Baptiste. Berthio has published two collections of caricatures: *Un Monde Fou* in 1961, and *Les Cents Dessins du Centenaire* in 1967.

"I try to make people laugh, to give them some consolation for the political events that make them suffer . . . It is important to make some people laugh and others groan."

Bickerstaff

Don Evans, born in Toronto in 1936, uses the *nom de plume* Isaac Bickerstaff, which was first employed by Jonathan Swift. He is best known for a series of books that he produced with author Mark Orkin, including the best-seller *Canajan, Eh?* Usually Bickerstaff's cartoons are more literary than political. He has produced caricatures for *Books in Canada* and *The Tamarack Review*.

Bierman

Born in Amsterdam in 1921, Bob Bierman did some work for various Dutch publications after the war before emigrating to Canada in 1950. In Toronto he picked up a job as doorman for a Yonge Street bar with instructions to keep the drunks out. Being about 5'8" and 140 lbs. he preferred letting the drunks in. Shortly thereafter he moved to BC. In 1954, while working as a draughtsman, he submitted a cartoon to the Victoria Times on a whim. The cartoon was published and, through some error, he was paid twice for it. Bierman felt he might be on to something and has been associated with the Times ever since.

Norris/Vancouver/Sun 2 February 1977

In June of 1978 he drew a cartoon of then Human Resources Minister Bill Vander Zalm pulling wings off flies, which was printed by the Times. Vander Zalm successfully sued the Times and Bierman for libel—the first time a politician has won such a suit against a political cartoonist in Canada or The British Commonwealth. The decision is presently being appealed.

"If this were a perfect world, cartoonists would be out of work...just like hangmen and judges."

Bing

During the Second World War, Bing Coughlin drew cartoons from the Italian front portraying Canadian troops in various humorous situations. These were printed in The Maple Leaf and later collected in a booklet.

Blaine

Blaine was born in Glace Bay, Nova Scotia in 1937. He drew his first political cartoons for The Cape Breton Post. Realizing that he was not going to make a living working out of Cape Breton, Blaine headed west in 1961 with three hundred hard-earned dollars. His first stop was Toronto, where he drew cartoons for The Globe and Mail while staff cartoonist Jim Reidford was on holiday. He then headed for the US, prepared to knock on every newspaper door in North America, if necessary, until he got a job as a full-time political cartoonist. Forty miles west of Toronto he knocked on his first door at the Hamilton Spectator. He was immediately hired and has been with the Spectator ever since, developing a large local following as well as being syndicated throughout Canada.

In 1963, Blaine won the Grand Prize at the first International Salon of Caricature and Cartoon in Montreal. In 1970, he was presented with the prestigious American award, The Reuben (named after

Blaine/Hamilton/Spectator

cartoonist Rube Goldberg) for being "the outstanding cartoonist of the year." Having produced two successful collections of his Spectator cartoons, Blaine was the recipient of The National Newspaper Award in 1974. Blaine has not confined his interests to cartooning. He has travelled extensively, producing illustrations and sketchbooks for The Spectator and other publications. Photography, portraiture, and painting have also become productive pastimes.

"One cartoon, without a caption, can sum up several thousand words uttered in Parliament."

Boothe

Jack Boothe was born in 1910 in Winnipeg. His first printed caricature, a drawing of "Kaiser Bill" appeared in the Winnipeg Tribune when he was eight years old.

After studying at The Chicago Academy of Fine Arts, famous in its day for producing political cartoonists, Boothe became the cartoonist for The Vancouver Daily Province in 1931. During the early years of the war, he produced two books under the guidance of the Province, Heeling Hitler and Accent on Axis. In 1943, Boothe moved to Toronto to become the cartoonist for The Globe and Mail, and by 1947 was reported to be the highest paid political

Toronto/Star/1937

tical cartoonist in the country at $7,000 a year. He won the first National Newspaper Award presented in 1949. In the early 1950s Boothe was employed by the Thomson newspaper chain. While with them, he worked on assignment in Korea during the war there. By 1957 he had moved to the Hamilton *Spectator*. In all of his cartoons, Boothe incorporated a small owl for secondary comments, and kept a stuffed owl in his office for inspiration. Eventually he moved back to Vancouver, where he died in 1973 while working on a book on Canadian political cartooning.

"I once thought that it might be possible to produce cartoons by way of a system or formula. It isn't."

Bourgeois

Albéric Bourgeois was born in Montreal in 1876. After studying at l'Ecole des Beaux-Arts he moved to Boston around the turn of the century and was hired by the Boston *Post* in 1902. He returned to Montreal in 1904 to work for *La Patrie*, moving over to *La Presse* one year later, an association that was to last for close to fifty years. Bourgeois was the first Quebec cartoonist to make a consistent living from the relatively new occupation of political cartooning in the French-language press. He created two stock figures, Baptiste and Catherine, whom he used in his cartoons throughout his career. Bourgeois' reputation grew, and he became a household word in Quebec. Bourgeois was also respected as a talented writer, creating popular cabarets and several radio scripts. He died in Montreal in 1962.

"Editorialists are often elevated to the Senate, but not caricaturists."

Brodeur

Georges Brodeur worked as a cartoonist for Montreal's *La Patrie* at the turn of the century. In 1904, a popular booklet entitled *Le Balai* was published containing his cartoons. These drawings dealt with the problems of the Tories gaining Quebec support and contemporary parochial rivalries in Quebec.

Bruce

Born in Scotland, Robert Randolph Bruce emigrated to Canada in 1887 and worked for the Canadian Pacific Railway as an engineer. Although he was an amateur, whose work was never published, his caricatures delighted many well-known Calgary personalities at the turn of the century, including the infamous Bob Edwards of *Eye-Opener* fame. Bruce served as Lieutenant-Governor of British Columbia from 1926 to 1931. He died in 1942.

Callan

Les Callan was born in Ignace, Ontario in 1905. In 1926 he studied briefly at the Chicago Academy of Art. He then headed for Winnipeg where he did some freelance work for the *Free Press*. He moved to Vancouver, where he was hired by the *Sun*. Callan stayed with the *Sun* until 1937, when he received a job offer from *The Toronto Star*. Except for three years during the Second World War, he stayed with the *Star* until 1961.

Callan joined the Army in 1942 and began sketching for *The Maple Leaf*, the Canadian Army's newspaper. He followed the invasion through France, Belgium, and Holland, recording both what he saw and humorous stories related to him by Canadian soldiers along the way. After the war his cartoons were collected and published as *Normandy and Beyond*. In 1963 he ran for the Ontario Legislature as a Liberal. Like most Liberals in Tory Ontario, he was unsuccessful. Callan is now retired and living in BC.

LaPalme/Le Canada/1949

"Unlike some cartoonists, who were in the position of having ideas supplied to them, I always came up with my own. But for the life of me, I still don't know where those thousands of ideas came from. They just happen somewhere in the back of your mind."

Cameron

Born in Calgary in 1912, Stew Cameron's two loves were horses and cartooning. As a youth he did a great deal of riding and back-packing in the foothills. After doing some work for several local publications, he took off for Hollywood to study and work as an apprentice at the Walt Disney Studios. While there, he worked on some of the animation for *Snow White and the Seven Dwarfs*. He returned to Calgary in 1936, where he got the job of staff cartoonist at the Calgary *Herald*. His arrival roughly coincided with the advent of Aberhart and his Social Credit government. Cameron started drawing Aberhart almost

232

Carless

Carless

Roy Carless was born in 1920 in Swansea, Ontario. Moving to Hamilton in the late 1940s, Roy became involved in union work and started drawing cartoons for the local's paper. One thing led to another and he began working for more publications on

daily at a time when political passions ran high in Calgary, and you had to be either for or against Social Credit. Refusing an office of his own, he worked in a large broom closet at the *Herald*. He entered and left the building by way of a back fire escape as he was afraid of being caught at the main entrance by the many people who had issued threats to get him. The *Herald* printed a collection of his Aberhart cartoons called *No Matter How Thin You Slice It*, which was immensely popular.

He joined the Army in 1942 and returned to the *Herald* after the War. In 1947 he accepted a job at the Vancouver *Province* with the stipulation that he got a case of India Pale Ale whenever he wanted it. He stayed at the *Province* for three years, where he worked, by choice, out of a flop house behind the newspaper building. Cameron died in Calgary in 1970.

From a letter to his father while a foot soldier during the Second World War: "I could be a hell of a lot more help to this country by doing cartoons than fucking around with a rifle!"

a free-lance basis, while keeping his regular job. With some encouragement from Duncan Macpherson, he continued to work for various labour publications—sometimes as many as twenty a month.

"I never draw anything that discriminates against working people," which includes damn near all of us . . . ."

Carlisle

William O. Carlisle was a topographer in the British Army stationed in Canada in the 1870s. He contributed caricatures in woodcut form to *The Canadian Illustrated News* and *l'Opinion Publique*. Back in England he published a book of drawings entitled *Recollections of Canada*.

Carr

Emily Carr, the well-known painter, produced political cartoons for a Victoria literary and political publication called *The Week*, in 1905 and 1906.

Chambers

The dean of Canadian political cartoonists, Bob Chambers is a Nova Scotia institution. Born in Wolfville, NS, in 1905 he started free-lancing in Halifax in the early 1920s for the princely sum of $2.50 per cartoon. He went to New York in 1924, where times were alternately good and bad. During the good periods he worked as an animator for Aesop's Fables (later Terrytoons) and as an illustrator for *New York Graphic*. He studied at the Art Students' League for a year, but the depression forced him to borrow the fare home to Nova Scotia in 1932.

In 1933 he was hired by *The Chronicle*, a liberal paper, to do cartoons attacking the Tories in power. The conservatives were defeated. Tory ex-premier Gordon Harrington was to say to Chambers later, "You know Bob, you libeled me twenty-three

times in twenty-three cartoons and I didn't sue you. But I sure thought about breaking your nose." In 1937, the rival Tory paper, *The Herald*, enticed him away with the promise of double the money. The two papers merged in 1948, and Chambers worked there until his retirement in 1977.

Recipient of the National Newspaper Award in 1953 and 1966, he also received an honorary doctorate from St. Francis-Xavier University in 1965. Chambers was elected to the Canadian News Hall of Fame in 1977.

"In the old days we drew things with balloons and labels all over the place. The new style is to avoid labels and I agree that it's a good thing. Still, when I draw a character who isn't easily recognized, I'll stick his name on his tie clip. Well, the other day a woman came up to me and I saw her staring at my necktie. I asked her what she was looking at and she said she was just trying to find my name."

Chambers/1973

Chapleau

Serge Chapleau was born in Montreal in 1945. He studied painting and graphic arts at the l'Ecole des Beaux-Arts. After graduation, he worked in many types of graphic design including the creation of posters, record covers, comic strips, and commercial

City of Montreal. During the same period he also worked as a political cartoonist and caricaturist for *La Patrie* and *Le Nationaliste*. His work proved very popular and he produced several collections of cartoons dealing with local political and social topics: the Church, the threatened French language, the Irish in Quebec, and Montreal Jews. Although his portrayal of the Jewish community would be unacceptable today, it did reflect prevailing attitudes of his time. In 1920, he moved to New York where he continued his career as a designer and illuminator of manuscripts, moving on to France in 1928. He returned to Montreal where he died in 1935.

Collins

work. Always interested in caricature, his first try was an immediate success. In 1973, *Perspectives*, the French-language edition of *Weekend* commissioned Chapleau to do a weekly full-page colour caricature of politicians and other public figures. The reaction to these drawings in Quebec was phenomenal, and eventually a portfolio of these collected drawings was published. This proved to be the first successful attempt to produce full-colour caricatures on a regular basis in Canada. Later, Chapleau moved to the tabloid *Montreal-Matin* where he continued to do full-page weekly drawings until the newspaper folded. Presently he free-lances for various publications and is experimenting in the area of caricature puppets and animation.

"Being a cartoonist in Quebec can be difficult. The population is small and so are the cheques."

Charlebois
Joseph Charlebois was born in Montreal in 1872. In 1897 he began a successful, twenty-three year career as a designer for the

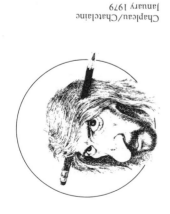

Chapleau/Chatelaine January 1979

Chic
Cartoons signed "Chic" appeared in *The Moon* during 1901 and 1902. This may have been a pen-name used by one of the numerous cartoonists working for daily newspapers in Toronto at the time.

Coallier
Jean-Pierre Coallier was born in Montreal in 1937. After studies at l'Ecole des Beaux-Arts, he began free-lancing as a political cartoonist in the early 1960s for *Le Nouveau Journal*. He was the full time editorial-page cartoonist for *Montreal-Matin* from 1969 to 1976. He is better known in Montreal, perhaps, as a radio and television personality.

Collins
John Collins was born in Montreal in 1917. With the retirement of Bob Chambers several years ago, Collins is now the longest-working editorial-page cartoonist in Canada. He moved to Canada with his family in 1920 and was studying at Sir George Williams University when he sold his first cartoon to the *Gazette* in 1937. He became the *Gazette's* first staff cartoonist

Charlebois

in 1939, and has remained with the paper ever since.

Collins' wartime cartoons proved to be very popular and were reprinted numerous times in *The New York Times* and other publications. Collins had a windfall in the 1950s with the CBC, the King and St. Laurent governments, the Petawawa horse scandal, and other topics of the day. He was drawing Defence Minister Brooke Claxton several times a week, ridiculing our supposed army in the cold-war days. Indeed, Claxton came very close to suing Collins and the *Gazette* for defamation of character.

It is hard to think of a Collins cartoon without his Uno Who, the figure of the little taxpayer who has appeared since the late 1940s. Collins won the National Newspaper Award in 1954 and 1973. He has published a collection of cartoons entitled *Cartoons 1955-1959 by John Collins*, which was printed by the *Gazette*.

"I think most politicians prefer being hated to being ridiculed."

Constable
Mike Constable was born in Woodstock, Ontario in 1943. After studying sculpture at the Ontario College of Art, he moved on to Carlton University in Ottawa where he studied Sociology. He was a co-founder of *Guerilla*, a Toronto underground newspaper from 1969 through 1974. He also free-lanced during that period for *The To-*

ronto Star, *Saturday Night, The Financial Post, Maclean's* and other Toronto publications. In 1977 he was one of the founders of Union Art Services, a co-operative mailing service of graphics and cartoons, which presently goes out to about forty-five labour publications.

> "Cartoonists work by the sweat of their hand and the work of their brow."

Côté

A pen-name sometimes used by J. W. Bengough in his humour publication *Grip.* Bengough used a different drawing style for these cartoons, which usually dealt with Quebec situations.

Côté

Jean-Baptiste Côté, born in Quebec City in 1834, is remembered there primarily as a talented wood sculptor who created numerous statues, reliefs of religious scenes, and figure-heads for ships. He was also French Canada's first cartoonist. As a youth he served as an apprentice architect and carver. In 1863, while still in his twenties, Côté founded and became editor, writer, and cartoonist of a satirical weekly publication called *La Scie* or *The Saw.* It was to last five short years, but was relentless in its attacks upon prominent Quebeckers of the day. Eventually Côté went too far in his portrayal of a Quebec civil servant's typical day and he was thrown in jail. The publication of *La Scie* ended and Côté returned to his wood-carving. He died in Quebec in 1907.

Côté/La Scie/21 January 1865

Cummings

Born in 1948 in St. Thomas, Ontario, Dale Cummings sold his first political cartoon to the London *Free Press* in 1968. He studied animation and illustration at Sheridan College in Oakville, Ontario. After doing some textbook illustration, Cummings became one of the chief animators in the production of *True North,* the first successful attempt to include animated caricatures in a documentary film on Canadian politics and life. The program was aired nationally on television in 1974, and this led to Cummings doing some animation for several *Sesame Street* productions. During a brief stay in New York he did some cartoons for the *New York Times.* He returned to Toronto in 1976, where he free-lanced for *The Last Post, The Canadian Forum, Maclean's, The Toronto Star, Canadian Magazine,* and *This Magazine.*

Courtesy of
Lindsay City Jail

Dale

Arch Dale was born in Aberdeen, Scotland in 1882. By the time he was seventeen he was working as a cartoonist for the local *Courier* and, shortly after, moved on to *The Glasgow News,* where he remained for two years. After free-lancing in London, he decided to try his hand at homesteading in Saskatchewan. When this venture failed, he moved to Winnipeg in 1907, selling his cartoons to the *Free Press* and the *Grain-Growers Guide.* His cartoons of this period summed up the discontent of the western farmer that led to the establishment of the new Progressive Party.

He also created a comic strip called *The Doo-Dads* at this time. He took it to Chicago in 1921 where it was syndicated to more than fifty papers. But Archie hated Chicago even more than the western winters, and returned to Winnipeg. He joined the staff of the Winnipeg *Free Press* in 1927 and worked out of a corner of the library for the next twenty-seven years. The thirties were a boon to Dale with the emergence of the CCF and Social Credit

> "Getting a start as a political cartoonist in this country is extremely difficult. It seems that you have to sit around waiting for somebody to die."

Daigneault

Robert Daigneault began drawing political cartoons for *Le Journal de Montréal* in 1963. Since that time he has worked on a free-lance basis for numerous publications throughout Quebec and for Ottawa's French-language newspaper *Le Droit* as their editorial-page cartoonist. He has also served as editorial-page cartoonist briefly at *La Tribune* in Sherbrooke.

Winnipeg/Free Press/1935

parties. But he was at his best and is remembered most for his portrayal of Tory opulence in the person of R. B. Bnnett during the depression. Working under J.W. DaFoe, the *Free Press* was probably the best paper in the country at the time, and Dale had a field day. Three books of his cartoons were published from the 1930s and early 1940s. Dale retired in 1954, and died in Winnipeg in 1962.

Delatri

Anthony Delatri was born in Pennsylvania in 1922 and has been a political cartoonist for *Le Nouvelliste* in Trois-Rivières since 1967. He grew up in rural Quebec, but returned to the US at the age of seventeen to join the Army and served overseas during the Second World War. Later he studied at the Newark School of Fine and Industrial Art, while drawing for several American publications. During this period, he also tried out as a pitcher for the New York Giants. By the 1950s, he was back in Quebec. He did occasional drawings for *Le Journal de Montreal*, *Montreal-Matin*, and *Dimanche Matin* until becoming the full-time cartoonist for *Le Nouvelliste* in 1967.

Donato

Andy Donato was born in Toronto in 1937. After working for various commercial art studios, nf the was hired by the Toronto *Telegram* in 1961 as a graphic artist, and he became the art director of one of The *Tely's* magazine inserts. Andy believes this period taught him to come to terms with a pressing deadline, one of the essential qualities of a successful political cartoonist.

Al Beaton, the staff cartoonist at that time for The *Tely*, encouraged him to pursue cartooning. As a result, Donato began to fill in on the editorial page while Beaton was on holiday. When *The Telegram*

Donato/Toronto/Sun

folded, Donato and several other members of the staff helped to found the *Toronto Sun*. There he started drawing daily political cartoons, and he has been at it ever since. His work is widely syndicated throughout Canada. Recipient of the National Newspaper Award in 1976, he has published a collection of cartoons from the *Sun*. Donato has also developed a reputation as a painter, and has had several successful exhibitions in Toronto.

"Like politicians, I have no politics of my own."

Douglas

In 1948, Joey Smallwood commissioned *Globe and Mail* cartoonist Jack Boothe to draw cartoons for *The Confederate*, which advocated Confederation with the rest of Canada. Boothe signed these cartoons "Douglas," his middle name.

Drew

Around 1912, numerous political cartoons appeared in *The Province* in Vancouver, which bore the signature Phil Drew. He used a small beaver in the corner of each cartoon and is one of a number of cartoonists who seemed to come and go during this period in BC.

Duggan

Frank Duggan was born in Montreal in 1904. He drew political and sports cartoons for the Montreal *Herald* from 1941 until the mid-1950s when the paper folded.

Duggan then worked in the art department of the Montreal *Star*. Presently he is retired and living in Montreal.

Dupras

Pierre Dupras was born in Montreal in 1938. He studied painting and majored in literature and art history at the Université de Montréal, where he presently teaches. For a short time in 1966 he drew editorial-page cartoons for *Dimanche Matin*, but his ideas were not consistent with those of his editors. In 1967 he began drawing for *Quebec-Presse*, a radical publication. In the same year, he produced a booklet of cartoons on the subject of de Gaulle's visit to Quebec, which sold out three editions in a few weeks. Dupras credits the book's popularity to the fact that he supplied the drawings while de Gaulle supplied the text. He produced a full-page comic strip for *Quebec-Presse* reflecting the turbulent political scene in Quebec in the early 1970s, until *Quebec-Presse* folded.

Edwards

The infamous publisher of the Calgary *Eye-Opener*, Bob Edwards drew many cartoons for his publication before he was in a position to commission professional cartoonists. His cartoons were not signed.

Feyer

George Feyer was born in Hungary in 1921. Suffering under successive Nazi and communist regimes, he forged papers which allowed him to flee his native country. By 1948 he was in Toronto working in a factory stuffing quilts, but within a year had sold his first gag cartoon to *Maclean's*. Showing a man being fitted for glasses, it was only after the cartoon had been published that the editors discovered that an eye chart in the background of the drawing spelled out some of the coarsest Hungarian words imaginable. Despite this, Feyer began appearing in *Maclean's* regularly. His reputation grew in the 1950s and he was working for any number of publications in Canada, the US, and Europe. He also did a great deal of live television work, patenting an animation process that is still used today. Despite being highly inventive and extremely prolific, much of Feyer's better work—reflections on religion, sex, and politics—still remains unpublished. In the mid 1960s, Feyer took his bizarre talents to Los Angeles. Although he was becoming established, he committed suicide there in 1967.

Fitzmaurice/Vancouver/Province

Fitzmaurice

J.B. Fitzmaurice, known simply as "Fitz" to his friends, was born in England about 1873. He came to Canada when he was sixteen and tried his hand at various occupations including farming and logging. Deciding it was "just too much hard work," he turned to commercial art, painting show-cards for various establishments. His talents came to the attention of the Vancouver *Daily Province* and he was asked to give cartooning a try. Fitz became the first cartoonist of any stature to work on a regular basis out of BC. In 1909 he was lured back east by the Montreal *Herald*, but BC was a part of him and he was back with the *Province* by 1916. During the First World War he was at the height of his popularity supplying a necessary light touch in worrisome times. He is also remembered for the fun he had with those who extolled the virtues of Women's suffrage and his pokes at "Bolsheviks" of the period. One of the wordiest cartoonists, he often used a comic-strip style that might contain hundreds of words. As Norris has done more recently, Fitz would often use domestic and social situations to comment on the political topics of his period. He died while still working for the *Province* in 1924.

Fons

Born in Holland in 1943, Fons Van Woerkom signs his work with his first name. After studying painting for eight years he graduated from the Jan Van Eyck Academy in Maastricht, Holland. Moving to Toronto in 1968, he began drawing striking cartoons for *The Toronto Star* over the next three years. One of these, a caricature of Israel's Moshe Dayan, won him the grand prize for Political Cartooning at the International Salon of Caricature and Cartoon. In 1971, he moved to New York where he has been doing some brilliant work for the op-ed page of the *New York Times*.

"The importance of my work lies in its ability to confront myself and others with our limitations."

Forrester

Very little is known about Charles H. Forrester. He was a Calgary sign painter in 1915 when Bob Edwards began using his cartoons in the Calgary *Eye-Opener*. He was still drawing for the paper after Edwards' death when his widow tried to carry on. It is thought that Forrester eventually moved to British Columbia.

Franklin

Born in Texas in 1921, Ed Franklin started his career working in the art department of the Houston *Press* in 1947, drawing occasional cartoons for the editorial page. Several years later he moved over to the Houston *Post*. By the mid-1950s, Franklin was in New York working as an illustrator for numerous magazines including *The Saturday Evening Post*, *Argosy*, and *True*. Fed up with New York, he decided it was time for another move and opted for Toronto, in 1959, feeling it would be a good place to bring up his kids. There he found

Globe and Mail

himself doing mainly commercial work and illustration, and hated it. On a whim, he called Jim Reidford, then the editorial cartoonist for *The Globe and Mail*, who suggested that Franklin at least get his feet wet and give cartooning a try. Free-lancing for the *Globe*, he moved over to *The Toronto Star* for a while, filling in for Duncan Macpherson. In 1968, he moved back to *The Globe and Mail* alternating on the editorial page with Reidford. Developing his own style as a fine caricaturist, he became the daily cartoonist for the *Globe* when Reidford retired in 1972. Probably remembering his experience with Reidford, Franklin has always been very encouraging towards younger cartoonists including Ted Jackman and, more recently, Tony Jenkins.

"One editor once told me, 'Look, it's easier to cut back on the cartoons than the editorials.'"

Gagnier

Jacques Gagnier was born in Montreal in 1917 and died there in 1978. He studied at l'Ecole des Beaux-Arts in 1934 and 1935, and spent most of his life working as a commercial artist. Having drawn caricatures for some publications such as *oLa Patrie*, he was hired as the political cartoonist for *Le Devoir* in 1960, after Normand Hudon left. He worked there for five years, but did not have the bite that both his predecessor and his successor, Berthio, were to bring to *Le Devoir*.

Gamboli

This pen-name, derived from the word 'gambol,' suggesting fooling around or having fun, is employed by Tony Harps, who was born in Montreal in 1937. Joining the Montreal *Star* in 1952 as an office boy, he ended up in the art department, where he drew occasional spot cartoons. In the early 1960s he branched out as a commercial artist, dabbling in film and becoming involved in many aspects of the plastic arts while free-lancing for the *Gazette*. Recently he was hired there as a staff artist and cartoonist.

"People are always asking how long it takes to draw a cartoon. They don't understand it takes a lifetime."

Gerrard

Canadian poet and novelist Margaret Atwood produces occasional political cartoons for *This Magazine* under the pen-name of Bart Gerrard.

Gibbs

Eric L. Gibbs was born in Edmonton in 1912. Working as a reporter for *The Toronto Star*, he drew a series of striking caricatures for the same publication in 1934. However, he did not appear to pursue his talent and no other record of his work exists.

Girerd

Jean-Pierre Girerd was born in 1931 in Algeria, where he studied art at l'Ecole Nationale des Beaux-Arts for five years. He won several local awards for both painting and cartooning. In 1956 he was hired as a political caricaturist for the *Journal d'Alger*. In 1961 being a *pied noir* in Algeria was not very comfortable, so Girerd decided to move to the US, where he worked for the Minneapolis *Star* as a cartoonist and illustrator.

Deciding that America was not for him, he settled in Paris. He came to Montreal on a holiday in 1964, and decided that he wouldn't mind living there, working in his

La Presse

native language. Before his holiday was up, he found a job. He worked for the newspaper *Métro Express* until it folded. He then worked as a cartoonist for *Le Petit Journal*, *Le Maclean* and *Perspectives*.

After Berthio left *La Presse*, Girerd was hired as their editorial-page cartoonist and has been working there ever since. At first, it wasn't easy. He found the Canadian scene rather confusing, not always knowing the difference between federal and provincial politics. Eventually he turned this to his advantage, as he could stand back and approach all subjects in an equally cynical and teasing manner.

A very prolific and fast cartoonist, he sometimes produces as many as a dozen cartoons a week for his paper. Often he

uses a dog named Dog (Chien) in his cartoons for secondary comments.

"Politicians do not always appear to know what they are doing in politics. Therefore, why should I pretend to?"

Glassco

Ivan Glassco's work began appearing regularly in the 1930s in the Hamilton *Spectator*. Considered one of the most promising young cartoonists in Canada, he died in 1941 while serving with the RCAF overseas.

Grassick

Bert Grassick was born in Victoria, BC in 1909. In 1929 he moved to Toronto to join his brother who was working in a commercial art studio. His first political cartoon appeared in *The Toronto Star* in 1935. His style evolved quickly; he developed a rapid brush technique initially influenced by the work of Sir David Low in England. His first drawings appeared in *Maclean's* in 1936. He drew about three cartoons per issue for that publication for well over twenty-five years. He also illustrated Blair Fraser's well-known column *Backstage at Ottawa*. While working for the *Financial Post*, Grassick was recognized in the 1940s as being "unexcelled as a draughtsman by any other Canadian cartoonist." During the 1950s, Grassick was

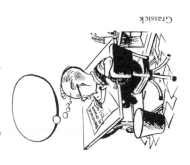

Grassick

certainly the most prolific cartoonist in Canada. In addition to his work for *Maclean's*, he drew six editorial-page cartoons a week for the Toronto *Telegram* between 1954 and 1962. He was also the political cartoonist for the *Canadian Forum* and freelanced for numerous other publications. He is now retired and living in Toronto.

"I remember, in the 1930s, drawing cartoons for the *CCF News* that poked fun at various financial interests. However, at the same time, I drew cartoons for the *Financial Post* that poked fun at the CCF!"

Graston

Mike Graston was born in Montreal in 1954. A graduate of the University of Western Ontario, he drew political cartoons for the university newspaper and, later, for the *Last Post*. He was hired by the *Ottawa Citizen* in 1977 as an office boy, but the editors discovered his artistic ability. Presently he draws editorial-page cartoons for the *Citizen* once a week and when their regular cartoonist, Rusins, is on holiday.

"It is very difficult to draw cartoons several days in advance. You should be right on top of the news for a cartoon to be effective. What's the point in dealing with a topic that people were talking about three days ago?"

Gosperin

The pen-name used in the mid-1800s by Quebec cartoonist Jean-Baptiste Côté in his humour publication *La Scie*.

Hall

Harry Hall was born near Hull, England in 1893 and studied for two years at the Manchester School of Art. He came to Canada before the First World War and settled in Moose Jaw, Saskatchewan, where he worked for the railway and drew cartoons as a hobby. He served overseas in the First World War and he became Welterweight Champion of the Canadian Army. He joined the Toronto *Telegram* in the 1930s, where he drew political and sports cartoons in addition to several comic strips that were syndicated to other Canadian papers. He died in Toronto in 1954.

Hawkins

Cartoons appeared in the weekly *British Columbia Saturday Sunset* in 1907 signed N.H. Hawkins. The publication was short-lived and his work did not appear in any other periodical of the time.

Hudon

Normand Hudon was born in Montreal in 1929. After studying at L'Ecole des Beaux-Arts with the son of Henri Julien, he received a grant to study in Paris for a year under the well-known painter Fernand Léger at l'Académie de Montmartre.

While a student in Montreal, he began doing some caricatures for the popular university publication *Le Quartier Latin*. After the war he began free-lancing for *Le Photo Journal*, *Le Petit Journal* and *La Patrie*, even though all three publications were rivals. In the late 1950s he began working full time for *Le Devoir*. In the early 1960s, Gerald Pelletier brought him over to *La Presse*, and later he moved to *Le Journal de Montréal*.

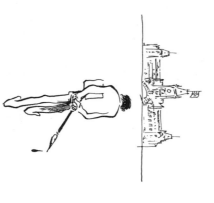

Hudon

In addition to a career as a political cartoonist, Hudon became a well-known television personality and also produced several humour publications. While at *Le Devoir*, Hudon succeeded Robert LaPalme in waging a strong campaign against the reigning Union Nationale party and its infamous leader, Maurice Duplessis. In many of his caricatures of the Premier, a vulture hovered somewhere in the drawing.

"The one time I met Maurice Duplessis, he claimed not to recognize himself in my caricatures. I assured the Premier that there was no need to worry as thousands of others did."

Humphrey

H. Humphrey is a signature found on cartoons produced occasionally in BC around the turn of the century.

Hunter, Gorde

Born in Winnipeg in 1925, Gorde Hunter studied at the Manitoba School of Fine Art before joining the Navy in 1942. After the war he joined the Winnipeg *Tribune* as a sports cartoonist and columnist. In 1953 he moved on to become the sports editor of the Calgary *Herald* and moved into radio work. He returned to cartooning in 1956 when he joined the Victoria *Colonist*. Presently he does two political cartoons plus four city columns for the *Colonist*. In addition, Hunter is a daily sports broadcaster for a local radio station.

Hunter, Raoul

Raoul Hunter was born in St. Cyrille de la Salle, Quebec in 1926. After attending l'Ecole des Beaux-Arts in Quebec City, he

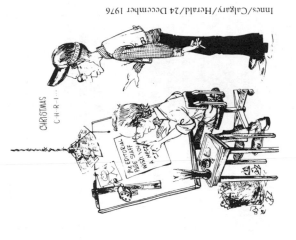

Innes/Calgary/Herald/24 December 1976

studied art history in Paris on a scholarship. Returning to Quebec, he began to make a name for himself as a sculptor while teaching at l'Ecole des Beaux-Arts. In 1956 *Le Soleil* was looking for a political cartoonist and approached the art school's director, asking if he might recommend someone. Always interested in caricature, Hunter applied for and got the job. Finding three careers rather hectic, he gave up teaching in 1969. Very much of the European school of simple line cartooning, Hunter draws eight cartoons a week for *Le Soleil* and its regional editions. Hunter won the National Newspaper Award in 1958 and 1967.

"My favourite cartoon is always the next one."

Hunter, Sam

Sam Hunter was born in Millbrook, Ontario in 1858. He worked as a cartoonist for numerous publications for close to sixty years. As a young man, he travelled through the west, producing a series of prints on Indian and western life. His first political cartoons appeared in Bengough's *Grip* in the late 1870s and he appeared to be firmly established in Toronto by 1885. Like most of the cartoonists in Toronto, his early cartoons were particularly critical of Laurier. Many of these appeared in the Toronto *World*, where he started on a daily basis in 1897, and stayed there for

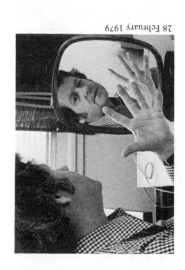

28 February 1979

almost twenty years. During the First World War he moved over to *The Globe*, producing cartoons that focussed on the Conscription Crisis and were very anti-Laurier and Quebec. After the war, Hunter switched to the *Toronto Daily Star*. A writer of the time referred to him as a great and gentle caricaturist. He died in Toronto in 1939.

Hyde

Graham Hyde was a political cartoonist for the *Vancouver Sun* in 1912. Using a crow as a symbol in all of his cartoons, Hyde was particularly severe on the provincial government of the time.

Innes, Jack

John or Jack Innes was born in London, Ontario in 1863 and educated in England at the Dufferin Military Academy. Always an adventurer, Innes' worked as a cartographer for a surveying party in the Canadian Rockies. Shortly afterwards his first cartoons appeared in the Calgary *Herald* in the late 1890s. Moving to Toronto to study art, he drew cartoons briefly for *The Mail and Empire* in the 1890s. Out west again, he developed a talent as a writer and helped to found several publications. By 1904 he was in South Africa as a war correspondent. In 1907 he was working as a staff artist for the Hearst Corporation chain in New York. He was back in Vancouver by 1913, drawing cartoons for the *Vancouver Sun*. This was his last known cartooning effort and he began to develop a national reputation thereafter as a painter of the Canadian west. He died in Vancouver in 1941.

Innes, Tom

Tom Innes was born in Salem, Oregon on November 30, 1923. His family migrated to Canada five years later and settled in the Calgary area. During the 1930s his family

moved to Vancouver, where he lived until the war broke out. In 1942 he joined the Navy. After the war he enrolled at the Calgary School of Technology and Art. He packed it in after two years and subsequently became, in turn, a pipefitter, ditchdigger, cement jockey, short-order cook, barn painter, hard-rock miner, diamond-drill operator and, eventually in 1956, a paste-up artist. While setting up his own commercial art operation, he was approached to submit several cartoons to the Calgary *Herald*. He then joined the staff as editorial-page cartoonist and has been with the *Herald* ever since.

"All cartoonists do have one thing in common . . . they can't spell worth a damn."

Jackman

Ted Jackman was born in Paris, Ontario in 1947. After studying at Queen's University he began drawing political cartoons for *The Globe and Mail* in 1972 on a freelance basis. More recently, he has been involved with Mike Constable in Union Art

Services, a co-operative that supplies labour publications with political cartoons and graphics.

Jacob

A pen-name sometimes used by Quebec cartoonist Albéric Bourgeois early in his career.

Jefferys

Charles W. Jefferys was born in England in 1869. He is remembered mainly as a historian as he produced numerous works illustrating Canada's past, particularly three volumes entitled *The Picture Gallery of Canadian History*. In the many tributes and obituaries when Jefferys died in Toronto in 1951, none made note of a short but interesting period of his life when he worked as a political cartoonist. In 1901 and 1902, he contributed cartoons to Toronto's short-lived humour publication *The Moon*. These drawings were at least as good as any cartoonist working at that period in Canada.

Jenkins

Jenkins

Tony Jenkins was born in Toronto in 1951, and presently is a staff cartoonist for *The Globe and Mail*. After graduating from the University of Waterloo, he began to free-lance for different newspapers and publications in Toronto including *The Toronto Star*. Encouraged by Ed Franklin, the editorial-page cartoonist for *The Globe and Mail*, he began working for *The Globe* in 1974, and was eventually taken on as a staffer to fill in for Franklin and draw cartoons for the op-ed page. Jenkins took a year's leave of absence in the fall of 1978 to travel throughout Asia. He is considered by many to be one of the handful of promising younger cartoonists presently working in Canada.

"Cartooning is an immediate form of communication. You need no previous knowledge of art for it to grab you."

Jueland

A signature found on some cartoons produced in 1948 for *The Independent*, a Newfoundland publication opposed to confederation with Canada.

Julien

Henri Julien was born in Quebec City in 1852 where, as a youth, he was intrigued by the woodcut caricatures produced by his neighbour Jean-Baptiste Côté in *La Scie*. Julien was to become the most accomplished draughtsman and the best-known Canadian cartoonist of his time. By 1868 he was in Montreal as a printer's apprentice on his way to becoming an expert engraver. Recognizing Julien's drawing ability, *The Canadian Illustrated News* sent him on a sketching tour of western Canada in 1874, during which he produced numerous drawings of Indian life on the plains. Established as one of the cartoonists for *The Canadian Illustrated News* and *l'Opinion Publique*, Julien contributed to numerous publications including *Le Farceur, Le Grelot, The Jester, Le Canard* and *Grip* in Canada as well as *Harper's* and *Le Monde Illustré* abroad. He was the first Canadian cartoonist to establish a reputation beyond our borders and the first to work as a full-time cartoonist for a newspaper. The Montreal *Star*, then the largest paper in the country, hired him in 1888. Julien spent much time in Ottawa sketching politicians from the Press Gallery in Parliament. Between 1897 and 1900, he produced his most famous caricatures, a series of drawings of Laurier and members of his cabinet portrayed as negro minstrels. These drawings were eventually published in a popular booklet entitled *The By-Town Coons*.

In addition to cartooning, Julien is remembered for his portraits, paintings, and drawings interpreting traditional Quebec life and politics. He died in Montreal in 1908. Thirty years after his death, The National Gallery in Ottawa held a major exhibition of his work, the first time that a cartoonist here has been so honoured. In Montreal, there is a street bearing his name.

Jump

Edward Jump was born in France in 1831, although he spent most of his working career as a cartoonist and portrait painter in San Francisco, Washington, and New York. However, he worked for a two-year period in Montreal from 1871 to 1873, producing a magnificent portfolio of caricatures of Canadian politicians for *The Canadian Illustrated News* and *l'Opinion Publique*. It is thought that he committed suicide in St. Louis.

Julien

Kahrs

A signature found on political cartoons that appeared in *The Daily Mail and Empire* in 1896. These cartoons are of particular interest as they were the first of many appearing in Toronto that were harshly critical of Prime Minister Wilfrid Laurier.

Kaleido

This cartoonist was active in Saskatchewan in 1908. It is not yet established if his cartoons were published or were the efforts of an enthusiastic amateur. What little of his work is available indicates that he drew flattering caricatures of local politicians.

Kamienski

Jan Kamienski was born in Poland in 1923. He studied art in Europe and worked full time in animation. He came to Canada in the late 1940s and he worked as a commercial artist in Winnipeg. When Lew Saw left the Winnipeg *Tribune* in 1958, Kamienski was asked to give it a try, and he has been there ever since. He won the National Newspaper Award in 1963 for his portrayal of the Social Credit Party running amok. The same cartoon won

first prize at The International Salon of Caricature and Cartoon the same year. In addition to his role as editorial-page cartoonist, Kamienski is the art-page editor and has done quite a bit of writing for *The Tribune*.

"If you hammer away often enough at a certain subject, cartoons will have as much impact on the public as persistent advertising does."

Kuch

Peter Kuch was born in Winnipeg in 1917. He studied Fine Arts with A.S. Musgrove before the Second World War broke out, whereupon he joined the Air Force. After

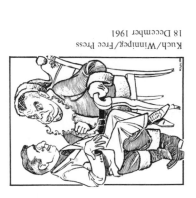

Kuch/Winnipeg/Free Press
18 December 1961

completing his tour of duty overseas, he joined the art department of the Winnipeg *Free Press* in 1946. When Arch Dale retired in 1952, Kuch took over as the editorial-page cartoonist of the *Free Press*, and has retained that position ever since. Kuch's interests range beyond that of cartooning. He has developed a reputation in the Winnipeg area as a portrait painter. He has also illustrated several books dealing with Manitoba, and collections of Ukranian folk tales.

"Name one other job in the world where a fellow can sit down and get so much venom out of his system in a few hours."

Kyle

J. Fergus Kyle was born in Hamilton, Ontario in 1876. He started his career as a reporter for *The News* in Toronto, and later became a cartoonist and illustrator for *The Globe*. At the turn of the century he contributed to *Saturday Night* and the short-lived humour publication, *The Moon*. Unlike most Toronto cartoonists of the period, Kyle was a Liberal and a strong supporter of Laurier, and drew several campaign posters for the party. However, with the election of Robert Borden, Kyle came into his own, and had a field day with the confusing naval policy of the Tories. Later Kyle moved over to *The Toronto Star*. He died in 1941.

Laforge

Jean-Marie Laforge was born in Belgium in 1946. He emigrated to Quebec in 1957. By 1973 he was contributing to *Le Quotidien du Saguenay* in Chicoutimi, and is presently its full-time cartoonist.

Landry

Jean Landry was born in Quebec City in 1927. There he studied at l'Ecole des Beaux-Arts and, later, at the Ecole des Métiers d'Art in Paris in the mid 1950s. He has been the caricaturist for *La Tribune* in Sherbrooke, Quebec since 1971.

LaPalme

Robert LaPalme was born in Montreal in 1908. As he tells it, there is a plaque on the building where he was born. It reads Hop Sing Lee Laundry. At the age of seventeen, he was refused entrance to l'Ecole des Beaux-Arts. Ironically, in 1972 he was decorated with the Order of Canada for his contribution to Canadian Art. In Montreal, he worked at a series of menial jobs and began drawing cartoons in his spare time. His first caricatures were cubist. He

Kamienski/Winnipeg/Tribune/1979

was hired, at eighteen dollars a week, to draw front page caricatures for the intellectual daily *l'Ordre*, through which LaPalme became a popular figure in the café society of Montreal. He worked for numerous publications starting with *Le Droit* in Ottawa in 1937. The following year he moved to Quebec City where he was drawing caricatures for *l'Evenment Journal, l'Action Catholique* and *La Patrie* and his work was reproduced in numerous publications throughout Canada. He also lectured at Laval University on the history of art. By 1943, he was back in Montreal drawing for *Le Canada*. This was the beginning of a busy period for LaPalme as he developed a name in the US and abroad as both a cartoonist and a painter. He participated in and organized several exhibitions, experience that was to prove of much value later.

In 1950 he joined *Le Devoir*, "Quebec's last fighting newspaper," as he called it at the time. In 1952 he won the National Newspaper Award. The period of the late 1940s and early 1950s was the zenith of LaPalme's career as a caricaturist. It seems that almost single-handedly, he carried on a vitriolic attack against Maurice Duplessis and his Union Nationale government. In 1959, with a move to the daily newspaper *La Presse*, he had worked for almost every important French-language publication. A turning point in his career came when he organized an exhibition of caricatures in 1963. This turned into an annual event and is now known as the International Salon of Caricature and Cartoon. Housed in a permanent museum, it exhibits cartoons from numerous countries, and has become the largest and most important exhibition of its kind in the world. In his role as curator, Robert LaPalme has set up channels of communication among cartoonists the world over. He is often referred to as the ambassador of political cartoonists.

LaPalme/Le Canada/July 1943

"I don't like everything I've drawn. Once I took 7,553 of my originals and filled up a compost heap with them. Some day it should make for an interesting archaeological dig."

"I give away original drawings to my friends . . . I sell them to politicians."

Larter

John Larter was born in Swift Current, Saskatchewan in 1950. From 1969 to 1971 he worked for *The Roughneck*, an Albertan magazine published for the oil industry that was also the training ground for Edd Uluschak and Vance Rodewalt. From 1972 to 1974 he worked for various Los Angeles publications. He returned to Canada and began doing political cartoons for the Lethbridge *Herald* in 1974. In 1977 he joined the staff of the newly founded Edmonton *Sun*.

Lawrence

George Lawrence worked in the 1920s for The Montreal *Herald* as a reporter, columnist, sports writer, and sometime cartoonist. During prohibition, he was once offered a job at the *New York Daily News*, which would have paid a great deal more than he could ever make in Canada. He refused to go on the grounds that he would never live in a country where he couldn't get a legal drink.

Leduc, Paul

Paul Leduc was a Montreal caricaturist who worked for *La Patrie* in the 1930s. He is remembered for his shrewd and amusing caricatures that usually dealt with the trials and tribulations of daily life.

Leduc, Robert

Robert Leduc was born in Montreal in the early 1930s and has spent most of his life working as a commercial artist. He took night courses at l'Ecole des Beaux-Arts and several other smaller schools. He supplied *La Patrie* with caricatures for seventeen years until the newspaper folded. Later he drew occasional cartoons for *La Presse*, *Montreal-Matin* and *Perspectives*. He has used collage effects in his cartoons.

Leroux

A. Leroux was a cartoonist and illustrator whose work appeared in *l'Opinion Publique* and *The Canadian Illustrated News* in the 1880s. Canadian art historian J. Russell Harper suggests that he may have been the painter A. Leroux who was born about 1833 in St. Eustache, Quebec and was known to be active in Montreal during the 1860s.

Le Messurier

Ernest Le Messurier was born in Hamilton, Ontario in 1894 and moved to Vancouver as a child. He worked for the Vancouver *Daily Province* as a political and sports cartoonist until 1920. Moving back east, he was a staff artist at different times for the Toronto *Telegram*, The Montreal *Star*, The *New York Journal* and *The New York Sun*. He died in Montreal in 1932.

Loth

Cedric Loth, born in St. Jerome, Quebec in 1955, presently works as a free-lance caricaturist in Montreal. He has contributed work to *Le Devoir* and *Le Soleil* in Quebec.

MacDonald

Wallace B. MacDonald was born in Espanola, Ontario in 1919 . After finishing school, "Mac" worked briefly as an accountant until catching on with the Toronto *Telegram* in 1932. His first assignment was to sketch a city council meeting. For close to forty years he drew caricatures for the paper at meetings, conventions, and various social functions of local and visiting dignitaries.

MacKay

James G. MacKay (sometimes spelled McKay), a native of Hamilton, Ontario, produced numerous political cartoons and illustrations for *The Canadian Illustrated News* in the 1870s and 1880s.

MacMellon

Jack MacMellon was born in Yarmouth, NS in 1911. At seventeen he ran away from school, eventually ending up in Philadelphia. There he became friends and apprenticed with Charlie Bell, a sports and editorial cartoonist for the Philadelphia *Inquirer*. Eventually, MacMellon returned to Nova Scotia where he ran a commercial art studio in Yarmouth. He joined the army during the war, and worked for several of the Armed Forces publications. Always interested in sports cartooning, he worked at this briefly after the war at the Halifax *Chronicle-Star*. In 1955 he joined the Moncton *Times-Transcript* and has had a cartoon in every edition of the paper since the day he was hired.

Macpherson

Duncan Macpherson, the celebrated cartoonist of *The Toronto Star*, was born in Toronto in 1924. He is recognized as the best cartoonist we have produced and has been instrumental in putting Canadian political cartooning on the world map.

Macpherson joined the RCAF in 1941, and served in England, where he took art courses and familiarized himself with British political cartooning. After the war, he studied Graphic Arts at the Boston Museum of Fine Art and graduated from The Ontario College of Art in 1951. Even before graduating he had established a reputation as a first-rate illustrator. *The Standard* (now *Weekend*) asked him to replace the late Jimmy Frise as illustrator of their regular Greg Clark stories in 1948. Later he moved over to *Maclean's* where he illustrated the popular Robert Thomas Allen stories through the 1950s. Pierre Berton, then an editor at *Maclean's*, moved to the *Toronto Star* and talked Macpherson into trying his hand at political cartooning for the *Star's* editorial page in 1958. Macpherson's success was instantaneous. Dealing with municipal, provincial, federal, and international politics, his scenarios of glad-handers, puppets, and any other number of satires tickled the funnybone of *Star* readers, parading day after day across the editorial page. His style was confident and unique, a first for cartooning in English Canada. He was also first to hire an agent to negotiate his salary with his editors. Being apolitical, he insisted on having enough room to express his 360° vision by striking out at the left, right, centre, or whoever else struck his fancy, without confining himself to the editorial viewpoint of the *Star*. Recognizing Macpherson's popularity, the *Star* was extremely accommodating. Undoubtedly Macpherson's strong, independent personality helped in establishing this relationship. Recognizing a cartoonist's limitations better than most, Macpherson insisted also on working at his own pace as opposed to drawing six cartoons a week for fifty weeks of the year. This worked to the benefit of other cartoonists in that the *Star* would use numerous other people on days when Macpherson was off. He would also satisfy his wanderlust by setting out on occasion to see the world. The *Star* benefited by sketchbooks from Parliament Hill, Cuba, Russia and, more recently, China. In addition to producing numerous annuals of his *Star* cartoons, he released a book containing sketches and watercolours created while wandering throughout Canada at different times.

Macpherson has won the National Newspaper Award an unprecedented six times in 1959, 1960, 1962, 1965, 1970 and 1972. In 1971 he received a $15,000 Molson Prize from the Canada Council, an honour presented for "a man's total career rather than any single work." In 1976 Macpherson was elected to the Canadian News Hall of Fame.

"I'm simply against the wrongness in public life."

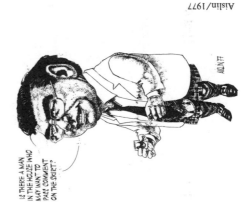

IS THERE A MAN IN THE HOUSE WHO MAY WANT TO PASS COMMENT ON THE SKIRT?

Aislin/1977

243

Mallette

Phil Mallette was born in Sault Ste. Marie, Ontario in 1955. After studying at The University of Guelph, he began freelancing in Toronto for various publications including *Books in Canada*, *The Last Post*, *The Canadian Forum* and *Maclean's*. When Tony Jenkins decided to take a year's leave of absence from *The Globe and Mail* in 1978, Mallette was taken on to do spot illustrations and fill in occasionally for Ed Franklin on the editorial page.

"If I wasn't a cartoonist I'd be an Edsel—swift, sleek, and years ahead of my time."

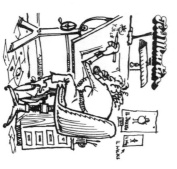

Martin/Toronto/Sun/25 February 1975

Martin

Ted Martin was born in Blackpool, England in 1938. After attending the Doncaster School of Art in Yorkshire, he joined the army at eighteen. Having visited Canada briefly in 1956, he returned permanently in 1962 where he joined the Toronto Telegram doing promotional art. While at the *Tely* he occasionally did some illustration and cartoon work. He moved to the *Toronto Sun* when the *Tely* folded, and started doing a daily socio-political cartoon. In addition, he filled in on the editorial page when Andy Donato was on holiday. In 1978 he started doing a syndicated daily cartoon for Universal Press Syndicate called *Pavlov*. Ted and his wife, Dawn, opened a cartoon gallery in 1975 in Toronto, the first of its kind in Canada, where they regularly exhibit the work of many Canadian cartoonists.

"Cartoonists are a unique breed when you consider that there are less of them around than there are brain surgeons."

Mayo

The pen-name of Harry Mayerovitch who was born in Montreal in 1910. An architect and graphic artist, in the 1930s and 1940s he contributed political cartoons to the *Montreal Herald*, *Le Jour*, *Authorité*, and other Montreal publications.

McConnell

Newton McConnell, born in Elgin County, Ontario in 1877, and, studied art at the Ontario School of Art and Design, graduating in 1900. Unlike many cartoonists of the time, McConnell made a living from cartooning almost immediately. His first drawings appeared in *Saturday Night* and *The Moon* and, shortly thereafter, he joined the staff of the *Toronto Daily News* where he worked for twenty-six years, fifteen as their editorial cartoonist. A very gregarious sort, Newt, as he was commonly called, became an institution at *The News* and was one of the most popular and prominent cartoonists of his period. He was one of the first Canadian cartoonists to be syndicated on a regular basis to the US and England. Although McConnell's style did not have the finesse of that of Julien and Hunter, he did have a lot more bite. Indeed he was credited at the time as being instrumental in the defeat of Laurier and his reciprocity policy in 1912. McConnell died in Toronto in 1940.

McKale

Daniel McKale was born in the small village of Pointe-Aux-Chênes, Quebec on either the fourteenth or fifteenth of January, 1951—no one seems to remember for sure. Studying at l'Institut des Arts Graphiques, he had his first cartoons published in the small newspaper *Le Carillon* in Hawkesbury, Ontario when he was eighteen years old. Shortly afterwards he moved to Montreal where he free-lanced for many publications including *La Patrie*, *Montreal-Matin*, *Quebec-Presse*, *Le Petit Journal* and *Perspectives*. In 1979 he became the political cartoonist for *La Tribune* in rural Sherbrooke, and recently became the full-time editorial-page cartoonist for Ottawa's French-language daily *Le Droit*.

"I am very fond of Sempé, Brétecher, Berthio, Girerd, and my wife."

McKee

Donald McKee was a political cartoonist for the Winnipeg *Telegram* in 1919, drawing daily front-page cartoons for that publication. Little else is known about him.

McKibbin

Ed McKibbin was born in Coleman, Alberta. Working briefly for the Walt Disney Studios in 1938, he returned from California and served overseas in the Canadian Army during the Second World War. After the war, he worked for several years as the editorial-page cartoonist for the Winnipeg *Tribune*.

McNally

Born in Fort William, Ontario in 1916, one of Ed McNally's first art-related jobs was

McNally

painting ten-foot high letters on the sides of grain elevators. After working briefly in a commercial art studio, he moved to Winnipeg where he drew wild flowers at two dollars a drawing. Even in those early days McNally was fast, and it was soon discovered that it would be cheaper to put him on staff for the *Free Press*. In 1941, he left Winnipeg and joined the Navy. After the war, he decided to settle in Montreal and have a go as a free-lance illustrator. With the help of Dick Hersey, then art director of the *Standard*, he developed a reputation as a superb illustrator. But, McNally wanted to become a cartoonist, and for six months worked on a unique style and approach drawing cartoons day after day. The Montreal *Star* took him on staff as their editorial-page cartoonist in 1960. Along with Macpherson he became one of the best-known Canadian cartoonists of the 1960s.

McNally won National Newspaper Awards in 1961 and 1964. In addition he won first prize for Political Cartooning at the third International Salon of Caricature and Cartoon in 1966. Although remembered as bearing little malice, a thorough look at his work reveals certain preoccupations: His drawings of Lester Pearson were right on target when Pearson proved to be quite difficult for many cartoonists. McNally was also quite the Canadian nationalist, and enjoyed taking a swipe at the Americans from time to time. But most of all, McNally despised privilege in any form, as is clearly seen in his social commentaries. He died suddenly in 1971.

"I became a great lettering man while painting silos out in Fort William."

McNally

McRitchie

Donald McRitchie was born in Cape Breton, NS in 1881. After leaving school, he worked for a coal company that transferred him to Boston, where he remained until 1904. During this period in the US he was exposed to American political cartooning and decided to pursue this as a career. Returning to Nova Scotia, he drew cartoons for the Sydney *Post* in 1904 and 1905. Over the next ten years he worked in every major Canadian city as a cartoonist, and managed to see the country at the same time. In 1906, he worked at the Ottawa *Journal*. He left and travelled through Toronto and the Lakehead, working for the Winnipeg *Telegram* in 1907. McRitchie was probably the first working political cartoonist in many of these cities. Later in 1907, he ended up working for Bob Edward's *Calgary Eye-Opener* where he stayed for five years. This was probably McRitchie's best period as a cartoonist, producing scurrilous drawings to suit the flavour of the publication. In Vancouver briefly, he returned to Montreal, where he worked as a cartoonist and illustrator until the First World War broke out. He joined the army and served overseas from 1915 to 1919. Returning to Halifax, he became the editorial cartoonist for the Halifax *Herald* where he worked for many years. McRitchie died there in 1948.

McTaggart

Ernest R. McTaggart was born in Kempville, Ontario in 1889, but his family moved to Vancouver while he was still a young child. He developed a reputation as a painter in BC and free-lanced as a political cartoonist for the Vancouver *Daily Province* in the 1920s after the death of J.B. Fitzmaurice. In the late 1930s, he moved over to the Vancouver *Sun*, where he drew cartoons through the 1940s. He died in Vancouver in 1958.

Meintjies

Jane Meintjies worked briefly as a free-lance caricaturist in the early 1970s for several Canadian publications. She produced one collection of caricatures of Canadian politicians entitled *The House on the Hill* in 1972.

Monks

Bob Monks is presently the political cartoonist for the *Windsor Star*. Born in Michigan in 1927, he worked as an illus-

Monks

trator in New York and Detroit before coming to Canada in 1955, where he taught art for nine years before becoming a cartoonist. Monks uses a simple linear style that is reminiscent of George Feyer and the European school of cartooning.

Moreau

C. Henri Moreau was born in France where he studied at l'Ecole Impériale des Beaux-Arts in Paris before emigrating to America. An officer in the Union Army during the American Civil War, he moved to Montreal in 1864 where he launched a short-lived publication called *Le Perroquet*. He drew cartoons against Confederation and in favour of Canada being annexed by the US. Returning to Paris, he died in 1837.

246

Moyer

Harry Moyer was born in Beamsville, Ontario in 1884. He worked as a cartoonist for the *Pittsburgh Despatch* until hired by *The Toronto Despatch* in 1908, where he worked as an illustrator and cartoonist.

Mozel

Born in Winnipeg in 1918, Mozel sold his first cartoon to a local paper when he was seventeen. After studying at art school for a year, he worked as a sign painter, display designer and mechanic's assistant. In 1938, he was hired as the editorial-page cartoonist for the *Winnipeg Tribune* where he worked until the mid-1970s.

Noax

Presumably a pen-name, this cartoonist was active in Regina, Saskatchewan from about 1915 to 1920.

Nokony

Denis Nokony was born in Oxbow, Saskatchewan in 1951. Working out of Regina as an illustrator and art teacher, he has contributed political cartoons to *Canadian Dimensions, This Magazine,* and various labour publications.

Norris

Len Norris was born in London, England in 1913 and moved with his family to Port Arthur, Ontario. In 1933 he drew his first cartoons—weekly comments on local events—which a local merchant hung in the window of his wallpaper shop. He moved to Toronto where he took night courses at The Ontario College of Art for one year. He worked as an art director for an ad agency from 1938 to 1940, when he joined the Army. Serving as a captain, he became editor, writer, and illustrator for the Canadian Army technical magazine *Cam.* For five years after the war he worked as an art director for Maclean-Hunter,

working on various magazines. Norris disliked the "Toronto rat race" and headed out to Vancouver, where he had been offered a job at the Vancouver *Sun.* "At first it was difficult," admits Norris, "because I tried to draw political cartoons the way everybody thought they should look . . . big labels and that sort of thing." Norris chucked this approach and, influenced by Giles, the brilliant English social cartoonist, began portraying local situations, types, and attitudes the way he saw them. The reaction to these cartoons was tremendous and his reputation sky-rocketed, not only in BC but across Canada. Norris won the National Newspaper Award the first year he entered, in 1951. He didn't enter again because he said that he didn't like the idea of losing.

The *Sun* produced annual collections of Norris cartoons for twenty-seven years. Walt Kelly, the creator of *Pogo,* referred to Norris as being "the best in the business." Hugh Hefner wrote Norris asking him to contribute to a new magazine he was starting. Len declined, which is probably just as well, as it's hard to imagine him cavorting about the *Playboy* mansion. Eventually Norris became as much a symbol of BC as the totem pole. In 1973 the University of Windsor granted Norris an Honorary Doctorate of Laws. Norris retired in 1978, but continues to draw two cartoons a week for

the *Sun.* He was elected to the Canadian News Hall of Fame in 1979.

"I should be allowed to make drawings of the government if they're allowed to spend my money."

Octavo

A Pen-name sometimes used by Henri Julien in the 1880s.

Palmer

Numerous cartoons appeared in Victoria's *The Week* around 1912, bearing this signature.

Vancouver/Sun

Parker

Lewis Parker was born in Toronto in 1926, where he studied art at the Central Technical School. In the army during the latter part of the war, he returned to Toronto to begin a career as an illustrator. At the time, Len Norris was an art director for Maclean-Hunter and was instrumental in getting Parker started. In the 1950s he worked with Duncan Macpherson and many other illustrators primarily for *Maclean's.* Continuing his work for *Maclean's* and other Toronto publications, Parker drew political cartoons occasionally for the editorial pages of both *The Toronto Star* and *The Globe and Mail* in the 1960s. Although Parker has worked as an illustrator,

Macpherson/Maclean's

cartoonist, and designer, his life-long love has been Indian life and folklore, and he is well known for his numerous paintings that deal with this subject.

"From a distance, I would say that what separates the men from the boys in the field of political cartooning is coming to terms with a daily deadline ... and at the same time retaining your creativity."

Passepoil
One of several pen-names used by Quebec cartoonist Albéric Bourgeois.

Patterson, C.R.
C.R. Patterson was a cartoonist for the *Victoria Times* in 1907.

Patterson, Russell
Russell Patterson was born in Omaha in the 1890s. As a child, his family moved to Newfoundland and then Montreal. After studying architecture at McGill University, he drew some cartoons, first for the *Standard*, and then *La Patrie*, where he also created a daily comic strip called *Pierre et Pierrette*. Rejected by the Canadian Army in 1914, he moved to Chicago to study. By 1920, his unique illustrations were appearing in *Harper's Bazaar*, *Cosmopolitan*, and *Life*. He became a great influence on the flapper fashion of the time; the "Patterson Girl" who appeared in his illustrations became to the 1920s what the "Gibson Girl" had been to the 1890s. He designed the sets and costumes for the 1922 Ziegfield Follies and continued a long and fruitful career in the US as a stage designer, interior decorator, illustrator, and comic-strip artist.

Pentridge
Well-known author and historian Bruce Hutchison drew political cartoons early in his career under this pen-name. His occasional full-page, full-colour cartoons appeared in the Vancouver *Daily Province*. He stopped cartooning as a side-line in 1935 after the defeat of R.B. Bennett's Conservative government.

Peterson
Roy Peterson was born in Winnipeg in 1936. He moved to Vancouver in 1948, and studied at the Vancouver Art School. One of his teachers there was the late cartoonist Al Beaton, who was then drawing for the Vancouver *Province*. Beaton told his wife, "There is this kid in my class who can draw circles around me and anyone I've ever seen. If he develops a political sense he's got it made!"

Peterson/Vancouver/Sun

He first began drawing for the *South Cariboo Advertiser* in 1956, sending his cartoons in by bus. He free-lanced for various publications and, after a brief flirtation with the Vancouver *Province*, began doing some work for the Vancouver *Sun* in 1962. His relationship with the paper flourished and he worked with Len Norris. His work has appeared in every major Canadian publication, numerous international publications such as *Punch*, *The Spectator*, *Time*, *The New York Times*, *The Washington Post*, *TV Guide*, and many others. His widest audience is through *Maclean's* where he has appeared on a regular basis for the last fifteen years. Peterson has also worked in conjunction with Stanley Burke on four books: *Frog Fables and Beaver Tales*, *The Day of the Glorious Revolution*, *Blood Sweat and Bears*, and *Swamp Song*. Peterson has been the recipient of two National Newspaper Awards, in 1968 and 1975. He also won first prize in Montreal's International Salon of Caricature and Cartoon for Editorial Cartooning in 1973.

"I draw with my shoes off."

Pic
This is the pen-name of Peter Pickersgill. Pic studied architecture and graduated from the University of British Columbia in 1971. Having done some caricatures and illustration for the Montreal *Star* and the Vancouver *Sun*, he moved to Ottawa in 1972 where he began working as the back-up cartoonist to Rusins on the editorial page of the Ottawa *Citizen*. Later, he experimented with animation, producing a daily political animated cartoon for Global Television.

Pilsworth, Eugene
Eugene Pilsworth was a cartoonist for the Victoria *Colonist* prior to 1912, when he apparently moved to San Francisco.

Pilsworth, Graham
Graham Pilsworth was born in Toronto in 1943. After graduating from the Ontario College of Art, he moved west in 1968 and worked as the editorial-page cartoonist for the Vancouver *Province* for two years. The *Province* went out on strike, so Pilsworth returned to Toronto, where he works as a free-lancer, particularly for *Saturday Night*, and *The Toronto Star*.

"I remember when I was a kid phoning up Duncan Macpherson and asking him if I could go down to the *Star* and watch him draw. He said, 'No!' and hung up."

248

Pier

Roland Pier was born in France in 1936. He came to Canada in 1965, travelled extensively, and had various jobs including construction and working at a gold mine. He spent time in cities throughout the country from Winnipeg to Vancouver, and as far north as Fort Nelson and Dawson City. He did not work as a professional cartoonist during this period, but would draw occasional caricatures of fellow employees. Arriving in Montreal in 1965, he began free-lancing for several publications including *La Patrie*. He was eventually hired by *Le Journal de Montréal* as a political cartoonist. *Le Journal* has since become the largest French-language newspaper in North America. As Pier's cartoons also appear in a sister publication, *Le Journal de Québec*, he is undoubtedly the most widely read cartoonist in Quebec today. Like Girerd and Berthio, he uses a simple European line style that is incisive and quickly understandable.

"I consider myself to be quite lucky to be a caricaturist and not a painter . . . I'm colour-blind."

Piper

Andrew W. Piper was drawing political cartoons for the Victoria *Colonist* as early as 1873.

Racey

Arthur G. Racey was born in Quebec City in 1870. While studying at McGill University, he developed a fondness for drawing caricature and his cartoons began to appear in the Montreal *Witness*, *Le Canard*, *Grip*, *The Moon*, and other publications of the day. In 1899, his first cartoons appeared in the Montreal *Star*, an association that was to last over forty years as Racey eventually succeeded Julien, who died in 1908. Like Julien, he became an institution at the *Star*. His work was reproduced in *Punch*, *Life*, *Le Monde Illustré* and in newspapers around the world. Racey often gave public lectures on the subject of Canadian Art and other matters. One lecture tour during the First World War raised $50,000 for the Red Cross. In 1927, Racey was one of seven judges for an international cartoon competition inaugurated in New York by *The American Art Student and Commercial Artist*. He produced two books, *The Englishman in Canada* and *Canadian Men of Affairs in Cartoon*. He died in Montreal in 1941.

Raine

Syd H. Raine was a cartoonist who was active in Saskatchewan in 1908.

Reeve

Alan Reeve was born in New Zealand in 1910. He developed a reputation as a political cartoonist there and in Australia in the 1930s, moving to London in 1939. In the early 1940s he was in Ottawa working as a cartoonist for *The Evening Citizen* and later became a war artist for the RCAF.

Reidford

Born in Glasgow, Scotland in 1911, James Reidford's family moved to Toronto when he was a baby. He studied at the Ontario College of Art and did a fair amount of commercial art work in Toronto in the early 1930s. He headed for Los Angeles in 1938 where he studied at the Chouinard Institute and worked for the Walt Disney Studios as an animator for several years. Returning to Canada, he landed a job as political cartoonist for the Montreal *Star* in 1941 after the death of A.G. Racey.

In 1951, he moved to *The Globe and Mail*, where he worked until his retirement in 1972. Here Reidford disproved the old theory about a cartoonist being a victim of his style. His first drawings were

Canadian/November 1900

heavy grease crayon cartoons filled with labels and symbols. However, by the time of his retirement, he had evolved a new and distinct linear style that was highly lyrical and filled with his own particular brand of light humour. Reidford won The National Newspaper Award in 1950, 1956, and 1957.

"Thankfully I never had a politician die on me between the time I lambasted him in a drawing and the time the newspaper hit the street."

Reynolds

Born in Iowa in 1877, Edward Reynolds spent most of his professional life on the west coast of the US, where he achieved a reputation as the "dean of cartooning." He had been working for the *Morning Oregonian* for fifteen years when he died in 1931. In his young days he drew for numerous west-coast newspapers, including the Vancouver *Province*, for two years from 1909 to 1911.

McLorinan/Globe and Mail
21 March 1958

Robson

James Robson was an artist who worked in Victoria in the 1870s and, with G.A. Walkem, produced some cartoons for the Victoria *Colonist*.

Rodewalt

Born in Edmonton in 1946, Vance Rodewalt's work expresses a strong western view. Although he won a scholarship to the Banff School of Fine Arts, he didn't bother to attend as he found himself far too busy immediately after finishing high school. Encouraged by Yardley Jones, who was then with the Edmonton *Journal*, Vance was free-lancing for *The Roughneck*, doing a great deal of ad work, and contributing regularly to several publications in New York and Los Angeles. He still contributes regularly to Marvel Comics in the US. After travelling around Europe, he began doing cartoons for the *Albertan*, where he has been ever since.

Calgary/Albertan

"It's fun drawing the two camps...the West with its new money, new pride, new confidence, and high aspirations on one hand, and the East with its old war chiefs, old money, and old ideas that seem to be crumbling away."

---

engraver with whom he was associated. Staples was born in Somerset, England in 1866, moving to Hamilton, Ontario as a child. He studied in Toronto and Philadelphia under Thomas Eakins. Although he worked for the Toronto *Evening Telegram* from 1885 to 1947, he ceased drawing political cartoons in 1908. His cartoons are best remembered for their vicious attacks on Laurier and the railway scandals of the time. Staples is best known as a landscape painter. He died in 1949.

Rodgers

D.L. Rodgers was a cartoonist active in Saskatchewan in the 1930s.

Roschkov

Vic Roschkov was born in Kiev in the Ukraine in 1941. After the war, his family moved to Canada, eventually settling in the Windsor area. Roschkov developed a love of billiards while in high school and decided

Toronto/Star

to drop out of the latter for the former. He knocked around until he landed a job with a silk screen company in London, Ontario. He discovered that he had an ability for caricature and put together a portfolio to show to newspapers. *Time* printed one of his drawings and, in 1972, the Windsor *Star* hired him as editorial-page cartoonist. He served a valuable apprenticeship there, drawing four cartoons a week and experimenting with various techniques including colour. In 1976, he moved to *The Toronto Star*, where he was hired as a political cartoonist and illustrator, filling in for Duncan Macpherson on the editorial page.

"Editorial meetings are necessary for the editorial writers, but seem to inhibit most cartoonists. Most of us feel that our time could be better spent alone at the drawing board where we belong."

Rostap

This was the pen-name used by Owen Staples. It is thought to be a combination of his own name and that of Robinson, an

---

Rusins

The pen-name used by Rusins Kaufmanis, editorial-page cartoonist for the Ottawa *Citizen*. Born in Riga, Latvia, in 1925, Kaufmanis came to Canada with his father in 1947. He was hired by Ontario Hydro as a labourer until his artistic talents were discovered. Subsequently, he worked for

Blaine

them as an illustrator for ten years. In the early 1960s, he drew occasional political cartoons for *The Globe and Mail* when Jim Reidford was on holiday. His work was noticed by the editors at the Ottawa *Citizen* where he was hired as the editorial-page cartoonist, and he has been there ever since.

"I tend to see things in shades as opposed to straight black and white."

Ryan

Alonzo Ryan was born in Montreal around 1868. He may have been the first Quebec caricaturist to use "Baptiste," a symbol of the average Quebecker that would be used by the following two generations of Quebec cartoonists. He was also one of the first cartoonists in Montreal to be used on a regular basis in newspapers. Ryan worked at one time or another for *Le Canada*, *Le Journal*, *The Witness*, *La Patrie*, the *Herald*, *Le Canard*, *Le Combat*, and many other publications.

Saw

Born in Western Australia in 1922, Lew Saw left school at fourteen to apprentice as a jeweller's engraver. He joined the Australian Air Force during the Second World War, and spent some time with his air crew training in Canada. After the war he became the editorial cartoonist for *The Perth Daily News* where he was given a free hand. As his wife was Canadian, he moved here in 1952, and travelled across the country applying at various papers. He caught on with the *Winnipeg Tribune*. Finding the prairie winters very difficult, he moved to Vancouver in 1957 where he did some free-lance work, eventually cartooning for the Vancouver *Province*. Disillusioned with the newspaper business and prevailing attitudes about the role of cartooning in comparison to his native Australia, he dropped political cartooning altogether and moved into animation.

"In my time, editors wanted cartoons to be illustrated clichés."

Schefield

Daily cartoons appeared on the front page of the short-lived Edmonton *Capital* in 1914 bearing this signature.

Vezina

Sebestyen

Ed Sebestyen, a native of Saskatchewan, originally worked as an engraver for the Saskatoon *Star-Phoenix* in the 1950s. He began submitting cartoon ideas to the editors there and became their full-time cartoonist in 1956. Sebestyen's work during Saskatchewan's Medicare crisis in the early 1960s is considered to be his strongest and best.

Shane

George Shane was born in Winnipeg in 1921. He now works as a cartoonist and free-lance animator for various companies and publications in Toronto. Always a free-lancer, he started cartooning before the war for the Calgary *Herald*, the Winnipeg *Free Press* and various other western newspapers. After serving in the Air Force during the war, he went to New York to study fine art and illustration. There he began doing some gag cartoons as they were much in demand at that time. Returning to Canada in the late 1940s, George worked for *Saturday Night* and *The Montrealer*, and illustrated a crime magazine. Opening his own commercial art studio, he worked with The Canadian Labour Congress. As a result of this, he became a cartoonist for numerous Canadian labour newspapers.

"I remember when I sold my first cartoon to the Calgary *Herald* in the late 1930s. They sent me a cheque for one dollar."

Shields

George S. Shields was born in Toronto in 1872. He was a printer's devil for the Toronto *Evening Telegram* by the time he was fourteen; later he became a cartoonist, and was associated with the newspaper for sixty-two years. Like the *Telegram*, Shields was a devoted conservative, and, with his newspaper, produced a booklet of cartoons that were highly critical of Mackenzie King's "five-cent speech" during the 1930 federal election. Shields signed his cartoons with a graphic of one shield in the shadow of another. Deeply interested in politics, he was elected to the Toronto City Council in 1923, and to the Ontario provincial legislature in 1926. He died in Toronto in 1952.

Skuce

Lou Skuce was born in Ottawa in 1886, where he started a long cartoon career with the Ottawa *Journal*. Moving to Toronto, he was employed by the *World*, the *Star*, *The Mail and Empire* and was the art editor of the *Sunday World* for fourteen years. In the 1920s, Skuce worked with J.K. Munro, the popular Ottawa columnist for *Maclean's* illustrating Munro's opinionated columns. A man of many talents, Skuce is also remembered for his sports cartoons. He was an avid athlete as a young man, as well as a playwright and actor. He gave public talks with a machine of his own invention called a Cartoonograph that would flash cartoons upon a screen at high speed. Skuce died at his drawing board in Toronto in 1951.

Sneyd

Born in 1933, Doug Sneyd found it tough going in the early years after graduating from high school in Guelph, Ontario. Working as a commercial artist and an illustrator of children's textbooks, he finally got his big break when he approached *Playboy*. Since then, he has drawn a regular full-page, full-colour "girlie" cartoon for the magazine. In the 1970s he decided to try his hand at political cartooning, ex-

Ting

This is the pen-name of Merle Tingley, political cartoonist for the London *Free Press*. Born and raised in Montreal, he studied art for one year and then worked briefly as a draughtsman until joining the army at the beginning of the Second World War. He worked as a staff cartoonist for two wartime publications, *Khaki* and *The Maple Leaf* in Europe. After the war he took a job at a Montreal ad agency but became tired of "drawing straight lines." Deciding that he would rather be a full-time cartoonist, he bought a used motorcycle and set off across the country with a portfolio, "often covering three hundred miles a day, spending many a night in the company of one cow or another in any convenient barn." Ting talked to thirty-one editors throughout Canada before he took a job retouching photographs for the London *Free Press* out of desperation. Drawing cartoons in his spare time, the paper printed one, then another, until he began on a full-time basis in 1948. He has a wide following in the western Ontario area.

Ting's cartoons always contain a pipe-smoking worm who was named Luke Worm by a *Free Press* reader. In addition to cartooning, Ting has written numerous articles and columns while on assignment in Korea, Formosa, the Congo, and the Middle East for the *Free Press*. Recipient of the National Newspaper Award in 1955, Ting has published several collections of

251

Besides assailing Government agencies and their treatment of Native People, Soop also criticized the oppressiveness of band councils and the foibles of his own people. Eventually, other Indian publications throughout North America began using Soop's cartoons. He also writes a column for *The Kainai News* in the same cutting and satirical vein. In 1979 a collection of the best of Soop's cartoons drawn over the last ten years was published.

"Indians are natural cartoon subjects . . . we are always losing."

Stokes

In 1908, cartoons bearing the signature W.H. Stokes appeared from time to time in Victoria's *The Week*.

Taylor

Richard Taylor was born in Fort William, Ontario in 1902. He studied at Toronto's Central Technical School, The Ontario College of Art, and The Los Angeles School of Art and Design. In 1927 he drew his first cartoons for *The Goblin*, a very popular humour publication produced in Toronto. By 1935, *The New Yorker* magazine picked up one of Taylor's drawings and he became a regular contributor to that magazine for many years thereafter. In the 1950s, he produced many cover drawings for *The Saturday Evening Post*.

Thom

Born in 1892 on St. Kitt's in the West Indies, Eric Thom moved to Montreal with his family around the turn of the century. For most of his life he worked as a commercial artist and joined the art department of the Montreal *Star* in the early 1940s. After Jim Reidford left the *Star* in 1950, Thom drew editorial-page cartoons for the *Star* for several years. He died in Montreal in 1977.

perimenting with several features for *The Toronto Star*. He used this experience as a stepping stone to syndicating his own feature entitled *Scoops*, a light-hearted daily political strip that is presently published by over one hundred newspapers in Canada and the US.

"Without Hugh Hefner, none of this would have been possible."

Soop

Everett Soop was born on the Blood Indian reserve near Cardston, Alberta in 1943. Incapacitated by muscular dystrophy as a youth, he overcame this to attend the Alberta College of Art in 1964, followed by a year at Brigham Young University in Utah. Studying journalism for several years at the University of Lethbridge, he took summer courses at The Banff School of Fine Arts. In 1968, Soop began drawing very popular political cartoons for *The Kainai News*, a newspaper that served the Indian community of southern Alberta.

Townshend

Brigadier General George Townshend was born in England in 1724. His godfather was George I. A man of rank and position, he also developed a reputation as one of the major caricaturists in London. It must be remembered that the caricatures of the time were not as we know them today; they were usually a pastime of the idle rich, and were attacks on one's political enemies. Educated at Cambridge, Townshend entered the British Army in 1745. Under the command of Major-General Wolfe, he participated in the siege of Quebec in 1759. He and Wolfe despised each other, and Townshend drew a series of devastating caricatures of his commander. The first caricatures drawn on North American soil, they survive today in the McCord Museum in Montreal and in collections overseas. Townshend returned to England where he served in various posts and continued his activities as a caricaturist. He died in England in 1807.

Uluschak

Edd Uluschak was born near Prosperity, Alberta in 1943. His family moved to Edmonton when he was ten years old. With no formal art training after high school, he began free-lancing in the Edmonton area, doing illustrations and working for a firm that published trade magazines. Some of his first cartoons appeared in *Roughneck*, an oil industry magazine that also spawned Yardley Jones, Vance Rodewalt, and John Larter. When Yardley Jones left the Edmonton *Journal* for Toronto, Edd replaced him as editorial-page cartoonist in 1968. The following year he won the 1969 National Newspaper Award. He has also won The Basil Dean Memorial Award for Outstanding Contributions to Journalism plus numerous international awards from exhibitions in Greece, Bulgaria, and Germany. Widely syndicated, his work has appeared in *Punch*, *Time*, *U.S. News and World Report*, *The National Review*, etc. The *Journal* has produced an annual collection of his cartoons since 1973.

cartoons including one covering twenty-five years of *Free Press* cartoons.

"When I tackle politics, I try to bring them into the viewer's back yard."

Uluschak/Edmonton/Journal

Vaughn-James

Martin Vaughn-James was born in Bristol, England in 1943. He moved to Toronto in 1969 where he drew occasional illustrations and political cartoons for *Saturday Night* and *The Toronto Star*. He has produced three books which he called visual-novels: *Elephant*, *The Projector*, and *The Park, a Mystery*.

"I love to kick pompous asses."

Vezina

Emile Vezina worked as an illustrator and caricaturist for several Montreal publications during the early years of this century. He was a contemporary of Charlebois, Ryan, and Brodeur. An accomplished draughtsman, his style lent itself more to illustrating social situations than hard-hitting caricature.

"What's the difference between a man squatting on a pile of dung and a refrigerator?"

Waghorn

Kerry Waghorn is one of the few contemporary Canadian cartoonists who has developed a career both here and in the U.S. Born in Vancouver in 1947, he did some work there for the *Georgia Straight* and other publications in the late 1960s. He worked on the fishing boats up and down the BC coast for three years, saving enough money to open a commercial art studio with a friend in Vancouver in 1972. Encouraged by Roy Peterson, he started cartooning again in 1975 on a full-time basis, and his work began appearing regularly in the Vancouver *Sun*. He also did some work for *Vancouver Magazine*, *Books in Canada*, and *The Canadian* magazine. By 1977, he was also working regularly for the *San Francisco Chronicle*. He began syndicating a feature with the *Chronicle* entitled *Faces*. These are topical caricatures of well-known Canadian and American political figures, and presently appear in newspapers in most Canadian cities in addition to many American papers. Waghorn acknowledges the early influence of Peterson and the well-known American caricaturist, David Levine, but his caricatures are beginning to take on their own unique look.

Walkem

George Anthony Walkem was born in Ireland in 1834. He emigrated to Montreal where he studied law at McGill University and was admitted to the bar. He moved to BC in 1862 and, with James Robson, a local artist, and drew some political cartoons for the Victoria *Colonist* in 1872. Walkem became premier of BC in 1874 and was instrumental in having BC join Confederation. He died in 1906.

Walker

Born in Ireland in 1831, John Henry Walker emigrated with his family to Montreal in 1842. On January 1, 1849 he published the first edition of *Punch in Canada*, our first humour publication. Walker drew a full-page cartoon for each issue. In 1850, the offices were moved to Toronto where *Punch in Canada* went weekly, but it folded within the year. Walker worked for many of the publications of the time including *The Dart, The Jester, Diogenes, Grinchuckle, The Canadian Illustrated News* and *l'Opinion Publique*. Rather than signing his cartoons, he substituted a small walking figure. A master designer and engraver, Walker designed many books and magazines in addition to being a landscape artist and portrait painter. He died in Montreal in 1899.

Walker

Werthman

Born in Germany, William C. Werthman emigrated to Newfoundland in 1951, where he eventually became the editorial cartoonist for the St. John's *Evening Telegram* from 1955 to 1959. Moving to New Brunswick in 1963, he joined the staff of *The Fredricton Gleaner* where he remained until 1970, also contributing occasional cartoons to the Ottawa *Journal*. Werthman received a Canada Council grant in 1964 to produce a book on Canadian Political Cartooning. Entitled *Canada in Cartoon*, it was published in 1977 and is the only known attempt at documenting the subject before the present volume.

"Art must be an expression of its time as seen by the artist himself. Our Canadian cartoonists have presented a remarkably true and unprejudiced account of the political, economic, and cultural development."

Weston

James L. Weston was thought to have been born in England around 1815. He was active as a painter in Montreal by 1840. In the 1870s, he was on the staff of *l'Opinion Publique* and *The Canadian Illustrated News* as an illustrator and cartoonist. Records show that he was teaching art in Montreal in the 1880s but by 1893 he was living in New York. He died about 1896.

Whalley

Born in Brockville, Ontario in 1921, Peter Whalley studied art at the Nova Scotia College of Art in Halifax, where he sold his first cartoon at the age of sixteen. After serving in the merchant marine during the war, he moved to Morin Heights in 1948, a small town some forty miles north of Montreal. He has been living there and working as a free-lance cartoonist ever since. During the 1950s and 1960s he did gag cartoons, illustrations, and political cartoons for *The Standard* (later *Weekend* magazine), *Maclean's*, and many other national publications. It was during this period that he illustrated his first book written by humourist Eric Nichol, *An Uninhibited History of Canada*, the first of several they produced together. Whalley won first prize for Political Cartooning at The International Salon of Caricature and Cartoon in 1965.

Although his illustrations were well known to Canadians in this period, there was a cynical side to the cartoonist that the reading public was not aware of. Pierre Berton considered Whalley to be one of the most inventive cartoonists he had ever run across. Max Newton, the late art director of *Weekend* magazine, called Whalley a man before his time in that, "He had a warped, poignant sense of humour that is finally coming into style." Indeed, this savage satire is reflected clearly in several limited edition books and magazines that Whalley produced privately such as *Hyperbole, Northern Blights,* and *Phap, the Pornographics of Politics*.

"I've managed to produce cartoons without the sponsorship of the Canada Council, Opportunities for Youth, Manpower, Winter Works Program, Information Canada, Affirmative Action Division of Fair Employment Practices Branch of The Department of Labour, L'Association des Chefs de Police et Pompiers de la Province de Quebec, The National Gallery of Canada and The Canadian Saltfish Corporation."

Wicks

Known to many Canadian newspaper readers, Ben Wicks produces a daily syndicated cartoon in addition to his daily comic strip, *The Outcasts*. Born in London, England in 1926, Wicks is proud of his Cockney heritage. During the war he claims to have held the Nazi horde at bay as a swimming pool attendant at a Canter-

"Working in both countries, I see a great deal of cartooning presently produced in both Canada and the States. I would have to say that the Canadian cartoonists have a definite edge when it comes to quality."

bury army camp. Preparing for his career as a cartoonist he became, in turn, a clog-boot maker, shipping clerk, and barrow salesman. Having learned to play the saxophone in the army, he toured Europe with a band that also had "Nine American showgirls and a homosexual pianist . . . the only show that had something for everyone." Later he was to play in the orchestra on the liner Queen Elizabeth.

Wicks moved to Canada in 1957, working as a milkman in Calgary and playing in a local Army band. He sold several gag cartoons to *The Saturday Evening Post* and never looked back. After drawing some political cartoons for the *Calgary Albertan*, he moved to Toronto in the early 1960s. There, he conceived his one-column political cartoon, which was picked up and syndicated by *The Telegram*. Drawing several cartoons daily aimed at both Canadian and international markets, the feature grew in popularity and eventually gained widespread use. He continues to draw this feature and it is now probably the most widely syndicated cartoon feature being produced in Canada today. Indeed, Wicks is our most prolific cartoonist. He has written and illustrated numerous books, has hosted his own television program, and has experimented in animated cartoons.

"Actually, I'm rotten at drawing."

Wicks/1979

Wieland

Well-known contemporary painter Joyce Wieland drew a series of political cartoons for *The Canadian Forum* in the late 1960s.

Willson

Frederick J. Willson, a Toronto painter, was one of a number of people who drew illustrations and cartoons for *l'Opinion Publique* and *The Canadian Illustrated News* in the 1880s.

Wilson

Cartoons in the Victoria *Times* in 1912 bearing the signature Wilson. These cartoons appear to be woodcuts.

Wright

Doug Wright, born in England in 1917, is well-known for his weekly cartoon feature *Doug Wright's Family* in the *Canadian* magazine. He has also dabbled at political cartooning over the past twenty years. Emigrating to Canada in 1938, Wright worked at a series of jobs until catching on with *The Standard* (now *Weekend* magazine) in 1948, working at various illustration jobs until he came up with his strip, *Nipper*. Wright moved from Montreal to Ontario in the 1960s, also moving *Nipper* from *Weekend* to the *Canadian* and renaming it *Doug Wright's Family*. In the late 1950s and early 1960s, Wright drew occasional political cartoons for the Montreal *Star*'s editorial page, often filling in for Ed McNally. Presently, he draws two a week for the Hamilton *Spectator*, which are used as back-up cartoons for their regular cartoonist, Blaine.

Yardley Jones

Born in Liverpool, England in 1930, John Yardley Jones grew up in Wales, where he became a boxer at fourteen. Between his 150 professional fights over a period of nine years, he studied some architecture and sold cartoons to various English publications on a free-lance basis. Deciding to emigrate to New Zealand, there was so much red tape involved in the procedure that he came to Canada instead, settling out west in 1957. Trying out at "a bewildering series of jobs," including salesman, printer, silk-screen artist, and sign painter, he free-lanced for both the Calgary *Herald* and Edmonton *Journal*. However, he credits his experience working for *The Roughneck*, an oil industry magazine, as being great preparation for his career as a political cartoonist. Being a small magazine, he was required to come up with a phenomenal number of cartoon ideas for each issue. *The Roughneck* proved a beginning for a whole generation of Albertan cartoonists including Edd Uluschak, Vance Rodewalt, and John Larter.

In 1962, he became the Edmonton *Journal*'s first staff editorial cartoonist and proved to be extremely popular there, producing a series of booklets with columnist Art Evans on local happenings and issues. After Al Beaton died in 1968, Yardley Jones was taken on at the Toronto *Telegram*. After the *Tely* folded, he worked with the *Toronto Sun*. Yardley won the National Newspaper Award in 1971. In 1973 he moved to the Montreal *Star* where he has been since. Syndicated throughout Canada, he hides a black cat in all of his drawings.

"I don't like meeting politicians. I might end up liking them."

Fiona Yardley-Jones
age 4

Zip

A signature found on cartoons published in various Saskatchewan publications in the 1930s.

Bibliography

_____. *Canadian Cartoon and Caricature.* Art Gallery of Ontario, Toronto: 1969.

_____. *Canadian Political Cartoons.* The Winnipeg Art Gallery, Winnipeg: 1977.

_____. *The Franco-Prussian War and the Commune in Caricature.* Victoria and Albert Museum, London: 1971.

_____. *A History of Canadian Journalism.* Canadian Press Association, Toronto: 1908.

_____. *The Image of America in Caricature and Cartoon.* Carter Museum of Western Art, Fort Worth: 1975.

_____. *War Cartoons and Caricatures of the British Commonwealth.* The National Gallery, Ottawa: 1941.

Allen, Robert Thomas. *A Treasury of Canadian Humour.* Canadian Illustrated Library. McClelland and Stewart, Toronto: 1967.

Ashbee, C.R. *Caricature.* Chapman and Hall, London: 1928.

Barbeau, Marius. *Côté—The Wood Carver.* Ryerson, Toronto: 1943.

Barbeau, Marius. *Henri Julien.* Ryerson, Toronto: 1941.

Becker, Stephen. *Comic Art in America.* Simon and Schuster, New York: 1959.

Bengough, J.W. *A Caricature History of Canadian Politics.* Grip, Toronto: 1886.

Bengough, J.W. *Chalk Talks.* Musson, Toronto: 1922.

Desbarats, Peter. *The Canadian Illustrated News—A Commemorative Portfolio.* McClelland and Stewart, Toronto: 1970.

Fauteux, Aegidius. *The Introduction of Printing into Canada.* Rolland Paper Company, Montreal: 1957.

Geipel, John. *The Cartoon—A Short History of Graphic Comedy and Satire.* A. S. Barnes and Company, New York: 1973.

George, M. Dorothy. *English Political Caricature.* Oxford University Press, Oxford: 1959.

Gombrich, E.H. *Meditations on a Hobby Horse.* Phaidon Press, London: 1928.

Harper, J. Russell. *Early Painters and Engravers in Canada.* University of Toronto Press, Toronto: 1970.

Harris, Eileen. *The Townshend Album.* National Portrait Gallery, London: 1974.

Hess, Stephen and Milton Kaplan. *The Ungentlemanly Art: A History of American Political Cartoons.* Macmillan, New York: 1968.

Hill, Draper. *The Satirical Etchings of James Gillray.* Dover Publications, New York: 1976.

Hill, Draper. *Charging the Line.* Privately published: 1972.

Hoff, Syd. *Editorial and Political Cartooning.* Stravon Educational Press, New York: 1976.

Hofman, Werner. *Caricature—From Leonardo to Picasso.* John Calder, London: 1957.

Holme, G. *—Caricature of Today.* The Studio, London: 1928.

Jones, Michael Wynn. *The Cartoon History of Britain.* Macmillan, London: 1971.

Kuch, Peter. *Arch Dale—The Pictorial Spokesman of the West.* Historical and Scientific Society of Manitoba, Winnipeg: 1964.

St. Hill, Thomas Nast. *Thomas Nast—Cartoons and Illustrations.* Dover Publications, New York: 1974.

Maurice, A.B. and F.T. Cooper. *A History of Caricature. Dodd, Mead and Company, New York: 1904.

Murrell, William. *A History of American Graphic Humor.* Cooper Square Publishers, New York: 1967.

Nevins, Allan and Frank Weitenkampf. *A Century of Political Cartoons: Caricature in the United States from 1800 to 1900.* Scribner's, New York: 1944.

Parton, James. *Caricature and Other Comic Art.* Harper and Brothers, New York: 1877.

Robidoux, Léon A. *Albéric Bourgeois—Caricaturiste.* Mediabec, Montreal: 1978.

Seguin, R. L. *L'Esprit revolutionnaire dans l'art québecois.* Parti Pris, Montreal: 1972.

Shikes, Ralph E. *Canada in Cartoon.* Brunswick Press: 1967.

Shikes, Ralph E. *The Indignant Eye.* Beacon Press, Boston: 1969.

Trepanier, Léon. *Images d'autrefois: caricatures du pays.* La Patire, Montreal: 1950.

Wardroper, John. *Kings, Lords and Wicked Libellers: Satire and Protest 1760-1837.* John Murray, London: 1973.

Wright, Thomas. *The Words of James Gillray, the Caricaturist.* Chattto and Windus, London: 1873.

255

Acknowledgements

The Glenbow-Alberta Institute, Calgary; Provincial Archives of Alberta, Edmonton; The British Columbia Archives, Victoria; Vancouver City Archives, Vancouver; The Saskatchewan Archives, Regina; The Vancouver Public Library, Vancouver; The Manitoba Archives, Winnipeg; The Winnipeg Art Gallery, Winnipeg; The Toronto Public Library, Toronto; The Art Gallery of Ontario, Toronto; The National Archives, Ottawa; The Parliamentary Library, Ottawa; La Bibliothèque de Montréal, Montréal; La Bibliothèque de l'Université de Montréal, Montréal; McGill University Library, Montréal; The Montreal Museum of Fine Arts, Montréal; The National Film Board of Canada Library, Montréal; The International Salon of Cartoons and Caricature Library, Montréal; The Westmount Library, Montréal; The McCord Museum, Montreal; The National Archives of Quebec, Quebec; La Musée de Québec, Quebec; The Public Archives of Nova Scotia, Halifax; Acadia University Library, Wolfville, St. Francis-Xavier University, Antigonish; The Newfoundland Archives, St. John's; The Provincial Archives of New Brunswick, Fredericton; The National Gallery, Ottawa.

Thanks to the libraries of the following newspapers:

The Victoria Times, The Victoria Colonist, The Vancouver Sun, The Montreal; Keith Mackenzie, Cartoon Vancouver Province, The Edmonton Journal, The Calgary Herald, The Winnipeg Free Press, The Winnipeg Tribune, The Globe and Mail, The Toronto Star, The Toronto Sun, The Montreal Star, The Gazette, La Presse, Le Devoir, Le Soleil, The Halifax Herald.

Special thanks to:

Robert LaPalme, Curator, International Salon of Cartoons and Caricature, Montreal; Keith Mackenzie, Cartoon Historian, The Daily Mail, London, England, Edith Firth, The Toronto Public Library, Toronto; Hugh A. Dempsey, Chief Curator, The Glenbow-Alberta Institute, Calgary; Draper Hill, Cartoonist and Historian, The Detroit News, Detroit, Michigan; Jack Yocum, The National Newspaper Awards, Toronto, for selected cartoons from his collection; Toivo Roht, The National Museums, Ottawa.